D0373136

Humor in the Advertising Business

Humor in the Advertising Business

Theory, Practice, and Wit

FRED K. BEARD

ROWMAN & LITTLEFIELD PUBLISHERS, INC.
Lanham • Boulder • New York • Toronto • Plymouth, UK

ROWMAN & LITTLEFIELD PUBLISHERS, INC.

Published in the United States of America
by Rowman & Littlefield Publishers, Inc.
A wholly owned subsidiary of The Rowman & Littlefield Publishing Group, Inc.
4501 Forbes Boulevard, Suite 200, Lanham, Maryland 20706
www.rowmanlittlefield.com

Estover Road, Plymouth PL6 7PY, United Kingdom

Copyright © 2008 by Rowman & Littlefield Publishers, Inc.

All rights reserved. No part of this publication may be reproduced, stored in a retrieval
system, or transmitted in any form or by any means, electronic, mechanical, photocopy-
ing, recording, or otherwise, without the prior permission of the publisher.

British Library Cataloguing in Publication Information Available

Library of Congress Cataloging-in-Publication Data

Beard, Fred K., 1957–
    Humor in the advertising business : theory, practice, and wit / Fred K. Beard.
        p. cm.
    Includes bibliographical references and index.
    ISBN-13: 978-0-7425-5425-2 (cloth : alk. paper)
    ISBN-10: 0-7425-5425-2 (cloth : alk. paper)
    ISBN-13: 978-0-7425-5426-9 (pbk. : alk. paper)
    ISBN-10: 0-7425-5426-0 (pbk. : alk. paper)
    1. Humor in advertising. I. Title.
    HF5821.B37 2008
    659.1—dc22   2007002332

Printed in the United States of America

⊚™ The paper used in this publication meets the minimum requirements of American
National Standard for Information Sciences—Permanence of Paper for Printed Library
Materials, ANSI/NISO Z39.48-1992.

Contents

Illustrations

TABLES

Acknowledgments

THE many people and companies acknowledged here answered questions, sent ads, helped with permissions, and otherwise made this book possible.

Rosie Ackred, New Business PA, Fallon London Ltd., for assistance in securing permission

Karen M. Barkas, Miller Brewing Company, Milwaukee, WI, for helping with permission

Glenn Barnett, Pot Noodle brand manager, Unilever UK, Ltd., UK, for permission

Denise Beard, Norman, OK, for 30 years of faith and inspiration

Peter Biggs, managing director, and Daniela Santilli, group account director, Clemenger BBDO/Melbourne, Australia, for helping with permission and for sending an ad

Corey Blake, actor, for corresponding about his performance in a funny ad for The Yard

Tom Bodett, humorist, Putney, VT, for passing on my inquiry to the folks at the Richards Group

Caroline Breakwell, brand marketing executive, *The Economist*, London, for permission

Josh Caplan, McCarthy Mambro Bertino Advertising, Boston, MA, for responding to my survey; for sending copies of The Yard TV spots; and for putting me in touch with Troll Subin, The Yard, and Steven Keenan, Backyard Productions

Gary Conway, VP-corporate marketing, Sprint Nextel Corp., Overland Park, KS, for permission

Ben Crane, The Trade Card Place, Wheaton, IL, for permission and for scanning two examples of late-nineteenth-century trade cards

Catherine Cusack, VP-brand programs, Staples, Inc., Framingham, MA, for permission to reproduce their radio spot

Mark D'Albis, actor, for returning my call and for approval

Bruce Delahorne, senior manager of national advertising, CDW, for granting permission

Rowena J. S. DeLeon, Duane Morris LLP, New York, NY, for help with permission

Joe Eberhardt, executive VP-global sales and marketing, DaimlerChrysler Corp., Auburn Hills, MI, and Kim Ray, DaimlerChrysler Intellectual Capital Company LLC, for permission

Kern Egan, the Richards Group, Dallas, TX, for sending Motel 6 radio spots on CD and for help with permission

Steve Ekdahl, brand manager, Holiday Inn Express, InterContinental Hotels Group, Atlanta, GA, for permission and for putting me in touch with the Fallon Minneapolis creative team

Carla Foster, paralegal, InterContinental Hotels Group, Atlanta, GA, for help with permission

Gene Goldschmidt, Findlay Market, Cincinnati, OH, for permission

Jo Graham, account director, Leo Burnett, London, for help with permission from client H. J. Heinz

Christopher Han, Singapore Cancer Society, Singapore, for permission

Jackie Hart, senior executive assistant, Ameriquest Mortgage Company, Orange, CA, for sending still images from the TV spot "Surprise Dinner"

Allen Hasken, Hobart, Troy, OH, for permission

Peter Keenan, Backyard Productions, Venice, CA, for help with permission

Sarah Longwell, communications director, Center for Union Facts, Washington, D.C., for permission

Abby Lovett, corporate affairs department, and Stephanie Pines, account executive, Leo Burnett USA, Inc., Chicago, IL, for assistance in securing permission

Kevin Lucido, director of marketing, Juniper Networks, Sunnyvale, CA, for permission

Patrick Malone, actor, for approval

Maria J. Martin, manager of intellectual property, Jim Beam Brands Co., Deerfield, IL, for permission

Suzanne McColl, artist representative, i2i Art Inc., Ontario, Canada, for helping to secure permission

John McFall, artistic director and chief executive officer, Atlanta Ballet, Atlanta, GA, for permission

Lex Medlin, actor, for returning my call and for approval

Mark Miller, 3rd Lair Skatepark/Skateshop, Golden Valley, MN, for permission

Jennie Moore, account supervisor, Fallon Minneapolis, Minneapolis, MN, for corresponding about the HIE STAY SMART® campaign

Melissa K. Murray, manager of corporate communications, Draft FCB, New York, NY, for help with permission

Tim Oden, executive VP and creative director, Ackerman McQueen, Oklahoma City, OK, for responding to the survey, for writing a great "Funny Business" piece, and for sending an ad for client Juniper Networks

John Pattison, HSR Business to Business, Cincinnati, OH, for responding to the survey, for sending numerous examples of funny ads, for helping with permissions, and for writing a great "Funny Business" piece

Steve Pederson, agency Wowza, Minneapolis, MN, for his assistance in gaining permission to reproduce ads for 3rd Lair Skatepark and for sending the ads

Phil, artist, for permission to reproduce his work in a TCM ad

Jeff Rabkin, agency Wowza, Minneapolis, MN, for contributing a "Funny Business" piece

John R. Renaud, counsel, Turner Entertainment Group, Atlanta, GA, for granting permission

Stephanie L. Ross, senior attorney, Leo Burnett USA, Chicago, IL, for help with permission

Nicole Sanda, Weru AG, Germany, for help with permission

Jon Schneider, client service executive, HSR Business to Business, Cincinnati, OH, for helping obtain permission from client Hobart

Leslie F. Schwartz, director, public relations, Mount Sinai Medical Center, New York, NY, for permission

Erica Shaffer, actor, Culver City, CA, for approval

Zelda Shute, executive assistant with Springs Global US, Inc., Fort Mill, SC, for helping to secure permission and for locating original copies of the classic Elliot White Springs ads

David T. Smith, the Workshops of David T. Smith, Morrow, OH, for permission

Carol Stack, for permission to print her picture of Clancy and Duncan

Dennis St. Aubin, manager of auto crime initiatives, Insurance Corporation of B.C., Vancouver, B.C., for assistance with permission

Duncan Stauth, executive VP, St. Michael's Majors Hockey Club, Toronto, Canada, for permission

Cyd Strittmatter, actor, for returning my call and for approval

Jeremy "Troll" Subin, president and founder, The Yard Fitness Center, Hermosa Beach, CA, for permission

David Tarpenning, advertising professor, Gaylord College of Journalism and Mass Communication, University of Oklahoma, OK, for serving early on as a co-advertising humor enthusiast

Roy Trimble, senior VP and executive creative director, JWT, Atlanta, GA, for answering questions about the CDW "Empathy" campaign and for writing a terrific "Funny Business" piece

Ellis Verdi, president and cofounder, DeVito/Verdi, New York, NY, for assisting with permission

Emily Hope Webster, Acme Talent and Literary, Los Angeles, CA, for assistance with approval

Fritz Widaman, National Thoroughbred Racing Association, Lexington, KY, for granting permission

Rany Xanthopoulo, executive director, Breast Cancer Society of Canada, Sarnia, ON, for taking my permission request to her board of directors

Kent York, Northern Star Council, Boy Scouts of America, Saint Paul, MN, for permission

Introduction

ABOUT 20 years or so ago, someone first said that most of us see around 3,000 ads a day. A more accurate estimate (one with an actual verifiable source) puts the number at something closer to 500.[1] But however many it is, it's a pretty safe bet that behind one-third to one-half of all those ads are advertisers who optimistically think they're going to make us laugh.

It's not as though we don't appreciate the effort. The ads may be the only genuinely funny thing we see during a typical broadcast of *Saturday Night Live*. In fact, it's almost become cliché to mention that the majority of the viewers tuning into the Super Bowl say they're doing it mainly to see the commercials. It's probably no coincidence that something like 90 percent of the 30-second spots (recently selling for somewhere around $2.5 million apiece) are obvious attempts at being funny.

Most people enjoy funny TV ads so much, in fact, that several companies have even made a profit repackaging them as videos[2] or, more recently, delivering them on the Web.[3] Thousands of people went to TBS's Web page in 2005 to cast their votes for the year's funniest commercial, and TBS has recently gone online with a permanent Web site titled veryfunnyads.com.[4] In addition, more than three million viewers tuned in to TBS's *Funniest Television Commercials of 2005* special and saw CareerBuilder.com's "Working with Monkeys" ad (featuring a human office worker employed with a bunch of chimpanzee coworkers) take first place. There seems little doubt the use of humor in advertising is popular, prevalent, and growing.

Why do U.S. advertisers spend what probably amounts to between $20 and $60 billion (yes, that's *billion!*) a year trying to make us laugh?[5] Surveys of advertising agency executives show they generally believe, among other things, that humor positively affects awareness for new products, establishes name registration, communicates simple copy points, and encourages brand switching. But more than anything else, advertisers hope humor will attract our attention and keep us from ignoring their ads.

Discouraging our page flipping, dial turning, channel surfing, and TiVo-ing helps explain almost all the earliest uses of humor and its especially widespread use in today's cluttered media. The continuing predominance of funny ads in most of the major remaining large-audience media spectacles, such as the Super Bowl and the Academy Awards, is a good example. In fact, this is one of those topics on which the advertising professional and academic researcher are in complete agreement. Many studies have shown that humor does a great job of attracting attention.

Advertisers also like to think being funny makes them seem more friendly and likable (and who doesn't?). Consequently, they believe that making us laugh will encourage positive thoughts and feelings toward their products and brands and put us in a receptive mood for their sales messages. In fact, advertisers in the 1970s often called humorous and other emotion-based ads "mood" advertising.

As with attention, researchers have found that positive feelings and attitudes toward an ad contribute to the likelihood we'll buy the product. A major study, with more than 15,000 subjects, found that our liking of an ad is a very strong predictor of the ad's ultimate sales success.[6] Advertisers also hope we'll see the entertainment value of their funny ads as a kind of reward for reading, watching, or listening.

But many advertisers agree there's a definite downside to the use of advertising humor. It seems to wear out quickly. It takes up time and space that could or should be devoted to selling. It can offend people. The ad can be remembered instead of the advertiser or message. But far worst of all, sometimes it simply isn't funny.

For every AFLAC, Geico, and Holiday Inn Express (successful advertising humorists all), there are many others like shoe marketer Just for Feet. Just for Feet's 1999 attempt at Super Bowl humor—in which a group of great white hunter-types drugged and then tagged a Kenyan distance runner with Nike shoes—was recognized by New York University's Department of Culture and Communication with a Schmio award for its racial insensitivity. The embarrassed company even tried to sue ad agency Saatchi & Saatchi Business Communications of Rochester, New York, for $10 million and malpractice—as if getting its client branded "Just for Racists" wasn't humiliating enough. The episode represents one of only two times that well-known advertising pundit Bob Garfield actually called advertisers before an ad ran to ask if they were aware of what a huge mistake they were about to make.[7]

Problems with advertising humor happen for lots of other reasons. Gilbert Gottfried sends some people scrambling for the TV remote (at least when he's not disguised as the AFLAC duck), and many others probably wish whoever killed Kenny would do the same thing to the people who produce the *South Park* TV show (at least actors Tom Cruise and Mel Gibson probably do). Which is just another way of recognizing that humor appreciation varies among different audiences. There's a reason why men howl at John Belushi's performance in *Animal House*, while most "chick flicks" have all the slapstick of a televised state funeral. Research consistently shows that men not only seem to appreciate humor more than women do but also definitely prefer different kinds of humor. Humor appreciation differs from culture to culture as well.

Advertisers have also long suspected that humor gets in the way of people remembering the information they want them to. Research supports this belief. During the 1990s, advertising researchers concluded that whether humor will work or not depends on lots of other factors, such as the type of product being advertised, the medium in which the ad appeared, program context, intensity of the humor, and whether the humor is related to the product or service in some relevant way.

The purpose of *Humor in the Advertising Business: Theory, Practice, and Wit* is to offer readers who study, create, approve, teach, or simply like to watch advertising a concise but thorough overview of the current state of knowledge about what advertising humor is and how it's believed to work. Humor is clearly a complicated topic, and no such summary and synthesis currently exists. In addition, if how advertising works has remained something of a mystery, adding explanations for the impact of humor suggests the problem could be next to hopeless. Fortunately, we have two places to go for help.

First, there are the collective rules of thumb and practical knowledge of the advertising professional, shared over the years in the pages of their biographies, advertising's many trade and professional journals, a survey or two, and the occasional proprietary study that manages to make its way into general circulation. Some advertising giants (and even a fair number of contemporary rank-and-file artists) seem to have figured humor out—as the many successfully funny examples presented in this book prove. And even if these creatively funny gurus often can't explain very well how they do it, watching an hour or so of TV on any given night shows they can consistently do it with a lot of success. Many of these advertising humorists share their thoughts and experiences throughout this book.

Second, many of the more puzzling aspects of humor in advertising have been explored and explained by the research findings of an army of scholars and researchers. Many advertising professionals, in fact, may be surprised to discover that the findings of typically academic researchers often confirm their own practical conclusions. Why surprised? Mainly because most advertising professionals don't spend much time with the academic literature on advertising. Which, of course, is mostly not their fault. Academic research is rarely written for a practitioner audience, and somewhere among the hypotheses, experimental designs, and structural equation models, all but the most masochistic nonacademic readers will decide the dog needs a walk.

Still, one freelance advertising copywriter was probably speaking for many when he recently observed that "unfortunately, there is little research on humor in advertising."[8] Not exactly! While this may have been true up until the early 1970s, today there's a large and growing body of research on advertising humor—nearly 50 studies published in scientific marketing and advertising journals between 1993 and 2005 alone. And these don't include many other nonadvertising books and articles produced by researchers and theorists in the fields of psychology, sociology, linguistics, education, and general communication. Many of these scholars have produced theories that not only stand up to rigorous empirical testing but have a lot of intuitive appeal as well.

This book, however, aims to be more than a dry, theoretical, and practical exploration of what advertising humor is and how it works. Readers who have chuckled or even laughed out loud at an advertiser's wit (and, really, who hasn't?) will find an homage here to what is probably the most widely appreciated form of sponsored communication. And although the many examples of funny ads in this book, almost all of which received top creative awards, were mainly chosen to illustrate certain types or characteristics of advertising humor, they definitely include many of the funniest ads and campaigns recently created by advertising's most gifted comedians.

Humor in the Advertising Business: Theory, Practice, and Wit is organized this way. Chapter 1 presents a history of advertising humor, exploring its evolution from creative outcast at the beginning of the last century to the popular workhorse it is today. Chapter 2 introduces a model of three theories or mechanisms that explain why we think some things are funny—incongruity-resolution, disparagement, and arousal-safety. This chapter explores what humor is, how we can recognize different kinds of humor, and how the humor in an ad can be related to the advertiser or product. Chapter 3 builds on Chapter 2 with a more thorough look at the mechanisms and the five types of funny ads they generate, with many award-winning examples of each from different advertising media.

Chapter 4 pulls together the theoretical and empirical knowledge of the academic researcher with the practical knowledge of the advertising professional, exploring in depth how and why humor in advertising is believed to work in various situations. Chapter 5 takes a slight detour by relating the topic of advertising ethics (no, not necessarily a contradiction in terms) with the long-standing question of whether or not humor is more likely to offend people than are other types of ads. Finally, Chapter 6 explores and interprets the commercial success of three funny advertising campaigns, using the concepts and principles from earlier chapters. Emphasized in this chapter are the message and media strategies that can lead to success when using humor in advertising.

So, now that you know where we're going and why, sit back, put your feet up, and let's explore the theory and practice of humor in advertising.

NOTES

1. Courtland L. Bovée and William F. Arens, *Contemporary Advertising*, 5th ed. (Homewood, IL: Irwin, 1995), 48.

2. "World's Funniest TV Commercials," 1990, 1991; "World's Funniest and Cleverest Commercials," 1989, 2004; "Leslie Nielsen's World's Funniest Commercials," 1994.

3. USATVADS.com; http://www.funnytvads.net (accessed March 18, 2004).

4. Find it at http://veryfunnyads.com.

5. Marc G. Weinberger, Harlan Spotts, Leland Campbell, and Amy L. Parsons, "The Use and Effect of Humor in Different Advertising Media," *Journal of Advertising Research* 35, no. 3 (1995): 44–56.

6. Russell Haley and Allan L. Baldinger, "The ARF Copy Research Validity Project," *Journal of Advertising Research* 31, no. 2 (1991): 11–31.

7. Bob Garfield, *And Now a Few Words from Me* (New York: McGraw-Hill, 2003).

8. Holger Enge, "Cockroach Farm," http://cockroachfarm.com (accessed March 16, 2004).

1

Historic Attempts at Advertising Humor

YOU can find humor in the print ads of the mid- to late 1800s, although you might not recognize it right off. Most of it looks quaint, if not downright strange, to our cynical and sophisticated twenty-first-century eyes. Advertisers occasionally used humor in the form of outrageous claims, limericks, slogans combined with "gag cartoons," and what critics of the day called a "flippant style of copy."[1] Advertisers also used what they apparently thought were hilarious racial and ethnic caricatures in their trade and show cards, such as the ones in Figures 1.1 and 1.2.[2] Historian Pamela Laird suggests the street criers of the latter nineteenth century gave advertisers another early option to use humor,[3] although advertising humor scholar Charles Gulas traces the earliest use of humor in sales messages even further back to the pub signs of sixteenth-century England.[4]

A little more familiar to us is the turn-of-the-century's mild, sentimental humor that often used illustrations of children. These early ads were designed to exploit what has been called "The Darlings!" reaction—"a phrase supposedly wrung from all normal women at the sight of such irresistible infants."[5] "Everyone," explained another writer, "has a tender spot for the children and likes to look at their pretty, innocent faces."[6] The Pears Soap ad in Figure 1.3 is a classic example of this warm and resonant humor.

But most of the serious-minded inventers of modern advertising—such as John E. Powers, Albert Lasker, John E. Kennedy, Claude Hopkins, and Ernest E. Calkins—rejected humor. Amuse and entertain buyers? What would

Figure 1.1 **This circa 1870s advertising trade card attempted to amuse with a racial stereotype. (Ad appears courtesy of Ben Crane, www.tradecards.com.)**

be the point of that? The smart advertiser would be better off if he (most early-twentieth-century advertisers were, of course, "he") stuck to the advice of influential advertising agent and pioneer George P. Rowell: "Be serious and dignified, but active and lively. Leave wit, however good it may be, entirely aside."[7]

Yet it's obvious that advertising humor is extremely popular among all kinds of advertisers and audiences today. Estimates of the use of humor range from 15 percent to as high as 46 percent in U.S. television advertising[8] and more than 30 percent in U.S. radio advertising,[9] with similar and even higher levels of use in other countries. Although humor doesn't appear to be quite as common in the print media, its use might range from 10 percent to as high as 20 percent in magazines[10] and up to 30 percent in outdoor advertising.[11]

How did this happen? What strange and twisting road did advertisers take to get from the belief that advertising was way too serious a business to allow for much levity to the belief that humor will work in situations as varied as creating awareness for financial services to reminding people that smoking causes lung cancer? This chapter presents a history of advertising humor that tackles this question. Its purposes are to explore how humor in advertising has been put to use, give us a sense of past successes and failures, and provide a historical context for the more in-depth explorations of humor you'll read later. Our goal is to understand how modern advertising got to where it is today—visibly dominated by successful (and frequently unsuccessful) attempts to make us laugh in the hope of making us buy.[12]

THE RATIONAL CONSUMER AND ATMOSPHERIC ADVERTISING: 1900–1917

Most historians agree that around 1900 was the beginning of what we consider "modern" advertising. Up to that point, advertisers mainly relied on either announcement advertising or the simple repetition of a product name and logo. But these techniques soon gave way to more persuasive efforts to sell, encouraged partly by the growing belief in "scientific advertising." About the same time, advertising agencies were taking over the job of writing copy, which, among other things, produced advertising that was much less product focused and more consumer focused.

Advertising lore credits successful freelance copywriter and former Canadian mounted policeman John E. Kennedy in 1904 or 1905 (the actual date seems to

Figure 1.2   Another in the St. Louis Beef Canning Co. campaign. (Ad appears courtesy of Ben Crane, www.tradecards.com.)

be in dispute) with the persuasion-oriented "salesmanship-in-print" approach. The story goes that Kennedy got a job at the Lord & Thomas agency by sending a note up to the main office from a saloon on the building's first floor. In his note, which was intercepted by junior partner and future advertising great Albert Lasker, Kennedy promised to reveal "what advertising is." You can see a reproduction of this famous note at the Center for Interactive Advertising Web site.[13]

Kennedy's belief that advertising could and should work as a surrogate salesman established once and for all that it should persuade as well as inform by giving consumers "reasons why" to buy a product. Advertising historians argue this influential "reason-why" school of advertising had actually been around for a while. For example, some suggest well-known copywriter John E. Powers—who

Figure 1.3   A major national advertiser tapped "The Darlings!" reaction with this warm, resonant humor from the 1890s.

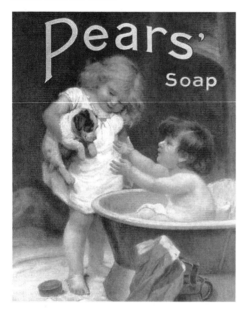

fathered the phenomenally successful and often imitated "Wanamaker-style" of advertising—also practiced the reason-why approach at least a decade earlier. Still, Kennedy coined a term something like "salesmanship-in-print," it resonated with Lasker and other advertising leaders, and Kennedy's place in history was guaranteed.

But neither the earlier announcement approach nor the reason-why approach relied much on humor. During this period advertisers frequently told each other, and anyone else who would listen, that people were more likely to be persuaded by a dignified appeal to logic than by the much-despised flippancy.[14] Nobody made this point more clearly than Claude Hopkins, in what is probably the most famous anti–advertising humor claim: "Appeal for money in a lightsome way and you will never get it. People do not buy from clowns."[15]

But the dignified hard sell wasn't the only approach popular at the dawn of modern advertising. The influential, image-oriented "atmospheric" style of Theodore F. MacManus—featuring lavish illustrations and emotional appeals— directly contradicted the hard-sell reason-why approach. By 1910, many advertisers of high-end products, such as the newfangled automobile, were using MacManus's soft-sell approach. But there wasn't any place for humor in atmospheric advertising, either. It was designed to deliver elitist impressions of "effortless quality and class."[16]

With retail advertising stuck in the announcement past and brand advertising either rationally persuasive or artistically imposing, it's easy to see why most advertisers during this period had few positive things to say about humor. One common criticism, still heard today, was that humor could easily violate standards of good taste. This is one of the main reasons many advertisers of branded consumer products were unwilling to risk offending people by lowering themselves to what they called "vulgar" attempts to be funny.

A second common and related criticism of humor was that it was undignified. Articles and books written by advertisers during this period strongly suggest they were preoccupied with dignity to the point of being unhealthily obsessed. And why would that be? First, they were trying to get past their professional embarrassment over the patent-medicine and P. T. Barnum–inspired "bombast and ballyhoo" advertising of the late nineteenth century. Second, they were deeply devoted to enhancing the professional status of advertising, with law and medicine the kinds of examples they wanted to follow.[17] And the professions and professionals who practice them, they reasoned, are dignified.

Although the language used to express these feelings about dignified advertising seems curiously old-fashioned, the point is clear: "Don't sacrifice dignity to misapply humor in copy," as one advertiser said. "Coarse jokes and ribald jests and vulgar slang in advertisements are not likely to cause buyers to open their purses."[18] Sharing the thoughts of Hopkins, another similarly observed: "It's all right to be a clown if you're connected with a circus."[19]

These rejections of humor also seem to be related to a general negativity toward cleverness and novelty in general. Although early advertisers were enormously concerned about attracting attention to their ads, they generally felt novelty was the wrong way to do it. They worried that it would distract readers from the message and, worse yet, threaten the advertiser's dignity by being perceived as "insincere." These objections to humor, novelty, and cleverness are clear in an institutional ad

Figure 1.4   The influential Lord & Thomas agency makes its position on humor absolutely clear. (Ad appears courtesy of Lord & Thomas, now Draft FCB.)

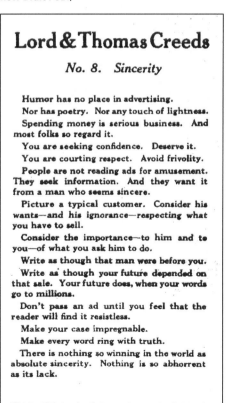

Lord & Thomas Creeds

No. 8.   Sincerity

Humor has no place in advertising. Nor has poetry. Nor any touch of lightness. Spending money is serious business. And most folks so regard it.

You are seeking confidence. Deserve it.

You are courting respect. Avoid frivolity.

People are not reading ads for amusement. They seek information. And they want it from a man who seems sincere.

Picture a typical customer. Consider his wants—and his ignorance—respecting what you have to sell.

Consider the importance—to him and to you—of what you ask him to do.

Write as though that man were before you. Write as though your future depended on that sale. Your future does, when your words go to millions.

Don't pass an ad until you feel that the reader will find it resistless.

Make your case impregnable.

Make every word ring with truth.

There is nothing so winning in the world as absolute sincerity. Nothing is so abhorrent as its lack.

This is the eighth of a series of business creeds to be published in Printers' Ink by Lord & Thomas. If you desire the set in card form address Lord & Thomas, Chicago, New York or Los Angeles

Figure 1.5   Jingles, like this one written by Earnest E. Calkins, eventually fell into disfavor because they "didn't sell."

(see Figure 1.4) for that prominent and influential bastion of the dignified hard sell, Chicago's Lord & Thomas agency, published in a 1916 issue of *Printers' Ink*.

But humor wasn't totally missing from advertising early in the twentieth century. Among a small handful of intentionally humorous ads were jingles and limericks—such as the hundreds written by Minnie Maude Hanff and Earnest E. Calkins for Force cereal (see Figure 1.5).[20] Their use, as well as other forms of "doggerel verse," was also related to increasing concerns advertisers had about attracting attention. As one advertiser said, "Whether they sold goods or not I cannot tell. But they surely performed the first function of the advertisement as we understand it—that of attracting attention."[21] But despite all this, it's important to point out that the use of limericks soon declined, repudiated even by Calkins, due to the belief they failed to sell products.[22]

Articles written by advertisers during this period also suggest the entertainment media were influencing their beliefs in favor of a less serious, lighter tone. This, of course, paved the way for the increasing use of humor. One advertiser proposed that "less dignity and more of the sort of jazz that enlivens the story pages of the magazine might not be amiss in the advertising pages."[23] Yet it's clear that even advertisers in favor of novelty, lighter copy, and limited humor never lost sight of what most advertisers agreed was the purpose of advertising—to make a sale. In the words of one innovative leader, "It's all right if your ads make people smile—provided also that they make them purchase from you."[24]

ENTERTAINING THE RABBLE: 1918–1940s

Advertising continued to become even more personal and consumer focused after World War I,[25] as advertisers concluded consumer behavior was less logical and more instinctive and nonrational than they had previously thought.[26] George Gallup's decisive research on advertising appeals and what people like to look at—which turned out to be the newspaper comics—supported advertisers' suspicions they were addressing a "tabloid" rabble that responded best to "unsophisticated, sensationalized, and frivolous entertainment."[27] The success of lowbrow publications such as *True Story Magazine* and the New York *Daily News* proved it beyond a doubt.

By the mid-1930s, influential advertisers, such as the president of the important N.W. Ayer & Son agency, were warning each other, "Remember that very few men are patient enough to untangle a heavy, involved or highly technical description of facts, however interesting the facts themselves might be."[28] The use of humor had become sufficiently common by 1922 to justify a freelance humorist's attempt to find new clients using a classified ad in *Printers' Ink* (see Figure 1.6). *Printers' Ink* was the most widely read advertising trade journal during the first half of the twentieth century.

But the hard-sell reason-why approach didn't fall completely from favor during this period, nor did its supporters change their minds about humor. Many advertisers continued to prefer the reason-why style and rejected impressionistic advertising. In 1925, the Lord & Thomas agency warned prospective clients against the excessive use of "cleverness" (see Figure 1.7).

Also, when the reason-why approach was adapted for radio a decade later by Frank Hummert, there was still little room for humor.[29] Like his mentor at the Lord & Thomas agency, Claude Hopkins, Hummert wouldn't use humor because he thought it would distract people from the message. As one historian summarized it, "The notable lack of humor in the Hummerts' serials can

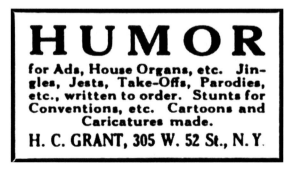

Figure 1.6   An early free-lance humorist advertises for clients.

Figure 1.7   This 1925 ad in *Printers' Ink* warned advertisers not to be too clever in their advertising. (Ad appears courtesy of Lord & Thomas, now Draft FCB.)

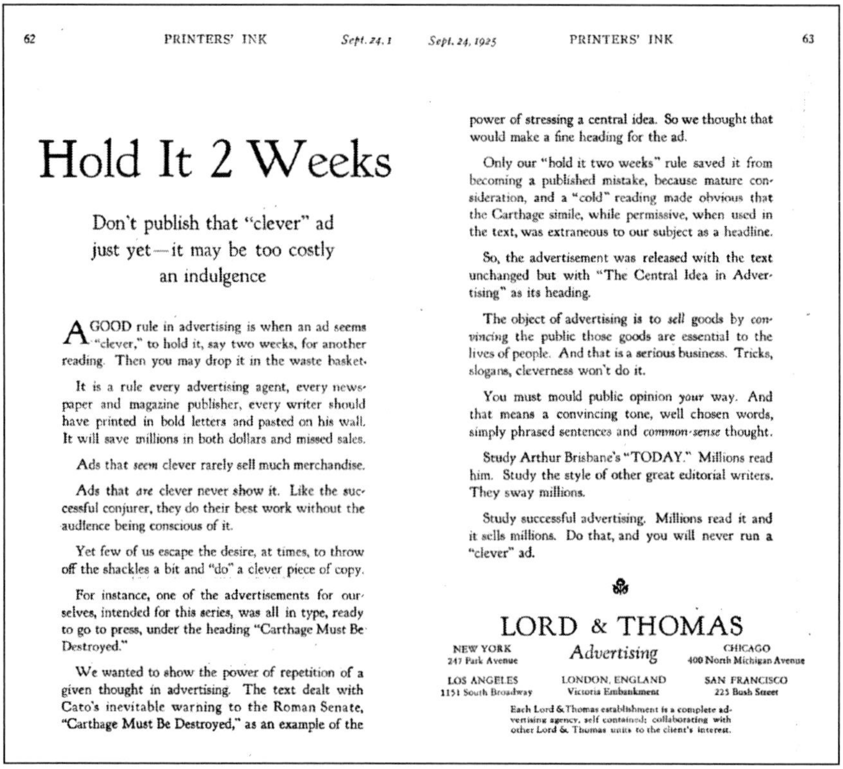

> 62   PRINTERS' INK   *Sept. 24, 1*   *Sept. 24, 1925*   PRINTERS' INK   63
>
> # Hold It 2 Weeks
>
> Don't publish that "clever" ad
> just yet—it may be too costly
> an indulgence
>
> A GOOD rule in advertising is when an ad seems "clever," to hold it, say two weeks, for another reading. Then you may drop it in the waste basket.
>
> It is a rule every advertising agent, every newspaper and magazine publisher, every writer should have printed in bold letters and pasted on his wall. It will save millions in both dollars and missed sales.
>
> Ads that *seem* clever rarely sell much merchandise.
>
> Ads that *are* clever never show it. Like the successful conjurer, they do their best work without the audience being conscious of it.
>
> Yet few of us escape the desire, at times, to throw off the shackles a bit and "do" a clever piece of copy.
>
> For instance, one of the advertisements for ourselves, intended for this series, was all in type, ready to go to press, under the heading "Carthage Must Be Destroyed."
>
> We wanted to show the power of repetition of a given thought in advertising. The text dealt with Cato's inevitable warning to the Roman Senate, "Carthage Must Be Destroyed," as an example of the
>
> power of stressing a central idea. So we thought that would make a fine heading for the ad.
>
> Only our "hold it two weeks" rule saved it from becoming a published mistake, because mature consideration, and a "cold" reading made obvious that the Carthage simile, while permissive, when used in the text, was extraneous to our subject as a headline.
>
> So, the advertisement was released with the text unchanged but with "The Central Idea in Advertising" as its heading.
>
> The object of advertising is to *sell* goods by convincing the public those goods are essential to the lives of people. And that is a serious business. Tricks, slogans, cleverness won't do it.
>
> You must mould public opinion *your* way. And that means a convincing tone, well chosen words, simply phrased sentences and *common-sense* thought.
>
> Study Arthur Brisbane's "TODAY." Millions read him. Study the style of other great editorial writers. They sway millions.
>
> Study successful advertising. Millions read it and it sells millions. Do that, and you will never run a "clever" ad.
>
> # LORD & THOMAS
> NEW YORK   *Advertising*   CHICAGO
> 247 Park Avenue   400 North Michigan Avenue
>
> LOS ANGELES   LONDON, ENGLAND   SAN FRANCISCO
> 1151 South Broadway   Victoria Embankment   225 Bush Street
>
> Each Lord & Thomas establishment is a complete advertising agency, self contained; collaborating with other Lord & Thomas units to the client's interest.

be attributed to reason-why advertising tenets. Reason-why proponents argued that humor, cleverness, or novelty might attract a listener or reader to an advertisement, but could not sell the product."[30] On the other hand, it's also important to recognize that Hummert and his contemporaries were among the first to hire comedians, such as Bob Hope and Jack Benny, to endorse products on the radio.[31] They seamlessly integrated entertainment and advertising, as they would later do on TV.

Although the majority of advertisers during this period were reluctant to abandon the reason-why approach, many others were experimenting with humor. As a result, they also began sharing some of the lessons they'd learned. For example, one business-to-business advertiser pointed out that making fun of your audience was probably a bad idea. "That's the 'catch' in it—if fun is to be had with anyone, let it be the customer, the rival in business, the advertiser himself—but never the person to whom the advertisement is addressed, save under propitious circumstances."[32] The same advertiser also pointed out that humor needed to be relevant, or related, to the product in some meaningful way. Many advertisers today agree with his position on the subject: "The purely irrelevant fun, dragged in by the heels to make a holiday of a headline, is certainly not good business."[33] See the sampling of current professional thought on the issue of relevance in Box 1.1.

The insecticide ad shown in Figure 1.8 represents an important trend in the use of humor that emerged during this period. Some advertisers were beginning to recognize that the reason-why approach might not work in every situation. As one advertiser said, "When dealing with a popular prejudice or superstition, for example, better results may be obtained by the use of gentle ridicule than by going after it with a club. This theory will doubtless be frowned upon among the more earnest thinkers, but there is a case in point."[34] The advertiser responsible for the Peterman's ad praised the campaign, noting that "humor made it possible to make even roach copy appealing, at least from a reading standpoint."[35]

Three other developments in professional thought during this period also help explain why advertisers were becoming more positive toward humor. First, and perhaps anticipating today's brand-image advertising, some advertisers proposed that advertising might accomplish something worthwhile without, if you can imagine, *selling at all*. As one advertiser wrote:

> For a reader doesn't necessarily buy a product because he remembers an advertisement. Nor is he necessarily sold by an advertisement because he remembers

---

Funny Business

Box 1.1. **KEEPING IT RELEVANT**

"Humor that *enhances* your selling message can be very effective. Humor that upstages or confuses your selling message is always disastrous." Hal MacDougall, vice chairman and chief creative officer, Christy MacDougall Mitchell Bodden, New York, NY

[What else would you like to tell me about humor?] "That the humor needs to be relevant to the product, to the audience and to the consumer/user of the product. Humor for humor's sake has no place in advertising." Peter Seronick, executive VP-creative, Allen & Gerritson, Watertown, MA

Figure 1.8 Peterman's used humor to make its roach powder advertising more appealing to female housekeepers in this 1927 ad (note the photo of dearly departed "Papa Roach" on the wall).

what product it advertised. He is sold and he buys because of the second re-
quirement of a good advertisement—that it make an impression, and a favorable one.[36]

The newspaper ad in Figure 1.9 for Van Dyk coffee is an early example of
advertising designed to do nothing more than produce favorable impressions.
As described in a *Printers' Ink* article about the campaign: "The jokes which appear in this campaign are run simply to produce smiles. There is no attempt to
have any one of them illustrate or suggest a sales point for Van Dyk coffee."[37]

Second, there's historical evidence that many advertisers were beginning to
recognize that the enjoyment of humor is a universal human trait.[38] As one of
them wrote, "Almost any person is susceptible to humor. It has an appeal which
is undeniably universal."[39]

Third, and as we saw in the previous period, the popular entertainment media were also having an influence on advertisers' decisions to use humor. As one
advertiser wrote, "Adventure, color and romance are taking their place in the best
sellers among books and magazines in place of the ultra-realistic stories of a few
years ago. This change in the character of words being written by the men who
appeal to the great masses, is, in my opinion, being reflected in the advertising
pages."[40] Another similarly observed, "The success of the comic strip in newspapers and of comedy acts in the movies, on the stage and over the air seemed to
this company to be convincing proof that nothing succeeds like laughter."[41]

Figure 1.9   This 1922 ad
shows that some advertis-
ers were aiming for posi-
tive brand impressions by
entertaining with humor.

It's hard to exaggerate the influence of cartoon and comic-strip advertising during the late 1920s and Depression years of the 1930s. As historian Roland Marchand points out, until then, advertisers had mainly rejected the comic-strip ad because it suggested frivolity and childish escape, and as we've already discussed, it also threatened dignity. All this changed with a comic-strip ad called "Suburban Joe" for General Foods Grape Nuts cereal. Advertisers, many outwardly embarrassed at their discipline's degeneration into frivolous entertainment, were soon responsible for a full-blown "comic-strip craze." Advertising space in Heart's Sunday *Comic Weekly* was selling for more than the *Saturday Evening Post* and *Ladies' Home Journal*, and a typical issue of the *Post* itself "was carrying as many as three full-page comic-strip ads per issue and at least a half-dozen other ads with balloons, sequence pictures, or other derivatives of comic-strip technique."[42]

The classified ad in Figure 1.10 from a 1927 issue of *Printers' Ink* shows that the use of both humor and cartoons had become sufficiently common to merit a freelance cartoonist's advertising of his talents.

Successful work for the Flit-gun by Theodor ("Dr. Seuss") Geisel led to a new client, the Chilton Pen Company, Inc., and a feature story in *Printers' Ink*. Chilton had hired Dr. Seuss to replace their traditional, nonhumorous advertising ("Formal, serious pictures illuminated formal, serious text") with humorous advertising of the type shown in Figure 1.11.[43] You can see many other Dr. Seuss ads, part of the Mandeville Special Collections Library at the University of California, San Diego, on the Web.[44] The comic-strip ad for two

Figure 1.10   A cartoonist advertised his services to prospective clients using this 1927 ad in *Printers' Ink*.

Figure 1.11   Dr. Seuss had a successful career drawing humorous ads, like this one for Chilton Pens, 1937.

Lifebuoy products in Figure 1.12 (originally developed for Lever Brothers by the Rauthrauff and Ryan agency) is another example of the popular comic format of this period.[45]

At the end of the 1940s, the self-proclaimed expert on "the tease," Elliot White Springs, established a highly risqué approach to humor that pushed the period's envelope of propriety and changed the course of humor in advertising. Barely out of his teens when he left college and entered military service, Springs became a World War I hero and the fifth-highest-ranked U.S. flying

Figure 1.12 This Lifebuoy ad represents a popular comic format of the 1930s. (Ad appears courtesy of Unilever United States, Inc.)

ace.[46] At the age of 35, he inherited the job of running the family business, Springs Cotton Mills.

The prolific author of nine books and dozens of short stories, Springs wrote all the copy for the company's advertising. It was in 1946, according to Goodrum and Dalrymple,[47] that Springs took the first steps toward his revolutionary style of humor. The ads in Figures 1.13 and 1.14 are samples of Springs's style, which combined racy, humorous illustrations with sexy puns and double entendre headlines. More samples—which were enormously successful at obtaining high levels of recognition and recall from consumers (and equally high levels of righteous outrage from other advertisers and consumers alike)—can be found in Goodrum and Dalrymple's excellent illustrated advertising history. One of Springs's raciest ads—the infamous "A Buck Well Spent" in Figure 1.14—placed 69th on *Advertising Age*'s list of Top 100 Advertising Campaigns of the 20th Century.[48]

Figure 1.13   WWI hero Elliot White Springs invented this risqué brand of humor in the 1940s to advertise his family's brand. (Ad appears courtesy of Springs Global US, Inc.)

Figure 1.14   This Springs ad is one of the most famous of all time. (Ad appears courtesy of Springs Global US, Inc.)

USP AND THE CREATIVE REVOLUTION: 1950s–1960s

The war between hard-sell rationalists and soft-sell impressionists continued into the 1950s and 1960s. Rosser Reeves, possibly the most sanctimonious of the period's hard-sell advocates, argued that a *unique selling proposition* (USP) was the most important part of a successful advertising campaign. The roots of Reeves's USP can be found in Kennedy's salesmanship-in-print; Reeves, in fact, "mentored in the Hopkins 'reason-why' tradition."[49] Reeves's decree that "at all costs, admen should avoid the most dangerous word of all in advertising—originality"[50] seems nearly as strange to us as the old-timers' fanatical vendetta against novelty—and strikingly similar to it.

Advertising icon David Ogilvy also relied on Hopkins's reason-why school. His inspiration, though, came from the image tradition of MacManus and Rubicam as well.[51] Regardless, in Ogilvy's first book, published in 1964, he offered his now famous warning that advertisers should avoid humor because it sells poorly. Advertising humorist Stan Freberg's reference to the beginning of this period as the "ice age of humor in advertising" also seems pretty revealing.[52]

On the other hand, this period also saw advertising's creative revolution. Leo Burnett's approach emphasized the "inherent drama" of products and services and often relied on humor and "critters."[53] Other Reeves opponents "wanted advertising to charm, amuse and entertain, along with the sales pitch."[54] Similarly, Bill Bernbach's revolutionary Volkswagen advertising of the 1960s—produced by Bernbach and written and designed by Julian Koenig and Helmut Krone—often included humor. Famous ads for Ohrbach's department store, which Bernbach worked on closely with designer Paul Rand, featured puns and wordplay, reinforced by a quirky combination of photos, illustrations, and logotype. Their approach was often "a practical headline juxtaposed with a frivolous visual."[55]

During this period, other famous advertisers helped launch the creative revolution and established once and for all that one of its chief weapons would be humor. Stan Freberg (who had nicknamed Reeves "the dean of the Gastro-Intestinal School of Advertising"[56]) produced humorous ads for Chun King and Pacific Airlines; Howard Gossage (who attracted Freberg to advertising) wrote "light-hearted copy"[57] for Rover cars and Eagle shirts; and Mary Wells created famous and humorous ads for Alka-Seltzer and Braniff Airlines.[58]

As advertisers during this period moved more and more of their advertising away from print and radio to TV, they often mentioned that advertising should be interesting and entertaining as well as sell the product.[59] Many advertisers also continued to experiment with ways to use tactical humor with reason-why strategies. Advertising written and designed by copywriter and humorous book author Ed Zern for the Nash automobile represents an excellent example of this combination. A writer in *Printers' Ink* praised the advertising for being "a light approach that mixes humor with selling points that get across all of Nash's important advantages for outdoor sportsmen"[60] (see Figure 1.15).

More evidence that advertisers' use of humor is related to positive economic times and changing perspectives of their audiences comes from no less an authority than motivation research guru Ernest Dichter:

> The old bromide that the average intelligence age of the consumer is 12 has been discarded. Advertisers are secure and they feel they can indulge in some self-kidding. . . . And that little old consumer is happy about the possibilities of the future; he is living and laughing it up while letting off steam accumulated over the past 10 years. Thus, the gaiety of the times reflects itself in the advertising of the times.[61]

Figure 1.15   Humorous book author Ed Zern mixed humor and hard-sell copy points in this 1951 ad for the Nash Airflyte. (Ad appears courtesy of DaimlerChrysler Corporation.)

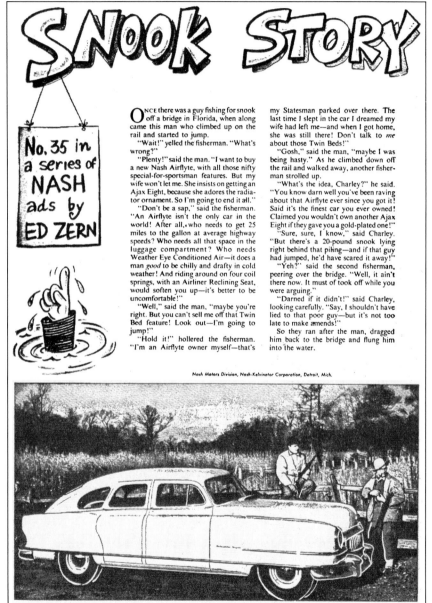

There Are 17 Nash Airflyte Models, in Three Great Series: The Ambassador, The Statesman and The Rambler.

By 1958, both events and writings suggest advertisers had become comfortable enough with the use of humor to bend their own rules. One early example of this was the *Alfred Hitchcock Presents* TV show. A writer described how one of the show's sponsors, Bristol-Myers, "allowed its commercials to be introduced over the CBS television network on Sunday evening prime time by a sardonic man who maligns the sponsor, insults the commercials, and chides the TV audience."[62]

Bristol-Myers wasn't the only Hitchcock sponsor whose commercials were insulted. But the show's consistently high ratings and the attention-getting value of Hitchcock's attacks apparently made the disparagement seem more tolerable. Ironically, a similar approach fell flatter than a three-day-old Pepsi 40 years later. Pepsico subsidiary Taco Bell couldn't run for the border fast enough after *Saturday Night Live* alum Dana Carvey premiered "The Taco Bell Dana Carvey Show" with a dancing taco and mission bell who sang: "We're paying him a fortune to use our name, 'cause he's a shameless whore!"

However, few, if any, advertising humorists in the 1950s and 1960s broke more rules than Stan Freberg—the self-styled "guerilla-satirist" of modern advertising. Freberg's classic campaign for Contadina Foods produced one of the most memorable and successful jingles of all time—"Who Puts Eight Great Tomatoes in That Little Bitty Can?" It also helped Contadina overtake a major competitor, while barely mentioning the product's name. Another Freberg campaign for Sunsweet Prunes ("Today the pits, tomorrow the wrinkles!") landed 63rd on *Advertising Age*'s list of the Top 100 Advertising Campaigns of the 20th Century.[63] Descriptions of many other similar breakthrough ads and campaigns can be found in Freberg's very readable autobiography, *It Only Hurts When I Laugh*.

BACK TO THE BASICS AND RINEY GOES SOFT: 1970s–1980s

By the early 1970s, the creative revolution was "dead, kaput,"[64] and in the latter half of the 1970s and throughout the 1980s, the hard-sell and soft-sell schools coexisted with the reason-why approach in a new form—positioning.[65] Some suggest advertising in the 1970s went "back to the 1950s hard-sell style,"[66] influenced partly by, once again, economic recession and changing perspectives of the audience. One writer in *Printers' Ink* (renamed *Marketing Communications* for the final few years of its publication) described the trend this way: "Turned off to today's consumer products is what's happening with many members of the younger set. . . . This generation, 'The Basics,' wants to know exactly what is in a product before buying it—more so than any previous generations."[67]

The Hopkins-influenced side of David Ogilvy caused him to exclaim, "Today, thank God, we are back in business as salesmen instead of pretentious entertainers. The pendulum is swinging back our way—the Hopkins way."[68] Yet, by the time he published his second book in 1985, Ogilvy revealed his soft side again and that he had changed his mind about humor.

> Conventional wisdom has always held that people buy products because they believe them to be nutritious, or labor-saving, or good value for money—not because the manufacturer tells jokes on television. . . . I think this was true in Hopkins' day, and I have reason to believe that it remained true until recently, but the latest wave of factor-analysis reveals that humor can now sell.[69]

There were also signs of another creative revolution in the 1980s, with the increasing use of emotional appeals, image advertising, and, of course, humor. The continuing influence of the Gossage tradition is evident in the work of agencies headed by Hal Riney; Jeff Goodby, Andy Berlin, and Rich Silverstein; and Dan Wieden and David Kennedy.[70]

Surprisingly, writings about humor in advertising's trade publications declined during this period. One of the few that appeared was written by influential copywriter John Caples, who began his career as a copywriter in 1925. Caples's status as an advertising legend was assured, also in 1925, when he wrote one of the most famous ads of all time for client U.S. School of Music (the ad placed 45th on *Advertising Age*'s list of the Top 100 Advertising Campaigns of the 20th Century): "They laughed when I sat down at the piano. But when I started to play . . ." In a 1975 piece summarizing his "Rules for Advertising," rule 18 states: "Avoid humor. You can entertain a million people and not sell one of them."[71]

Other statements about humor during the period, however, are generally positive and link humor with the belief that it humanizes advertising and possibly the sponsor as well. "Humor needs to come out of human interest—not from vaudeville, not from slapstick, not from sophomoric jokes, not from Madison Ave. 'in' jokes, not from slob characters."[72] Freberg expressed the same notion in the following way: "If a company does a funny spot, it's obviously not taking itself too seriously, right? It must have a good product or else it couldn't afford to kid around. That's the theory."[73]

In the 1980s, Hal Riney's influential soft sell often relied on humor, yet it was generally wry and understated, serving primarily to evoke a mood.[74] Riney's use of humor is related to his rejection of the hard sell.

We're asking advertising to depend too much on the rational, and much less, or not at all, on the effective element of our business, which is emotion. The rational element is often merely what people use to justify emotional decisions. Knowing when and how to use emotion is the most important part of an advertising person's job.[75]

The first "sneaker wars" peaked in 1990 with a Wieden + Kennedy–produced Reebok ad that was supposed to be aggressively funny but also foreshadowed where funny advertising was going to go in the next decade. The ad showed two bungee jumpers leaping from a bridge. The one wearing Reebok "Pump" shoes has a successful jump. The other, wearing Nikes, presumably falls to his death on the rocks below. The point, apparently, was that jumper number two should have thought that footwear decision over a little more carefully. According to a trade article written at the time, this attempt at advertising *humor noire* backfired, and Reebok stopped running it after parents complained.[76]

As in earlier periods, advertisers acknowledged that the entertainment media influenced their use of humor. As one advertiser said, "Television has changed mass communication more than most people realize. You can look at the guy when he's saying it and see if there is a smile on his lips or a twinkle in his eye. And the visual situation may have a human interest humor all its own that the printed word cannot easily convey."[77] Freberg made the connection more directly: "Why not make the sponsor's message as interesting as the show itself?"[78] Still, Freberg sounded conspicuously similar to earlier critics of atmosphere when he also observed that advertising, as an art form, doesn't make a worthwhile contribution unless it "succeeds at the point of sale or has solved some marketing problem."[79]

ADVERTISING HUMOR GETS AGGRESSIVE: 1990s–2000s

Advertisers in the 1990s often said they were worried about advertising's effectiveness, and the century-old debate between hard and soft sell continued. The 1990s version of the debate has been described as a basic disagreement between those who believe advertising should directly sell "by giving consumers just the facts" and those in favor of building "an emotional bond between consumers and brands that goes beyond product attributes."[80]

Advertisers often discussed humor in the pages of their trade magazines and journals during this final period. By this time, several earlier conclusions about the use of humor in advertising had become widely accepted. The belief that everybody, to a certain extent, enjoys humor was clearly made by a creative director for Leo Burnett Worldwide: "Comedy is kind of a universal language. It's a way to get everybody who's watching to sort of engage with your brand."[81] Advertisers also frequently mentioned the belief that humor can attract attention and create a positive mood. According to a commercial film editor, "Make people laugh and they like you. If people like you, they pay attention, and attention is what advertisers are paying for."[82]

As we saw during earlier periods, advertisers in the 1990s argued that they should adapt their use of humor to changing societal factors, such as "the mood of the times and the economy in general."[83] The president of the W.B. Doner & Co. agency stated this belief in the following way:

> Humor is what we took in 1929, during two world wars, Korea, Vietnam and the recession of the 70s. And it's what we will take today. We in the business of selling will employ humor or we'll run the risk of driving consumers to dejection and depression, and away from our products and our stores.[84]

This theme became especially apparent after the terrorist attacks of September 11, 2001. And perhaps like *Saturday Night Live* executive producer Lorne Michaels and his cast, advertisers may have been waiting for New York mayor Rudy Giuliani's declaration that it was okay to start being funny again, which he did on the show's October 1, 2001, broadcast.

As the chairman of one of the country's largest advertising agencies wrote in an *Adweek* column about the same time: "Given the current mood, now is the time to prove as never before that advertising that sells can also celebrate humanity and mutual affirmation. And that humor, the great sales tool of the ages, does not have to be coarse. It just has to be funny."[85] The CEO of the Doner agency similarly explained the decision to continue with a funny advertising campaign for PNC Financial Services Group shortly after 9/11, noting that the campaign's humor was "gentle" rather than "edgy."[86]

Other things advertisers said about humor after 9/11 were also consistent with earlier periods regarding inappropriate humor. Many advertisers predicted the attack would especially affect the use of aggressive humor. For example, a creative director for the Cliff Freeman & Partners agency described why a commercial for Mike's Hard Lemonade in which an ironworker falls off a building and is impaled on a huge spike wouldn't be seen again. "There are certain things you just don't want to go near now."[87]

TV commercials for Cliff Freeman & Partners client Outpost.com—in which gerbils are fired from a cannon or a pack of hungry wolves is turned lose on a high school marching band—are also examples of the kind of aggressive humor that began appearing in the late 1980s and that has become especially prevalent in today's advertising. Even more recent examples are the award-winning TV spots shown in Figures 1.16 (titled "Coverage") and 1.17 (titled "Dressed for Dinner"). Created in 2001 for JC Advertising client Yard Fitness and produced by Backyard Productions, these are great examples of this period's aggressive humor. Although the ads' potential for causing offense is high (an issue we'll explore in greater depth in Chapter 5), their popularity is undeniable. Exposure via e-mail, TV shows featuring funny ads, and Web site links have no doubt far surpassed the original media buys. You can see these hilarious ads online at www.backyard.com (follow the links to the work of director Kevin Smith).

Many advertisers, however, believed the effects of 9/11 on humor would be short term—and they were clearly right. As summarized by one writer, "According to a number of top creative directors asked to appraise the state of advertising creativity at the six-month anniversary of the terror attacks, comedy came back faster

Figure 1.16 A basketball player (played by actor Corey Blake) is comfortable in his own skin. (Ad appears courtesy of Backyard Productions and The Yard.)

than initially imagined."[88] In fact, many Super Bowl XXXVI ads, only a few months after 9/11, were intentionally funny,[89] although most of the humor had "softened edges."[90] By Super Bowl XXXVIII, aggressive humor had possibly exceeded its pre-9/11 levels.[91]

Other writings on the topic of humor during this period were also consistent with those from earlier periods. For example, observations about the relationship between advertising and entertainment reveal the continuing belief that some advertising needs to be entertaining in order to be effective. An executive vice president and creative director for BBDO New York observed that humor is "a good way to get people to let their guard down and enjoy the story rather than feeling something is being shoved down their throat."[92] Another advertiser made a similar point: "If there was ever a time when advertising and entertainment needed to converge, it's now. . . . With 'their worst nightmare' on their minds, we need to entertain to break through. Ads that entertain are like oxygen: a moment to breathe, a release from the events of the day."[93] Box 1.2 offers a sampling of current thought about humor and its entertainment value.

As in earlier periods, writers linked the characteristics of advertising humor with those of the entertainment media. "Almost by instinct we follow the lead of events and entertainment," one

Figure 1.17   Dinner guests are greeted by friends who are comfortable in their own skins. (Ad appears courtesy of Backyard Productions and The Yard.)

advertiser wrote.[94] Another advertiser proposed the aggressive humor of this period was influenced by earlier *Saturday Night Live* ad parodies.[95] The frequent use of extreme "frat boy" humor in the latter part of the 1990s has been attributed to MTV and youth-oriented films such as *Scary Movie*.[96]

Funny Business

Box 1.2. **HUMOR AND ENTERTAINMENT**

"Humor is entertaining. In a world of clutter, you must entertain before you educate." Arnie DiGeorge, creative director, R&R Partners, Las Vegas, NV

"The average consumer just wants to be entertained. Full-stop." Mark Tutssel, regional director creative (North America), Leo Burnett USA, Chicago, IL

"Humor is a form of entertainment and works not only to keep consumers from changing channels, but also help them remember the advertiser. If the advertisement is funny enough for people to talk about, you just got a lot more for your money." Steve Slais, cocreative director, Kupper Parker Communications, Inc., Saint Louis, MO

Finally, and quite appropriately, advertisers during this period expressed concerns similar to their predecessors about the effective use of humor and whether it's consistent with the goals of advertising. Stan Freberg often made this point, with statements such as: "Just to keep people from zapping you is not reason enough to do something that is totally irrelevant to what you're selling."[97] Referring to humorous TV commercials for Rice Krispies Treat Bars, the director of the commercials noted: "We didn't do this work just to have fun. . . . We did it to execute a *business* [italics in original] objective, which was to appeal to teens and become a relevant brand in their lives."[98]

SO HOW DID WE GET HERE?

During the first decade or so of the past century, the majority of U.S. advertisers were committed to rational advertising appeals with a serious and dignified tone that were delivered to a likewise serious-minded audience. Or at least that's what they said when they talked about their beliefs. Humor should be avoided, they argued, because it was undignified and often in poor taste—a painful reminder of the "humbug" entertainment and patent-medicine advertising of the previous century.

Humor was also seen as inconsistent with what was believed to be effective advertising—that which sells products directly. The criticism that "humor doesn't sell" continued throughout the twentieth century. So how did advertising end up where it is today—delivering a near-constant barrage of jokes, puns, pratfalls, and sentimental comedy?

It seems clear that humor became increasingly acceptable to early advertisers as they worried more and more about attracting attention. They eventually convinced each other that attention-getting advertising would have to be less dignified, lighter, original, clever, novel, and, yes, even funny. That humor is a great way to attract attention was mentioned frequently and consistently by advertisers throughout the twentieth century.

This chapter's history offers other clues to why humor has become so prevalent in today's advertising. Professional thought in favor of humor evolved along with (1) the more frequent use of emotional appeals of all kinds; (2) the changing perspectives of audiences and their characteristics (from serious, dignified buyers to lowbrow sensation seekers); (3) the recognition that advertising might help achieve marketing objectives other than selling products directly; (4) the rediscovery that advertising should, in certain situations, entertain; (5) the changes in the content and tone of the entertainment media; (6) the emergence of the broadcast media, first radio and then TV; and (7) the slowly evolving belief that humor and novelty need not necessarily be distracting if they are related somehow to the product and its uses.

And it wouldn't do to ignore the unique and influential role cartoons and comics played in the history of advertising humor. Consistent with Gallup's finding that people prefer to read cartoons and comics, their use encouraged the more frequent (if not entirely respectable) use of humor during the 1920s and 1930s. It shouldn't be surprising that the emergence of the broadcast media also paved the way for even more humor. Surveys of advertising agency executives and creative gurus consistently show that radio and TV are believed to be the media best suited for funny ads.[99] Consequently, it's also no surprise to find the use of humor is highest in these media.

Although humor is often linked with emotional appeals and the soft sell, it's interesting to note that advertisers as early as the 1920s were combining tactical humor with rational, reason-why-style selling points. This discovery is consistent with survey research (which you'll read much more about in Chapter 4) that shows contemporary advertisers believe humor can enhance the recognition and recall of simple copy points. It also helps explain another unexpected discovery. Despite the professional taboo that business-to-business advertisers should avoid humor, among the earliest uses of humor was in ads targeting trade and business audiences. The use of humor in this type of advertising was found throughout the last century.

Now that we've learned how and why humor in advertising has become so popular, we're ready to look more closely at how theorists and researchers in such diverse fields of study as advertising and linguistics believe it works. That's the subject of Chapter 2.

NOTES

1. Frank Presbrey, *The History and Development of Advertising* (Garden City, NY: Doubleday, 1929).

2. Ben Crane, "The Trade Card Place," http://www.tradecards.com (accessed March 16, 2004).

3. Pamela Laird, *Advertising Progress: American Business and the Rise of Consumer Marketing* (Baltimore, MD: Johns Hopkins University Press, 1998).

4. "Gulas Co-Authors Book on Humor in Advertising," *Dialogue: A Newsletter for Wright State University*, http://www.wright.edu (accessed March 10, 2006).

5. Frank Rowsome, Jr., *They Laughed When I Sat Down: An Informal History of Advertising in Words and Pictures* (New York: McGraw-Hill, 1970), 76.

6. Merle Curti, "The Changing Concept of 'Human Nature' in the Literature of American Advertising," *Business History Review* 41 (Winter 1967): 335–357, 342.

7. George P. Rowell, cited in Presbrey, *The History and Development of Advertising*, 276.

8. Cordruta Catanescu and Gail Tom, "Types of Humor in Television and Magazine Advertising," *Review of Business* 22, no. 1/2 (2001): 92–96; J. Patrick Kelly and Paul J. Solomon, "Humor in Television Advertising," *Journal of Advertising* 4, no. 3 (1975): 31–35; Dorothy Markiewicz, "The Effects of Humor on Persuasion" (PhD diss., Ohio State University, 1972); Paul S. Speck, *On Humor and Humor in Advertising* (PhD diss., Texas Tech University, 1987); Mark F. Toncar, "The Use of Humour in Television Advertising: Revisiting the US-UK Comparison," *International Journal of Advertising* 20, no. 4 (2001): 521–540; Marc G. Weinberger and Harlan Spotts, "Humor in U.S. versus U.K. TV-Advertising," *Journal of Advertising* 18, no. 2 (1989): 39–44.

9. Marc G. Weinberger and Leland Campbell, "The Use and Impact of Humor in Radio Advertising," *Journal of Advertising Research* 31 (December–January 1991): 44–52.

10. Lynette S. McCullough and Ronald K. Taylor, "Humor in American, British, and German Ads," *Industrial Marketing Management* 22, no. 1 (1993): 17–29; Marc G. Weinberger, Harlan Spotts, Leland Campbell, and Amy L. Parsons, "The Use and Effect of Humor in Different Advertising Media," *Journal of Advertising Research* 35, no. 3 (1995): 44–56.

11. Mukesh Bhargava, Naveen Donthu, and Rosanne Caron, "Improving the Effectiveness of Outdoor Advertising: Lessons from a Study of 282 Campaigns," *Journal of Advertising Research* 34, no. 2 (1994): 46–55.

12. Portions of this chapter previously appeared in Fred Beard, "One Hundred Years of Humor in American Advertising," *Journal of Macromarketing* 25, no. 1 (2005): 54–65. ©2005 Sage Publications.

13. ciadvertising.org, "John E. Kennedy: Advertising Copywriter," http://www.ciadvertising.org/studies/student/96_fall/kennedy/JEKennedy.html (accessed March 16, 2006).

14. Curti, "The Changing Concept of 'Human Nature,'" 338.

15. Claude Hopkins, cited in Rowsome, *They Laughed When I Sat Down*, 138.

16. Stephen Fox, *The Mirror Makers: A History of American Advertising and Its Creators* (New York: Vintage, 1984).

17. Laird, *Advertising Progress*; Roland Marchand, *Advertising the American Dream: Making Way for Modernity, 1920–1940* (Berkeley: University of California Press, 1985); Richard W. Pollay, "The Subsiding Sizzle: A Descriptive History of Print Advertising, 1900–1980," *Journal of Marketing* 49 (Summer 1985): 24–37; Rowsome, *They Laughed When I Sat Down*.

18. "Editorial," *Printers' Ink* 45, no. 11 (1903): 34.

19. John S. Grey, "The Crude in Advertising," *Printers' Ink* 63, no. 12 (1908): 35.

20. Earnest E. Calkins, *And Hearing Not* (New York: Scribner, 1946).

21. J. W. Schwartz, "About Jingles," *Printers' Ink* 34, no. 7 (1901): 16.

22. Daniel Pope, *The Making of Modern Advertising* (New York: Basic, 1983).

23. Frank H. Williams, "Copy Writers, Won't You Please Liven Up?" *Printers' Ink* 107, no. 9 (1917): 45–47.

24. "Editorial," *Printers' Ink*, reprint from *White's Sayings* 38, no. 10 (1902): 10.

25. Laird, *Advertising Progress*; Marchand, *Advertising the American Dream*.

26. Curti, "The Changing Concept of 'Human Nature.'"

27. Fox, *The Mirror Makers*.

28. Wilfred W. Fry, "Why Advertising Must Have Human Approach," *Printers' Ink* 275, no. 7 (1935): 40.

29. Fox, *The Mirror Makers*; William Meyers, *The Image-Makers: Power and Persuasion on Madison Avenue* (New York: Times Books, 1984).

30. Meyers, *The Image-Makers*, 122.

31. Meyers, *The Image-Makers*.

32. A. L. Townsend, "How to Use Humor in Advertising to the Dealer," *Printers' Ink* 125, no. 3 (1923): 81–88.

33. Townsend, "How to Use Humor," 88.

34. John P. Wilder, "Fighting a Trade Bogie with Ridicule," *Printers' Ink* 120, no. 1 (1922): 87–88.

35. J. T. O'Connor, "Liven Up That Technical Copy with a Little Humor," *Printers' Ink* 140, no. 7 (1927): 10.

36. W. J. Weir, "Sir Veigh, Ad-Critic," *Printers' Ink* 170, no. 9 (1935): 19–24.

37. "Advertising Coffee with a Joke a Day," *Printers' Ink* 152, no. 11 (1930): 103.

38. Viktor Raskin, *Semantic Mechanisms of Humor* (Boston: Reidel, 1985), 2.

39. Townsend, "How to Use Humor," 84–86.

40. Roy Dickinson, "An Idea Plus Romance as a Copy Formula," *Printers' Ink* 145, no. 9 (1928): 5, 73–76.

41. "Advertising Coffee," 103.

42. Marchand, *Advertising the American Dream*, 115.

43. "It's a Real Pen Name Now," *Printers' Ink* 181, no. 2 (1937): 24–26.

44. The Dr. Seuss Collection, Mandeville Special Collections Library, http://orpheus.ucsd .edu/speccoll/seusscoll.html.

45. John W. Hartman Center for Sales, Advertising & Marketing History, Duke University Rare Book, Manuscript, and Special Collections Library, Ad*Access On-Line Project, Ad #BH0966, http://scriptorium.lib.duke.edu/adaccess (accessed February 12, 2004).

46. "Legacy of Leadership: Elliott White Springs," My ETV, http://www.myetv.org (accessed February 21, 2007).

47. Charles A. Goodrum and Helen Dalrymple, *Advertising in America: The First 200 Years* (New York: Abrams, 1990).

48. "The Advertising Century," AdAge.com, http://www.adage.com/century/campaigns.html (accessed February 13, 2006).

49. Ann Maxwell, "From Advertising to Marketing," in *Advertising and the Business of Brands*, eds. Bruce Bendinger and Jim Avery (Chicago: The Copy Workshop, 1999).

50. Rosser Reeves, cited in Fox, *The Mirror Makers*, 193.

51. Maxwell, "From Advertising to Marketing."

52. Stan Freberg, *It Only Hurts When I Laugh* (New York: Times Books, 1988), 272.

53. Fox, *The Mirror Makers*.

54. "Ad Pioneer Reeves, 73, Dies; Proponent of Hard Sell, USP," *Advertising Age* 55, no. 4 (1984): 4, 84.

55. Maxwell, "From Advertising to Marketing," 75.

56. "Ad Pioneer Reeves, 73, Dies," 4.

57. "How Humor Wins Reader Response," *Printers' Ink* 275, no. 7 (1961): 40.

58. Maxwell, "From Advertising to Marketing."

59. "Local Ham Jousts National Brands on TV," *Printers' Ink* 267, no. 4 (1959): 53.

60. Edward J. Dever, "Humor Mixed with Facts Sells General Product to Special Market," *Printers' Ink* 237, no. 5 (1951): 53–54, 58.

61. N. Keline, "Tongue-in-Cheek Ads: New Copy Craze," *Printers' Ink* 254, no. 3 (1956): 28–30.

62. "Bristol-Myers' Alfred Hitchcock: His 'Personality' Sells What He Derides," *Printers' Ink* 264, no. 3 (1958): 63–68, 63.

63. "The Advertising Century" AdAge.com, http://www.adage.com/century/campaigns.html (accessed February 13, 2006).

64. Jerry Della Femina, "The Death of the Creative Revolution," *Marketing Communications* 299, no. 2 (1971): 16.

65. Al Ries and Jack Trout, *Positioning: The Battle for Your Mind*, rev. ed. (New York: McGraw-Hill, 1981).

66. Maxwell, "From Advertising to Marketing," 84.

67. Ted Angelus, "New Product Payout," *Marketing Communications* 299, no. 1 (1971): 51–52.

68. David Ogilvy, cited in Maxwell, "From Advertising to Marketing," 84.

69. David Ogilvy, *Ogilvy on Advertising* (New York: Vintage, 1985), 103.

70. Juliann Sivulka, *Soap, Sex, and Cigarettes* (Belmont, CA: Wadsworth, 1998).

71. John Caples, "50 Things I Have Learned in 50 Years in Advertising," *Advertising Age* 46, no. 38 (1975): 47–48, 48.

72. Harry Wayne McMahan, "So Funny It Ain't Funny: Sort of a Serious Look at Humor," *Advertising Age* 47, no. 37 (1976): 72.

73. Stan Freberg, cited in Cary Bayer, "A Laugh a Minute," *Madison Avenue* 25, no. 11 (1984): 100–110.

74. Joseph M. Winski, "He Swims against the Tide," *Advertising Age* 53, no. 18 (1982): M1–M6.

75. Hal Riney, cited in Winski, "He Swims against the Tide."

76. Michael McCarthy, "Rivals Scramble to Topple Nike's Sneaker Supremacy," *USA Today*, April 3, 2003, Money section, B1.

77. McMahan, "So Funny It Ain't Funny," 72.

78. Freberg, cited in Bayer, "A Laugh a Minute," 106.

79. Freberg, cited in Bayer, "A Laugh a Minute," 110.

80. Bob Kuperman, cited in Anthony Vagnoni, "Creative Differences," *Advertising Age* 68, no. 46 (1997): 1, 20, 28, 20.

81. Bob Akers, cited in Bill Dunlap, "Funny Business," *Shoot* 41, no. 31 (2000): 19–21, 20.

82. Angelo Valencia, "Cutting Sense of Humor," *Shoot* 42, no. 37 (2001): 4–5, 4.

83. Polly Devaney, "Cheerful Super Bowl Ads Mask a Deeper Malaise," *Marketing Week*, February 28, 2002, 36.

84. Herbert Fried, "Humor Is Our Best Tool," *Advertising Age* 62, no. 15 (1991): 26.

85. Keith Reinhard, "Now Is the Time," *Adweek* 42, no. 41 (2001): 12.

86. Tanya Irwin, "Doner Keeps Humor in PNC Ads," *Adweek* (Midwest edition, Chicago) 42, no. 44 (2001): 4.

87. Eric Silver, cited in Richard Linnett, "Ad Creativity Feels Pressure," *Advertising Age* 73, no. 36 (2002): 6.

88. Anthony Vagnoni, "Fear of Funny Abating," *Advertising Age* 73, no. 10 (2002): 8, 42.

89. Devaney, "Cheerful Super Bowl Ads Mask a Deeper Malaise."

90. Linnett, "Ad Creativity Feels Pressure," 6.

91. Tim Goodman, "Super Bowl Ads Strain for Cheap Laughs," *San Francisco Chronicle*, February 2, 2004, A2.

92. Bill Bruce, cited in Dunlap, "Funny Business," 19.

93. Steve Novick, "Advertising, Pure and Simple," *Advertising Age* 72, no. 46 (2001): 29.

94. Fried, "Humor Is Our Best Tool," 26.

95. Valencia, "Cutting Sense of Humor."

96. Scott Donaton, "No Laughing Matter: 'Frat-Boy' Humor Spreads into Advertising," *Advertising Age* 70, no. 47 (1999): 36; Dunlap, "Funny Business."

97. Stan Freberg, cited in Bob Garfield, "Freberg: Humor's No Laughing Matter," *Advertising Age* 63, no. 3 (1992): 52.

98. Jim Tozzi, cited in Dunlap, "Funny Business," 20.

99. Fred Beard, "Practitioner Views of Humor in Advertising: A Twenty-Year Update" (paper presented at the annual conference of the Society for Marketing Advances, Nashville, TN, November 2, 2006); Tom Madden and Marc G. Weinberger, "Humor in Advertising: A Practitioner View," *Journal of Advertising* 24, no. 4 (1984): 23–29.

2

Theoretically, What's So Funny?

*T*HE TV commercial opens with Dad on the phone. The voice-over tells us *he's ordering Domino's pizza and Cheesy Dots and that shortly he'll be spending some quality time with his son. The commercial cuts to the little monster in question, who's in the front yard spraying passersby with a garden hose. It cuts again to Mom and Dad, who are soberly observing this outrage from the living room window. Mom hands Dad some baseball equipment, and the voice-over tells us that Dad's quality time will include playing baseball with the monster—* lots and lots *of baseball.*

My wife and I look at each other. "What do you think the point of that was," she asks. We ponder. "I think they mean Mom and Dad have a real problem on their hands, and they hope Domino's pizza and an afternoon of playing catch can make up for years of neglectful parenting." But then the second question: "Do you think they were trying to be funny?" Sadly, I answer: "Yes, I do."

We should be clear up front that this cheesy (sorry!) ad is no great disaster for Domino's. It's nowhere as lame, for instance, as the Just for Feet "bag 'em and tag 'em" catastrophe described in the introduction to this book. It's not even a waste of money, as advertising goes. Domino's has Cheesy Dots, you can add some to your pizza order for only 99 cents, and what's not to like about pieces of baked pizza dough covered with Colby and Monterey Jack cheese? That's probably what Domino's executives had in mind when they or their advertising agency made the spot. Our real interest is in how Domino's journey from point A (let's make a funny ad) to point B (an actual funny ad) went so wrong. In other words, why should it have been funny, and why wasn't it?

What you'll find in this chapter are several theories that help explain why we think things are funny. We'll be using the model of advertising humor in Figure 2.1 as a roadmap. The model starts with three "classical" humor theories—incongruity-resolution, arousal-safety, and disparagement. I call them classical theories because of their extensive development and use across many fields of study. You'll also see them called *humor mechanisms* because they create (or *generate*) the characteristics or features of humor. This is important because we think about, or process, different kinds of potentially funny messages in different ways.

The theoretical mechanisms in Figure 2.1 are important for a couple of reasons. First, they show that the things we think are funny have definite identifiable characteristics. Second, these characteristics are consistent across almost all humorous situations and scenarios. Once you can recognize these characteristics and how they're related to each other, you can use them to understand why things, including ads, should be funny or not.

But just because a joke, funny story, or ad has these characteristics, it doesn't guarantee that it's going to be funny. There are what researchers call *boundary conditions* on the relationship between humor characteristics as a cause and funny as an effect. Two of the most important conditions are called *sufficiency* and *necessity*. Theoretically, the humor characteristics generated by the mechanisms might not be *sufficient* to cause humor, because a story, joke, or ad can have them and still not be funny. On the other hand, these theoretical characteristics are still useful and important because they are *necessary*—something simply can't be funny without at least one of them.

Figure 2.1   Humor mechanisms, humorous ad types, and relatedness.

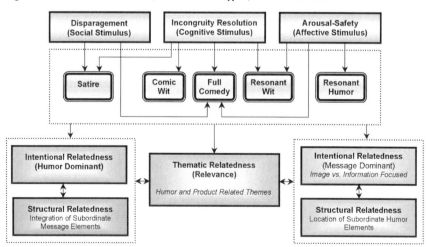

The model in Figure 2.1 shows that the three mechanisms work sometimes alone and sometimes together to generate the humor in five types of humorous ads—satire, comic wit, full comedy, resonant humor, and resonant wit. An advertising scholar named Paul Speck produced the original work on these funny ad types.[1] Research by advertising humor scholar Harlan Spotts and his colleagues also contributed substantially to our understanding of the model and these ad types.[2] Briefly, satirical ads are generated by a combination of the incongruity-resolution and disparagement mechanisms. These ads look a lot like satire when it's used in other forms of communication or entertainment and often involve an attack on somebody (criticism or a put-down). Comic wit ads, though, are generated entirely by the incongruity-resolution mechanism. They include jokes, parodies, visual or verbal puns, comic exaggeration, or just plain silliness. Full comedy ads are generated by all three mechanisms.

Resonant humor ads, on the other hand, are generated entirely by the arousal-safety mechanism. They often present warmly sentimental or mildly negative images or circumstances. When the emotional elements of a resonant humor ad are combined with an incongruous element (e.g., a pun, exaggeration, understatement, or punch line), we get a resonant wit ad. My colleague David Tarpenning and I decided to call these ads "resonant" because of the way they seem to resonate with people on an emotional level. Chapter 3 is devoted to looking at the five types of humorous ads generated by the three mechanisms in much greater depth, with award-winning examples of each.

Finally, the model presented in this chapter includes three types of advertising humor *relatedness*. The three mechanisms apply to humor in general, but relatedness is mainly a concern to those of us interested in advertising. The most important kind of relatedness, thematic relatedness, explains how the humor in an ad can be related somehow to the advertiser or the product being advertised.

Let's face it: Humor is complicated. So the theories that explain how it works are complicated, too. Still, to encourage you not to skip Chapter 2—or just look at the funny ads and not read the text—it comes with a guarantee. When you're finished, you'll be able to (1) identify different types of humor, (2) explain why most funny things are funny, and (3) understand how the humor in an ad can be related.

INCONGRUITY THEORIES

Some psychological theories propose that we often laugh when we see or hear something we don't expect.[3] For example, most of us will smile and maybe even chuckle at the unexpected sight of two dogs, one very large and one very small, posing for a picture together (see Figure 2.2). Just the difference, or *incongruity*, in size between these four-legged buddies is enough to produce a pleasantly mild arousal that we experience as humor. These theories are called *one-stage incongruity theories*. We *cognitively process* (or think about) the message in a single stage that includes three parts—interruption (what's that?), perceptual contrast (there's something incongruous and unexpected here!), and playful confusion (what's it mean?)."[4]

Other incongruity-*resolution* theorists argue that an unexpected or incongruous message or stimulus is not always enough by itself to be funny.[5] They agree with the incongruity theorists that humor begins when a single message simultaneously presents two elements that are normally incompatible. Incongruity-resolution theory, though, also says that the incongruous parts have to overlap in meaning in some way or have two meanings, both of which make sense. We think it's funny when a *punch line* suddenly (and often surprisingly) switches us from the first meaning to the second, making it possible to resolve the incongruity. These theories have been called *two-stage incongruity-resolution theories* because they add a second cognitive processing stage—the resolution of the confusing incongruity.

This popular playground joke shows how incongruity-resolution works:

Zoo visitor to zookeeper: "Excuse me, but can you tell me why gorillas have such big nostrils?" The first line of the joke is consistent with an expected zoological or physiological explanation or interpretation—perhaps their hubcap-size nostrils enable them to smell a bunch of bananas from some ridiculous distance?

Figure 2.2 Clancy and Duncan demonstrate incongruity humor. (Clancy and Duncan appear courtesy of Carol Stack.)

Zookeeper: "Yes, sir, it's because they have such big fingers." The first line of the joke is also consistent with a second, less expected, and incongruous meaning—that of gorillas as excessive nose-pickers—and the punch line switches us suddenly to that interpretation. At first, the answer in the punch line doesn't seem to *logically follow* the main idea in the question (which is, basically, what *incongruous* means). But as we puzzle over the playful confusion caused by the incongruity, we realize suddenly that it does (if we get the joke). It's the resolution of this incongruity—the *Ah ha!*—that produces the pleasurable psychological arousal and release that we experience as humor.

Incongruity-resolution theorists say we get two kinds of pleasure from a joke like this. The first is playful confusion caused by the incongruity all by itself (or stage one). The second kind of pleasure results from recognizing and mastering that confusion (or stage two).[6]

The psychological theories of incongruity and incongruity-resolution are very important in helping us understand why things are funny. They propose that almost everything we think is funny has an incongruity. The father of psychoanalysis himself, Sigmund Freud, argued that all humor is based on our ability to recognize similarities between dissimilar things.[7] But there's another piece of the incongruity puzzle that's still missing at this point. We have to consult a linguist to learn what it is.

A SEMANTIC THEORY OF INCONGRUITY HUMOR

One of the most influential nonpsychological humor theories (and one that has been used quite a bit in the study of funny advertising) is the *semantic script theory of humor* (SSTH) developed by Victor Raskin. Raskin's theory is a linguistic theory, but it works a lot like the psychological incongruity-resolution theories. Scientists like it when different theories, especially in different fields of study, point to the same conclusions. When that happens, it suggests someone is on the right track.[8]

Like the psychological theories, Raskin's linguistic theory proposes we'll find a joke or other potentially humorous message funny when the message itself (what linguists call a *text*) is fully or partially compatible with two opposite, or contrasting, situations or realities (what linguists call *scripts*). The SSTH also proposes that a punch line (or what Raskin calls a *trigger*) makes it possible for us to resolve the incongruity by switching us from the first, generally expected situation to the second, generally unexpected one.

The piece of the incongruity-resolution puzzle that Raskin's theory offers is that it explains how the two situations brought to mind by a single message can be opposites (or incongruous) from each other. These types of oppositeness not only help explain incongruity-based humor but give us a way to categorize it, too.

In Raskin's theory, all jokes or incongruously funny stories describe a "real" situation and an "unreal" situation. Not real in the sense of the "real world," but real in the context of the joke. For example, in the gorilla joke, the real situation is that there is no zoological explanation for the size of gorillas' nostrils—they're the way they are because gorillas spend a lot of time with their fingers in them. The unreal situation is that there's a zoological explanation for their large nostrils, and a zookeeper is the most likely person to be able to tell somebody what it is. Our recognition of the playful oppositeness between these two contrasting scripts or situations, combined with our knowledge about the kinds of unpleasant things we often see primates doing at the zoo, is what generates the humor in the joke.

But the point is that this real situation (in the context of the joke), although incongruous and unexpected, is also fully compatible with the text of the joke—Why do gorillas have such big nostrils? Incongruity happens when the contrasting situations are both at least partly compatible with the joke or story, and resolution happens when the trigger helps us recognize the oppositeness between the two situations. This is, of course, exactly what the psychological incongruity-resolution theorists say, too. This notion of real and unreal situations is also consistent with humor theorist D. H. Monro's observation that incongruity humor often consists of finding "the inappropriate within the appropriate."[9]

So what are the categories of oppositeness? According to Raskin, all such real versus unreal humorous opposites (or *contrasts*) fall into three categories: (1) actual situations versus nonactual, nonexisting situations; (2) normal, expected situations versus non-normal, unexpected situations; and (3) possible situations versus fully or partially impossible situations.

Actual versus Nonactual Contrasts

According to Raskin, if the blanks in the following statement can be filled in with two opposing statements involving the characters or the actual setting of the joke, then it's an actual versus nonactual contrast: *It is the case that _____, and it is not the case that _____*. This is easiest to see if we're talking about puns or other forms of wordplay. For example, a Conoco/Phillips 66 gasoline billboard recently punned, "We fight dirty." In the context of this joke, the *actual* (or real) situation is that its gas fights dirty buildup in car engines. The *nonactual* (and not real) situation is that Conoco/Phillips 66 fights engine buildup in a not entirely fair or sporting way. Or, and using Raskin's statement, *it is the case that* Conoco/Phillips 66 fights engine buildup, *and it is not the case that* it fights others in a way that's unsportsmanlike.

Normal versus Non-normal Contrasts

The second type of Raskin contrast, normal versus non-normal, describes contrasting situations in which one script is normal and expected and the other is abnormal and unexpected, but still true or factually possible (or based in *reality*). The TV spot for Sprint Nextel in Figure 2.3 (titled "Dance Party") is a good example of this type of contrast. It's *normal* for technology geeks who completely have things under control to hang around the office and try to think of things to do (that's the expected state of affairs). It's *non-normal* and unexpected for them to kill time by practicing their hip-hop dancing.

But there's also warm, resonant humor here in the silly behavior of these characters. In fact, this is one of those ads that just doesn't seem to wear out. That probably helps explain why, when

Figure 2.3   Sprint Nextel's "Dance Party" geeks demonstrate a normal versus non-normal contrast. (Ad appears courtesy of Sprint Nextel Corp.)

I asked top advertising creatives in the survey you'll read about in Chapter 4 what their favorite recent funny ads were, more of them mentioned this one than any other. The comments about the ad in Box 2.1 also confirm that the

> **Funny Business**
>
> Box 2.1. **WHAT'S YOUR FAVORITE FUNNY AD?**
>
> "Nextel 'Dance Party.' Boss asks three employees where someone else is. They're grooving and dancing to a boom box. 'No worry,' they say and locate him instantly vis-à-vis the Nextel tracking device. They resume dancing. This is a good example of using humor to demonstrate the benefits of a product." Michael Faulkner, executive VP and creative director, Daily & Associates, West Hollywood, CA
>
> "Currently I like the Nextel spot with three geeks practicing their hip-hop dancing in the office only to be interrupted by a panicked supervisor. . . . Where's the shipment, etc. The geeks have split-second responses using Nextel technology then immediately go back to their hip-hop dance practice. The spot communicates the product's ability to relieve stress and anxiety and does it in a humorous way." Steve Slais, cocreative director, Kupper Parker Communications, Inc., Saint Louis, MO
>
> "Nextel 30-second TV spot. Geeks dancing in office, boss enters demanding answers to three critical big problems. Music stops, they use their phones to get immediate answers. Go back to dancing. Why? Great casting!" Bruce Waters, VP-creative, Al Paul Lefton Co., Philadelphia, PA

humor is thematically related to the benefits of using Sprint Nextel (you'll read about thematic relatedness a little later).

Possible versus Impossible Contrasts

Raskin's third type of contrast is just like the normal versus non-normal contrast, except the unreal or contrasting reality is *fantasy based* and impossible. Another successfully funny spot for HIE (from a campaign you'll read more about in Chapter 6) is a good example. In the spot, a Clint Eastwood–type cowboy arrives on the scene to rescue a tourist who's been bitten by a snake (see Figure 2.4). "You," he says authoritatively to one of the tourists, "suck out the poison while I start a fire to cauterize the wound." This, of course, is not unexpected given the state of affairs. What's unexpected is that he's no real cowboy—he's a movie actor (complete with a back full of faux arrows). How does he know how to help the victim? That's the impossible, contrasting reality: He stayed at a Holiday Inn Express the night before.

In summary, the incongruity and incongruity-resolution theories, along with Raskin's script-based humor theory, go a long way toward helping us understand the cognitive structures and characteristics of many humorous situations and scenarios, including ads. The criteria for recognizing incongruity-based humor and Raskin's three types of contrasts are summarized in Box 2.2.

It's also important to keep in mind, as Raskin mentions, that the boundaries between his three types of contrasts are not completely airtight.[10] But even though Raskin developed his theory to explain mainly verbal humor (he's a *linguist*, after all) and we can run into some overlap problems, the types definitely hold up well enough to be useful for understanding the incongruent contrasts we find in funny ads, whether verbal or visual. You'll see how useful they are in Chapters 3 and 6.

DISPARAGEMENT THEORIES

The disparagement mechanism in Figure 2.1 is based on another

Figure 2.4 A phony cowboy demonstrates a possible versus impossible contrast. (STAY SMART® ad appears courtesy of InterContinental Hotels Group.)

group of psychological theories. These theories have also gone by various names, including hostility, superiority, malice, aggression, and derision theories.[11] Humorous disparagement is based originally on the ideas of such profound thinkers as Plato, Aristotle, and Thomas Hobbes, and it's probably the oldest explanation for why people laugh. Several scholars have reviewed the

> ## Box 2.2. INCONGRUITY-BASED HUMOR AND RASKIN CONTRASTS
>
> ### Identifying Incongruity-Based Humor
> - A single message element is consistent with two interpretations.
> - The message element stops us and produces momentary and playful confusion.
> - A punch line switches us from one interpretation to another, encouraging resolution and mastery of the confusion.
> - The two interpretations of the single text are opposite from each other in a way described by at least one of Raskin's three types of contrasts: (1) actual versus nonactual, (2) normal versus non-normal, or (3) possible versus impossible.
>
> ### Identifying Actual versus Nonactual Contrasts
> - The text consists of wordplay (e.g., a pun or double entendre).
> - Opposing propositions involving the characters or actual setting of the text fit the following statement: *It is the case that* _____, *and it is not the case that* _____.
> - The punch line emphasizes an opposition in literal meaning. One contrasting reality renders the other *not true or nonexisting*.
> - The text doesn't rely on anything else—such as a normal versus non-normal or possible versus impossible contrast—for its humor.
>
> ### Identifying Normal versus Non-normal Contrasts
> - The contrasting situations involve the state of affairs or the way situations or circumstances are expected to be at a certain point in time.
> - The contrasting reality or situation is unlikely, unexpected, or inappropriate (but still possible or reality based), given the expected state of affairs.
>
> ### Identifying Possible versus Impossible Contrasts
> - The contrasting situations involve the state of affairs or the way situations or circumstances are expected to be at a certain point in time.
> - The contrasting reality or situation is outright impossible (or fantasy based), given the expected state of affairs.

literature exploring this theoretical and literary tradition, which proposes we laugh because of our unfortunate tendency to enjoy feeling we're better than other people.[12] Humorous disparagement, then, has to do with the social context in which humor occurs.

Disparagement theories definitely seem to help explain why humor is often thought of as not being very nice. Many people have pointed out that a lot of humor actually seems to be thinly veiled hostility. In fact, one influential scholar argues that ridicule stemming from victory in hand-to-hand combat was actually the first kind of humor employed (and apparently enjoyed) by man.[13] This is probably why humor doesn't always reflect positively on its users or isn't always appreciated by its targets.

Even the origins of the colloquial idiom "pulling your leg" are pretty sinister. Some believe it originally referred to the practice of allowing the friends of public hanging victims to pull mercifully on the victim's legs if things didn't move along quickly enough. Others propose it refers to the practice of street thieves tripping their victims so they could steal their stuff. That's why today we use the term to refer to making a joke by tricking or confusing someone.[14] Obviously, from this point of view, humor has its roots in hostility, ridicule, and, to a certain extent, violence. Disparagement as a theoretical mechanism, then, also seems to help explain much of the notoriety William Hung received for his *American Idol* performance of "She Bangs."

Disparagement works a lot like incongruity-resolution in the sense there's a stimulus of arousal. In this case, though, the stimulus is the ridicule of somebody or something else—a person, group, institution, or even idea—instead of a puzzling incongruity. Likewise, there's an arousal state or tension, but instead of playful confusion, it's a mixture of pleasure and anxiety—pleasure caused by feelings of superiority and anxiety caused by the feeling that it's just not very nice to enjoy somebody else's ridicule. We have a word to describe this feeling—it's called *guilt*! Finally, and also similar to incongruity-resolution humor, there's a release of the arousal state or tension. With disparagement, though, the tension (or guilt) is not resolved cognitively, but through a process called *misattribution*.[15]

Misattribution simply means we can rationalize our enjoyment of someone else's ridicule—and relieve our guilt—by attributing it to something other than our own failure as a human being. One thing we can use to relieve our guilt is thinking about how much the disparaged person or group has been made fun of by others. For example, many of us enjoyed such disparaging observations as "You might be a redneck if . . . you think a chainsaw is a musical instrument"[16] because redneck humor was widely popularized by comedian

Jeff Foxworthy in his stand-up comedy, books, and popular TV show, and, more recently, with his comedic buddies Bill Engvall, Ron White, and Larry the Cable Guy on the *Blue Collar Comedy Tour*. Once the tension is relieved by misattribution, we are free to enjoy the ridicule of people who live in rural Arkansas and other parts of the southern United States without a serious threat to our sense of fair play.

Misattribution frees us from the ethical and social consequences of enjoying the disparagement of other people in several other ways: (1) The person being ridiculed is beyond our control (and, consequently, not our personal responsibility), (2) the victim deserves it, (3) it's unlikely anyone else will think less of us for enjoying it, and (4) we can tell ourselves we're enjoying the wittiness of the put-down and not the ridicule itself.[17]

Most of these types of misattribution apply very well to disparagement advertising. For example, none of us really feels personally responsible if Coca-Cola's feelings are hurt because Pepsi says only losers drink Coke, and no one will probably think less of us if we laugh at an ad that says this. The second item in the list just given suggests another important point about disparagement and whether we'll think it's funny. Our attitudes and feelings toward the object of the disparagement also determine whether we'll perceive a put-down as funny. That's why we generally respond most favorably to disparagement when our friends are making fun of our enemies and least favorably when our enemies are making fun of our friends.[18]

Disparagement was pretty rare in mainstream brand advertising up until the 1970s. Before that, a lot of people agreed with advertising great David Ogilvy, who argued that it didn't make much sense to create awareness for a competitor's product by even mentioning it in an ad, and people have a tendency to come away from a disparaging ad with the feeling that the disparaged competitor is the good guy and the advertiser is the bad guy. But during the 1970s, direct-comparison advertising became more acceptable, and comparisons with "Brand X" disappeared forever. (You'll read much more about comparative advertising in Chapter 3.) The exception to this rule, of course, is political advertising. Candidates and political parties—and now "527" organizations such as MoveOn.org and SwiftVets.com—have been ridiculing and shamelessly heaving buckets of mud at each other since organized politics began and will probably keep doing it as long as it seems to work.

Today, product and brand advertising with elements of disparagement is probably more common than it's ever been. In fact, it's easy to find examples of at least mild disparagement in brand advertising in several very competitive product categories, including soft drinks, beer, and athletic shoes. For example, Reebok fired a satirical salvo in the sneaker war early in 2004 with its parody of Nike's Shox streaker TV spot, created by the Arnell Group. You can read all about this incredibly funny spot, and several others in the campaign, online at Wikipedia (http://en.wikipedia.org). The spots themselves can also be found in many places on the Web.

Watching the spot, we're completely duped into thinking we're seeing a sequel to Nike's famous TV spot, as a flamboyant streaker in nothing but Nike Shox and a long, wooly muffler successfully eludes pursuing security officers during a soccer game. Duped, that is, up to the point where he stops to swivel his hips for the crowd and Reebok's popular "Terry Tate the Office Linebacker" appears from off-screen and ferociously tackles him. After knocking him down, Tate stands over the flattened streaker and mocks Nike's "Just Do It" slogan— "You went and did it, so I had to hit it! Wooo!"

The criteria for recognizing disparagement-based humor in advertising are summarized in Box 2.3.

AROUSAL-SAFETY AND RELEASE THEORIES

Arousal-safety is one of a group of similar psychological theories that can be conveniently referred to as *release* or *relief theory*. The idea behind tension-release and arousal theories is that the release from physiological or emotional strain, tension, or anxiety that we get by laughing is something we naturally do in order to return ourselves to a comfortable and steady state (scientists call this state *homeostasis*). These theories describe how people respond emotionally, so the stimulus of arousal is called *affective*. Several researchers have also reviewed these theories.[19]

Box 2.3. **RECOGNIZING DISPARAGEMENT-BASED HUMOR**

- Something or someone is being attacked or ridiculed.
- The message encourages us to believe that something or somebody (including us) is better or superior to something or somebody else.
- The message encourages us to attribute our enjoyment to something other than the disparagement (i.e., it encourages misattribution).
- The message consists of satire, a put-down, sarcasm, or self-deprecation.

Remember the difference between one-stage incongruity and two-stage incongruity-resolution theories? Release theories work a lot like that. Some release theories propose that humor results simply from arousal. Others, though, argue that arousal is not the key, but how we interpret and resolve it is.

Humor scholar Mary K. Rothbart is credited with the arousal-safety version of release theory. Arousal-safety theory proposes that we find something funny when we experience a state of anxiety or uncertainty for the safety or well-being of ourselves or someone else. The tension is relieved when we can make a *safety judgment* either that the object of the anxiety is safe or the negative consequences insignificant. As Speck notes, arousal-safety responses "generally involve an outpouring of sentiment or goodwill for people (or personified creatures) that we consider cute, warm, friendly, or familiar. In its fullest form, arousal-safety involves an empathetic bonding with someone who narrowly avoids disaster."[20] These theories explain why we laugh when someone slips on a banana peel or after some other near catastrophe, but not until we know for sure there's no real harm. Writer, actor, and film director Woody Allen clearly understands this aspect of arousal-safety humor: "If it bends, it's funny; if it breaks, it's not funny" [Alan Alda in *Crimes and Misdemeanors*].

As with disparagement theory, there have been several names for theories with similar characteristics, such as tension-release theory,[21] arousal theory,[22] and freedom theory.[23] Like arousal-safety theory, these similar theories all propose an initial tension or emotional arousal followed by a release, which we experience as a kind of humor. In addition, though, to arousal-safety humor that produces feelings of warmth and goodwill toward the object of our anxiety, arousal-safety theory also explains a kind of negative-humor-generating arousal caused by the violation of social standards, conventions, norms, and taboos. The obscene language of some stand-up comedians is a good example of this type of aggressive humor. Arousal-safety theory predicts we'll be shocked initially at the language, experience tension and anxiety at the violation of society's standards, but then make a safety judgment that it's OK in that context, and this release allows us to laugh (uncomfortable laughter though it may be).

Two other things seem worth mentioning about these explanations for arousal-safety humor. First, in the situation just described, some people won't be able to resolve the tension. They'll decide the bad language isn't appropriate, they'll be offended, they won't laugh, and they may even head for the door. Second, it also seems fairly obvious that as society's norms and conventions change regarding what kind of language is appropriate in certain situations, obscene language alone becomes progressively less shocking (tension arousing) and, consequently, less funny.

In advertising, arousal-safety humor often consists of sentimental themes, uncomfortable situations, or mildly embarrassing personal problems. The print ad for the Boy Scouts of America in Figure 2.5—with its cute cartoon illustration and gentle encouragement for kids to step away from their video games and get active—is a good example of this type of humor.

But ads don't always have to present an "entire arousal-safety sequence" to produce an affective response. "Sometimes it's enough just to depict a critical image, such as a family celebration, a child laughing, or a cartoon character, to evoke the response. In such cases, there is still a play signal and a safety judgment, but there is no arousal or tension directly related to the message."[24]

On the other hand, arousal-safety

Figure 2.5 This ad uses mild arousal-safety humor to encourage kids to quit playing video games and join the Scouts. (Ad created by Carmichael Lynch and appears courtesy of the Northern Star Council, Boy Scouts of America.)

humor can also include much more aggressive messages, such as shockingly graphic images, explicit sexual innuendo, or violence. The Tate-inflicted annihilation of Nike's streaker in Reebok's TV spot, for example, has an element of arousal-safety. Society's standards usually dictate that we're not supposed to enjoy a hearty laugh when someone is physically assaulted (naked or not). As I mentioned in Chapter 1, such aggressive humor in advertising has become increasingly common since it first started to emerge in the late 1980s, and a lot of it is generated by the arousal-safety mechanism. We'll take a closer look at this trend and its implications in Chapter 5.

The criteria for identifying arousal-safety-based humor in advertising are summarized in Box 2.4.

OTHER FACTORS

As I mentioned earlier, not all incongruity, disparagement, or arousal-safety stimuli generate humor. It depends on at least three other things that need to happen at about the same time along with a potentially humorous message or image. First, Raskin's theory, like other semantic and psychological theories,

---

Box 2.4. RECOGNIZING AROUSAL-SAFETY-BASED HUMOR

- Something or someone experiences or narrowly avoids disaster.
- The message portrays an uncomfortable or embarrassing social situation, fear appeal, a shocking graphic image, or an explicit sexual innuendo.
- The message stimulates arousal and affective uncertainty in the form of physiological tension or emotional anxiety.
- There is a play cue that allows you to make a judgment that the object of the tension or anxiety is going to be all right or that the consequences don't really matter (i.e., a safety judgment).
- The message includes elements that encourage sentimental feelings, goodwill, or empathy.

---

proposes there must be a switch from a *bona fide communication* mode to a playful, nonthreatening communication mode. Bona fide communication is the serious, ordinary, everyday communication we use to tell each other important things. As Raskin explains, bona fide communication is ruled by the *cooperative principle*. The cooperative principle states that when we're talking to other people, we're committed to being truthful and relevant; the people we are communicating with know this, so they'll expect our speech to be truthful and relevant.

Obviously, then, if someone is telling you a joke, and you don't understand that he or she is in a non–bona fide communication mode (which includes joke telling, as well as lying and play acting), you'll try to interpret the joke as serious, truthful, and relevant communication. The result will be confusion, and you probably won't get the joke. Or it will throw off the timing, at the very least. Mode ambiguity or confusion can also produce some other interesting possibilities, such as when we're attempting bona fide communication but the person we're talking to thinks we're in the joke-telling mode.

The difference between bona fide and non–bona fide communication modes also suggests why the notion of humor as an expression of play is a second important factor. Some psychological theorists say there needs to be a *play cue* to help us recognize that a situation is not real and is meant to be taken playfully.[25] In funny ads, these play cues can be seen in the setting of the ad, its visuals, its music, and its sound effects (in TV and radio) or by the behavior of the characters. The laugh tracks added to TV situation comedies function as this kind of play cue.

Since people generally assume advertising is, or should be, bona fide communication, the problem of mode ambiguity looks as if it would be a serious one for advertising humorists. Clearly, the serious inventors of modern advertising described in Chapter 1 thought advertising should always be bona fide communication. So this expectation might also help explain why some people don't appreciate humor in advertising or why it frequently falls flat. Fortunately, the second most socially acceptable form of communication is joke telling and humor.[26] That means that when we are unable to accomplish a bona fide communication interpretation for what someone is saying or doing, we generally and fairly quickly assume the communicator is involved in non–bona fide communication and probably trying to be funny. So confusion over mode ambiguity shouldn't, on the average, last very long.

Finally, if incongruity-resolution humor is involved, it won't be funny if it takes too long to resolve the incongruity or if it's too difficult. In other words, the longer we have to try to figure it out, the less likely we'll find it funny or "get the joke." All but the most incompetent humorists know that once they need to start explaining why their jokes are supposed to be funny, they're doomed.

ARE WE RELATED?

Advertisers and advertising researchers have been worrying about the relationship between the funny and nonfunny parts of ads for a long time. A couple of early scholars originally talked about the "direction of humor" in advertising.[27] They argued that if humor is associated with the product or if the product is, in fact, used to create the humor, then the humor is directed toward the product. If the humor in an ad could have existed without the product or any connection to it, it's not directed toward the product.

Today, most people in advertising refer to the relationship between humorous and nonhumorous message elements as either *relatedness* or relevance. As I mentioned in Chapter 1, early advertisers were especially concerned that humor should be related to the product or its use in some way, or what they more commonly thought of as humor relevance. In addition, surveys show that nearly 90 percent of the creative people in top advertising agencies agree that humor should be related to the product.[28] Research also suggests that related humor is more effective.[29]

The model in Figure 2.1 accounts for three types of message-humor relatedness. First, *intentional relatedness* refers to the relationship between humor and how an advertising message will be recognized and processed as information. Second, *thematic relatedness* (or what I also simply call relevance) refers to the relationship between humor and product-related themes. And third, *structural relatedness* refers to the relationship between humor and message elements within an ad.

Intentional Relatedness
Intentional relatedness is based on the branch of semiotics (the general theory of signs) called *pragmatics*. Pragmatics describes the relationship between signs and the people using them to communicate (i.e., how we use language). Intentional relatedness, then, describes how audiences recognize and process the humorous information in an ad.

Intentional relatedness is associated with information processing because, depending on what we think the advertiser's intent is, we process information differently. Will we process the ad as reality or fantasy, as bona fide communication or non–bona fide communication? Humor in an ad is intentionally related if we recognize the advertiser's intent to be funny and to entertain us. Intentional relatedness, then, is used to describe the level of humor (or *dominance*) in an ad.[30] If humor is dominant, then the intent of the ad is obvious. This doesn't refer, though, to how funny the humor is. The humorous elements of ads that are not humor dominant can be extremely funny. Instead, it refers to how much of the ad consists of humorous compared with nonhumorous content.

In humor-dominant ads, the humor dominates (or is *superordinate* to) the nonhumorous parts. Put another way, it means an ad's product-related elements are presented within a mainly humorous message structure that controls and shapes our overall experience of the ad. Speck calls this the "message-within-humor structure."

Normally, a play cue signals we should process an ad as humor and not reality (or bona fide communication). But that's not always the case. Take Geico insurance TV spots that parody TV shows (e.g., nature documentaries) and even ads for other products. In one of their ads a white-coated character tells us: "Hi, I'm Dr. John Parker. Hair loss is an all too common problem, but now there's good news." When a hair-challenged character asks if the good news is that Dr. Parker has discovered a cure for hair loss, he says no, of course. "I just saved a bunch of money on my car insurance by switching to Geico." Even though there's no initial play cue, this ad is humor dominant. In fact, the parody doesn't work unless we accept the premise that we're watching a hair system ad and not a Geico ad. In addition, the key to recognizing a humor-dominant ad is that the advertising message no longer makes sense if the humor is removed, which is also the case with the Geico ad. If we removed the humorous part of the message—the "I just saved a bunch of money on my car insurance by switching to Geico" punch line—the advertising message could no longer be understood.[31]

On the other hand, in message-dominant ads, the humor is secondary (or *subordinate*) to the overall message. This means the humor elements are embedded in a message that is basically nonhumorous. Speck calls this the "humor-within-message structure." In message-dominant ads, there isn't an initial play cue, so we process them as reality-based, bona fide communication.

There are two types of message-dominant ads—image focused and information focused. In image-focused ads, the funny parts are used to reinforce the image or reputation of a product or advertiser. On the other hand, with information-focused ads, the humor focuses more on tangible product features, benefits, or price. In both cases, if the humor is removed, the ads still make sense.

As an example, the radio spot for Staples in Figure 2.6 is message dominant and information focused. There's a cue early in the spot (the voice of a stereotypically testy female teacher) that tells us it should be processed playfully. But the key to recognizing this spot as message dominant is that the humor could be removed with no serious damage to the message. Without the teacher character, what we'd have would be Staples' announcement that its stores have everything we need for school, followed by the recitation of a list of supplies to prove it and concluding with a guarantee that we can get them at a competitively low price. The humor is information focused because it's used to reinforce specific product offerings (e.g., notebooks, backpacks, folders, and paper clips).

A radio spot for Mike's Hard Iced Tea, on the other hand, is message dominant and image focused. The spot's copy begins this way: "Creating a drink as delicious as New Mike's Hard Iced Tea took the hard work of every employee. From the master craftsmen who perfected the recipe to the men who clean the tanks, everyone contributed. Except for Matt Bijarski in accounts receivable. He didn't really do that much. Unless you count sitting on your ass all day making personal calls. Which we don't."

There's no initial play cue in the Mike's spot, and we begin processing the ad as though it were a relatively serious one about product quality. The humor is embedded in the middle and, more important, could be removed without harm to the ad's message. The humor is image focused because it reinforces Mike's aggressive, in-your-face brand image.

The criteria for recognizing different types of intentional relatedness are summarized in Box 2.5.

Figure 2.6   This Cliff Freeman & Partners radio spot for Staples is message dominant and information focused. (Ad appears courtesy of Staples, the Office Superstore, LLC.)

ANNOUNCER:	Staples has everything you need to go back to school.
TEACHER:	I'm Ms. Kupermacher, and I hope you're all prepared for math.
ANNOUNCER:	Notebooks.
TEACHER:	Advanced geometry.
ANNOUNCER:	Protractor, graph paper, notebooks.
TEACHER:	Here's your syllabus.
ANNOUNCER:	Wastebasket.
TEACHER:	And your textbooks.
ANNOUNCER:	*Seven-gallon* wastebasket.
TEACHER:	You're expected to read every word.
ANNOUNCER:	Highlighter.
TEACHER:	There will be homework.
ANNOUNCER:	Folders.
TEACHER:	*Lots* of homework.
ANNOUNCER:	Backpacks.
TEACHER:	*Tons* of homework!
ANNOUNCER:	Hand truck.
TEACHER:	And there will be pop quizzes.
ANNOUNCER:	Pencils.
TEACHER:	Every week.
ANNOUNCER:	Pencil sharpener.
TEACHER:	And a final examination.
ANNOUNCER:	Calculator.
TEACHER:	There will be no calculators!
ANNOUNCER:	Small calculator.
TEACHER:	I expect your work to be neat.
ANNOUNCER:	WiteOut.
TEACHER:	Organized.
ANNOUNCER:	Paper clips.
TEACHER:	And legible.
ANNOUNCER:	600 dot-per-inch laser printer.
TEACHER:	I will not tolerate tardiness!
ANNOUNCER:	Alarm clock.
TEACHER:	And don't forget . . .
ANNOUNCER:	Post-it notes.
TEACHER:	You can easily be removed from this class.
ANNOUNCER:	*Thank-you* notes.
ANNOUNCER:	Staples has everything you need to go back to school. The guaranteed low price on over 7,000 items. Staples. Yeah, we've got that.

Box 2.5. **RECOGNIZING INTENTIONAL RELATEDNESS**

Humor Dominant

- There's an initial play cue (source, stimulus, social context, or behavior of others) that encourages us to process the ad as fantasy or play instead of as reality.
- Product information is embedded within a humorous structure (incongruity, disparagement, or arousal-safety) that controls and shapes our overall experience of the ad.
- If the humor is removed, the ad can no longer be understood.

Message Dominant, Information Focused

- A humorous element is embedded in a basically nonhumorous message.
- The humor focuses primarily on tangible features, benefits, claims, or the price of the product or service.
- If the humor is removed, the ad can still be understood.

Message Dominant, Image Focused

- A humorous element is embedded in a basically nonhumorous message.
- Humor is used to reinforce the less tangible image or reputation of a product or advertiser.
- The humor is visual and closely related to the product or user.
- If the humor is removed, the ad can still be understood.

Thematic Relatedness

The relatedness of humor to product-related themes is called thematic relatedness. Thematic relatedness is based on the branch of semiotics called *semantics*, which describes the relationship between signs and what they represent. The history presented in Chapter 1 strongly suggests thematic relatedness is what advertisers have been referring to all these years when they said that humor should be relevant. In thematically related ads the humor is related to the product and its uses, benefits, brand name, or typical users.[32] Humor may also be related to negative consequences caused by not using the product or, in the case of satire, to negative characteristics of competitors or the people who use their products. On the other hand, in thematically unrelated ads, humor is not related to the product or any product-related claims. You'll see unrelated humor most often in locally produced ads for cars, furniture, and appliances. I found one car dealer's use of a lip-synching chimpanzee particularly annoying.

The award-winning ad for Turner Classic Movies in Figure 2.7 is a great example of thematic relatedness. The second line of copy—"WHEN YOUR PLANE BARELY MISSES YOU, that's CLASSIC"—is related not only to TCM as a cable channel but also to what it shows: classic movies.

Structural Relatedness

The relationship between humor and the message elements contained within an ad is called structural relatedness. Structural relatedness accounts for differences on the syntactic level. *Syntactics* is the branch of semiotics that deals with the formal relationship of signs to each other, as opposed to the relationship between signs and sign users described by pragmatics.

As we already know, in humor-dominant ads, subordinate product- or brand-message elements are embedded in a humorous message. In this case, structural

Figure 2.7 This print ad for Turner Classic Movies is thematically related. (©2005 Turner Classic Movies LP, LLLP.)

relatedness refers to how closely connected these message elements are with the humor. In the case of incongruity-resolution, is the product message part of the incongruity? In the case of humorous disparagement, is the product message part of the disparagement? In the case of arousal-safety, is the message part of the perception concerning the object of the anxiety or empathy?

For example, the product message in the Geico hair system parody is completely integrated with the humor. In this case, the "I just saved a bunch of money by switching to Geico" punch line not only delivers the advertising message but also makes it possible for us to resolve the incongruity and get the joke.

On the other hand, in a message-dominant ad, humor is embedded in a message that is basically nonhumorous, so structural relatedness refers to where the subordinate humor elements are located relative to the dominant message elements. Is the humor located at the beginning of the ad? Is it embedded in the body of the ad? Or is it placed at the end as a tag or finale?[33] For example, in the Staples radio spot in Figure 2.6, the funny elements are embedded throughout—starting in the second line of the spot and then alternating every other line until almost the very end. Similarly, in the Mike's Hard Iced Tea radio spot, the sole humor element (ridicule of lazy accounts receivable employee Matt Bijarski) is embedded in the middle.

APPLYING THE THEORY

We now have some answers to the main question we started with—what is humor? Humor is what we think is funny. And theoretically, what we think is funny are incongruous, disparaging, or anxiety-inducing messages or images that produce a cognitive, social, or affective tension that is suddenly relieved, producing pleasure. The classical humor theories in the model account for all these humor-generating possibilities. We also gained an appreciation for the critical roles that communication modes and the hypothetical world of play perform as preconditions for humor. Finally, we can also explain how the humor in an ad can be related.

Can we apply this chapter and its theories to help explain why the Domino's ad we started with should have been funny and, maybe, why it wasn't? Let's see. First of all, we'd probably categorize the spot as full comedy—a product of all three mechanisms. Is Dad actually ordering pizza and Cheesy Dots and looking for the baseball equipment so he and the monster can enjoy some wholesome family fellowship? Not really. The pizza and baseball may, with any luck, be enough to keep his warped offspring from moving on to more destructively antisocial activities, such as setting the neighbor's cat on fire. Note the Raskin-type actual versus nonactual contrast.

Second, Junior's potentially psychopathic behavior is fairly aggressive arousal-safety humor. There's pending disaster here for both Mom and Dad—we are, in fact, witnessing a parental train wreck. Third, we also have mild disparagement, with the implied ridicule of incompetent parents who need to rely on pizza delivery to maintain some kind of control over their sadistic offspring.

What does this tell us about why the ad scored low on the funny scale? One big problem is that it takes some effort to resolve the incongruity—why is Dad really ordering Domino's pizza, and what did the voice-over mean by that *lots and lots* of baseball remark? Not only does this problem violate an incongruity-resolution humor rule—it takes too long to resolve the incongruity—but once we get there, the destination isn't worth the trip.

What about the arousal-safety humor? One problem with this negatively aggressive arousal-safety message is that we don't get what we need to make a safety judgment. Pizza and baseball aren't going to solve this disaster—who doesn't know that the more you try to bribe obnoxious kids with pizza, the more obnoxious they get? In addition, the ad doesn't encourage warmth or sentimentality because it's difficult to feel empathy for the parents of the hose-spraying kid.

As for disparagement, many of us should (and perhaps some do) derive a little pleasure from our feelings of superiority over hapless Dad and desperate Mom. But the put-down isn't very obvious, and, the fact is, the subtle ridicule of people for being bad parents just isn't all that clever or witty.

It's important to keep in mind, as we've recognized elsewhere in this book, that successful humor is almost entirely in the eye of the amused or unamused. And a lot of advertising humor isn't appreciated, not because it didn't have the characteristics of recognizable humor but because it was delivered to an audience for which it was not intended—a problem we'll explore again in Chapter 5. And while it's possible to identify certain ads as near-perfect examples of different types of humor, others are sometimes more difficult to categorize. As Speck points out, two people might view the same ad as two different kinds of humor, partly due to different humor preferences.

But despite these and other limitations of the body of classical humor theory presented in this chapter, knowing what the absolutely necessary conditions are for something to be funny goes a long way toward helping us understand why an ad is funny or why it's not.

NOTES

1. Paul S. Speck, "On Humor and Humor in Advertising" (PhD diss., Texas Tech University, 1987).

2. Harlan E. Spotts, Marc G. Weinberger, and Amy L. Parsons, "Assessing the Use and Impact of Humor on Advertising Effectiveness: A Contingency Approach," *Journal of Advertising* 26, no. 3 (1997): 17–32.

3. John E. Morreall, *Taking Laughter Seriously* (Albany: State University of New York Press, 1983); Goran Nerhardt, "Incongruity and Funniness: Towards a New Descriptive Model," in *Humour and Laughter: Theory, Research, and Application*, eds. Antony J. Chapman and Hugh C. Foot (London: Wiley, 1976), 55–62.

4. Speck, "On Humor," 7.

5. Dana L. Alden and Wayne D. Hoyer, "An Examination of Cognitive Factors Related to Humorousness in Television Advertising," *Journal of Advertising* 22, no. 2 (1993): 29–37; Paul S. Speck, "The Humorous Message Taxonomy: A Framework for the Study of Humorous Ads," in *Current Issues and Research in Advertising*, eds. James H. Leigh and Claude R. Martin Jr. (Ann Arbor: University of Michigan, 1991), 1–44; Jerry M. Suls, "A Two-Stage Model for the Appreciation of Jokes and Cartoons: An Information-Processing Analysis," in *The Psychology of Humor: Theoretical Perspectives and Empirical Issues*," eds. Jeffrey H. Goldstein and Paul E. McGhee (New York: Academic, 1972), 81–100.

6. Speck, "The Humorous Message Taxonomy."

7. Sigmund Freud, *Der Witz und seine Beziehung zum Unbewussten* (Leipzig, Vienna: Dueticke). English translation: *Jokes and Their Relation to the Unconscious* (Harmondsworth, NY: Penguin, 1976).

8. Raskin's original theory was later broadened and renamed the general theory of verbal humor (GTVH) by Raskin and colleague Salvatore Attardo.

9. D. H. Monro, "Theories of Humor," in *Writing and Reading across the Curriculum*, 3rd ed., eds. Laurence Behrens and Leonard J. Rosen (Glenview, IL: Scott Foresman, 1988), 349–355.

10. Viktor Raskin, *Semantic Mechanisms of Humor* (Boston: Reidel, 1985), 112.

11. Lawrence LaFave, "Humor Judgments as a Function of Reference Group and Identification Classes," in *Psychology of Humor*, eds. Jeffrey H. Goldstein and Paul E. McGhee (New York: Academic, 1972), 195–210; Joanne R. Cantor and Dolf Zillman, "Resentment toward Victimized Protagonists and Severity of Misfortunes They Suffer as Factors in Humor Appreciation," *Journal of Experimental Research in Personality* 6 (1973): 321–329.

12. D. H. Monro, *Argument of Laughter* (Melbourne: Melbourne University Press, 1951); Patricia Keith-Spiegel, "Early Conception of Humor: Varieties and Issues," in *The Psychology of Humor*, eds. Jeffrey H. Goldstein, Hans J. Eyesenck, and Paul E. McGhee (New York: Academic, 1972), 3–39; Dolf Zillman and Joanne R. Cantor, "A Disposition Theory of Humour and Mirth," in *Humour and Laughter: Theory Research and Application*, eds. Antony J. Chapman and Hugh C. Foot (London: Wiley, 1976), 93–116; Morreall, *Taking Laughter Seriously*.

13. Albert Rapp, *The Origins of Wit and Humor* (New York: Dutton, 1951).

14. The Word Detective, http://www.word-detective.com (accessed January 15, 2004).

15. Zillman and Cantor, "A Disposition Theory of Humour and Mirth."

16. "You Might Be a Redneck If," *Jokes Magazine*, http://jokesmagazine.com (accessed March 1, 2004).

17. Speck, "On Humor," 72.

18. Zillman and Cantor, "A Disposition Theory of Humour and Mirth."

19. Keith-Spiegel, *Early Conception of Humor*; Paul E. McGhee, "The Role of Arousal and Hemispheric Lateralization in Humor," in *Handbook of Humor Research*, vol. 1, eds. Paul E. McGhee and Jeffrey H. Goldstein (New York: Springer-Verlag, 1983), 13–38; Morreall, *Taking*

Laughter Seriously; Mary K. Rothbart, "Psychological Approaches to the Study of Humour," in *It's a Funny Thing, Humour,* eds. Antony J. Chapman and Hugh C. Foot (Oxford: Pergamon, 1977), 87–94.

20. Speck, "The Humorous Message Taxonomy," 6.

21. Max Eastman, *Enjoyment of Laughter* (New York: Simon and Schuster, 1936).

22. Daniel E. Berlyne, "Humour and Its Kin," in *The Psychology of Humor: Theoretical Perspectives and Empirical Issues,* eds. Jeffrey H. Goldstein and Paul E. McGhee (New York: Academic, 1972), 43–60.

23. Harvey Mindess, *Laughter and Liberation* (Los Angeles: Nash, 1971).

24. Speck, "The Humorous Message Taxonomy," 6–7.

25. Hyongoh Cho, "Humor Mechanisms, Perceived Humor and Their Relationships to Various Executional Types in Advertising," *Advances in Consumer Research* 22 (1995): 191–197; Paul E. McGhee, *Humour: Its Origin and Development* (San Francisco: Freeman, 1979).

26. Raskin, *Semantic Mechanisms.*

27. J. Patrick Kelly and Paul J. Solomon, "Humor in Television Advertising," *Journal of Advertising* 4, no. 3 (1975): 31–35.

28. Fred Beard, "Practitioner Views of Humor in Advertising: A Twenty-Year Update" (paper presented at the annual conference of the Society for Marketing Advances, Nashville, TN, November 2, 2006); Tom Madden and Marc G. Weinberger, "Humor in Advertising: A Practitioner View," *Journal of Advertising* 24, no. 4 (1984): 23–29, 27.

29. Marc G. Weinberger and Charles Gulas, "The Impact of Humor in Advertising: A Review," *Journal of Advertising* 21, no. 4 (1992): 35–59; Marc G. Weinberger, Harlan Spotts, Leland Campbell, and Amy L. Parsons, "The Use and Effect of Humor in Different Advertising Media," *Journal of Advertising Research* 35, no. 3 (1995): 44–56.

30. Spotts et al., "Assessing the Use and Impact of Humor on Advertising Effectiveness."

31. Spotts et al., "Assessing the Use and Impact of Humor on Advertising Effectiveness."

32. Spotts et al., "Assessing the Use and Impact of Humor on Advertising Effectiveness."

33. Speck, "On Humor," 188.

Why Typology Is a Funny Word

THIS chapter starts with a look at some of the many ways researchers have categorized different types of humor and funny ads. We'll examine how they match up with the three classical humor theories we talked about in Chapter 2. We're also going to focus on why Paul Speck's *humorous message taxonomy* (HMT) continues to be the definitive approach for categorizing funny ads. Returning to the humor model in Chapter 2, we're going to look more closely at how the three humor mechanisms generate humor in the HMT's five types, with several award-winning examples of each. When you're finished with this chapter, you'll be able to identify any funny ad you see as one of the five types and understand why it's funny.

We'll also look at the available evidence suggesting how people typically respond to the five types. This will suggest some ways the use of humor might be fine-tuned to produce the most effective ads possible. Finally, in this chapter you'll meet some talented and award-winning advertising professionals. They talk about some of their own funny ads and what they think it takes to be a successful advertising humorist.

HUMOROUS AD TYPOLOGIES

One of the first things researchers or scientists do when they start studying something is see if they can classify or categorize it into different types. The general idea is that you can learn a lot about something simply by figuring out whether it's made up of just one universal type or several different types. Whatever set of categories you end up with is called a *typology* or *taxonomy*. Often criticized for being less than a theory—and, consequently, not as useful—a typology is one of the first steps toward understanding a phenomenon.

As you may recall from Chapter 2, humor is a difficult thing to define and categorize. But that certainly hasn't kept people from trying. As you also know, we've adopted what I call classical humor theory—the incongruity-resolution, disparagement, and arousal-safety theories and mechanisms—as the most useful way to define and understand funny ads. This body of theory accounts for just about everything people find funny, both in terms of content and technique.

Table 3.1 summarizes some of the typologies researchers have created to describe different types of humor. The table emphasizes how all the humor types are related to the three classical humor theories. A couple of the typologies listed in Table 3.1, like Speck's, also start with the classical humor theories, although others categorize humor and humorous ads along two other dimensions—*content* or *technique* (or humor *devices*).

As I mentioned in Chapter 2, the model in Figure 2.1 shows that the incongruity-resolution mechanism generates a type of funny ad called comic wit when used alone. The arousal-safety mechanism produces a type of humorous ad called resonant wit, when combined with incongruity, and resonant humor, when used by itself. Arousal-safety humor is especially important because it's the most aggressive type of humor and, consequently, the most likely to cause audience offense. You'll read more about that issue in Chapter 5.

Disparagement appears in advertising only when it's combined with an incongruity—a combination that generates satire. When the three humor mechanisms are used simultaneously, they generate a type of funny ad called full comedy.

Speck originally called the ad types generated by arousal-safety "sentimental humor" and "sentimental comedy," but the term *resonant* does a better job of capturing the kind of affective arousal they produce. My colleague David Tarpenning and I borrowed the *resonance* concept from media guru Tony Schwartz. According to Schwartz, an ad resonates with people when its creator understands the kinds of experiences and feelings audience members have and the exact way that an emotional (or affective) message evokes those feelings.[1] In the case of arousal-safety humor, then, ads that arouse sentimentality, empathy, or negative anxiety are resonant in much the same way. You can read more about legendary mass communicator Schwartz (he created the famous "Daisy" political ad for Lyndon B. Johnson's 1964 presidential campaign) at www.tonyschwartz.org.

According to Speck, arousal-safety ads often "tap middle-class values: family members helping each other, fathers taking time to participate in their chil-

Table 3.1. Humor Theories, Mechanisms, and Typologies

Typologies	Incongruity/ Incongruity-Resolution	Arousal-Safety	Disparagement
Speck	Comic wit, resonant wit, full comedy, satire	Resonant humor, full comedy	Satire, full comedy
Goldstein and McGhee	Nonsense	Sexual	Aggressive
Freud	Nontendencious wit	Tendencious wit	Tendencious wit
Kelly and Solomon*	Pun, understatement, joke, something ludicrous, irony		Satire
McCullough and Taylor	Nonsense, pun humor	Sexual, warm humor	Aggressive
Cho	Negativity, subtle complexity, perceptual interest	Negativity, slice-of-life, subtle complexity, miniaturization	Negativity ludicrousness, slice-of-life, perceptual interest, miniaturization
Stern	Verbal comedy, satiric comedy	Romantic comedy	Satiric comedy, physical comedy
Catanescu and Tom	Comparison, personification, exaggeration, pun, silliness, surprise		Sarcasm
Toncar	Pun, understatement, joke, ludicrous, irony, satire		Satire
Buijzen and Valkenburg	Slapstick, clownish humor, surprise, misunderstanding, parody	Slapstick	Slapstick, satire, irony

*Kelly and Solomon's "humorous intent" type is not generated by any of the mechanisms.

dren's lives, children learning the value of hard work, and people acting responsibly."[2] This is a great description of positive, warm arousal-safety humor. Although most experts agree humor and warmth aren't the same thing, they often show up together in advertising. Ads that present families, kids, and small animals are classic examples of "warmth." Unger points out that another major area where warmth and humor overlap is in the portrayal of common problems, which also encourages empathy.[3]

More important, though, while the notion of "sentimentality" accounts nicely for arousal-safety humor in a positive and warm tone, it doesn't explain very well the more aggressive (and occasionally shocking) examples of arousal-safety humor. For example, there's no way anyone is ever going to feel "warm and sentimental" about Reebok's "Terry Tate the Office Linebacker," at least not while he's flattening streakers or coworkers. So this is another reason I call the humor types based on the arousal-safety mechanism *resonant humor* and *resonant wit*.

Finally, Dana Alden and his colleagues added significantly to our understanding of the incongruity-resolution mechanism and the types of funny ads based on it. As you learned in Chapter 2, their work focuses on the presence and humorousness in ads of the three Raskin-type contrasts—actual versus nonactual, normal versus non-normal, and possible versus impossible.

Two early and important humor researchers, Goldstein and McGhee, surveyed the humor literature published between 1950 and 1971. They found that humor had generally been categorized in terms of content as aggressive humor, sexual humor, or incongruity (nonsense).[4] These three categories of humor match up with Sigmund Freud's earlier typology, which consists of two types of humor—aggressively or sexually *tendencious* humor and *nontendencious* (nonsense) *wit*.

An early mixed typology of funny ads, developed by Kelly and Solomon, consists of seven types: a pun, an understatement, a joke, something ludicrous, satire, irony, or humorous intent (i.e., an audience's perception that an advertiser intended to be funny).[5]

For their study of American, British, and German trade magazine ads, McCullough and Taylor used a typology of five humor types that mixes content and technique—aggressive, sexual, nonsense, warm humor, and pun humor.[6] Unfortunately, they also concluded more research needs to be done because their typology didn't explain a quarter of the ads they studied.

Cho extended work based on the three classical humor mechanisms. However, his analysis produced six types of funny magazine ads instead of five. His use of multiple regression analysis made it possible to identify which of the three humor mechanisms contributed most to the six types.

What Cho calls "negativity" is primarily disparagement because it consists mostly of "cynicism about morals, pessimistic attitudes, exchanges of retaliative jokes, and sarcasm,"[7] although it's also partly influenced by incongruity and arousal-safety. "Slice-of-life" ads are mainly determined by the arousal-safety mechanism and are very similar to the warmly sentimental ads described earlier, although Cho's also includes some disparagement. "Ludicrousness" is entirely disparagement in Cho's typology; it includes ads in which people act foolishly or adults do undignified or immature things.

What Cho calls "subtle complexity" is determined mainly by incongruity because it includes "various levels of complexity, metaphor, indirect situation, and tricky allusions in the message delivery."[8] But because these ads also tend to be "subtle, inoffensive and sophisticated," they also include some arousal-safety humor. "Perceptual interest" includes both disparagement and arousal-safety and consists of "contrast between verbal and visual elements, visual puns, and perceptual displacement."[9] "Miniaturization," which is also affected by both the arousal-safety and disparagement mechanisms, "portrays children or animals struggling to get through seemingly complicated situations."[10]

Stern took a different route and proposed a typology of funny ad types based on drama theory. In her typology, advertising humor is called "comedy," and the audience response to it is called "laughter."[11] The typology is based on Henri Bergson's theory of laughter, which categorizes comedy into four types along two dimensions: (1) verbal versus physical and (2) romantic versus satiric. Stern notes that physical comedy is often considered "low" comedy or "farce," while verbal comedy is often called "high" comedy or "wit." Examples of wit include the familiar humor techniques or devices we've already seen in other typologies, including puns, irony, and double entendres.

Let's digress for a second and talk about double entendres. A double entendre is an incongruous figure of speech, similar to a pun, in which the message can be understood in two different ways. The actual, or literal, meaning is typically an innocent one, while the second (or nonactual) meaning is often aggressively risqué. Note the Raskin-type actual versus nonactual contrast—descriptive of all puns, double entendres, and parodies. The double entendre can be very funny when intended and embarrassing when not (but still funny). An unintentional double entendre has gotten more than a few people in trouble, including advertisers. Take a look at the Burger King examples in Box 3.1 and decide whether you think they were actually caused by a "software malfunction."

Stern's romantic versus satiric comedy types distinguish between two types of audience responses—"laughter with the characters and laughter at them."[12]

Box 3.1. **BURGER KING OF THE DOUBLE ENTENDRES?**

A day after going live with a Web site devoted to its parody scratch metal band "Coq Roq" (featuring lead singer "Fowl Mouth"), Burger King removed what appeared to be at least two extremely aggressive double entendres. Deleted from Coqroq.com (designed by Subservient Chicken creators Crispin Porter & Bogusky) were captions under pictures of fictional female fans that read "Groupies love the Coq" and "Groupies love Coq." A BK spokesperson blamed the placement of the captions on a Flash and XML programming malfunction and reported the company had received no complaints. According to BK, the target for their advertising is the 18- to 34-year-old, usually male "super fan," who eats fast food as often as every other day.

Sources: David Kiley, "Burger King's Coq Roq Site Stirs Pot. But Will It Sell Greasy Chicken Fries?" http://www.businessweek.com (accessed July 11, 2006); Dan Beucke and Brian Grow, "Burger King: Raunch with Those Fries?" *Business Week*, August 15, 2005, 9.

In romantic comedy, audiences are encouraged to feel warmth and empathy (there are those terms again) toward the characters, the tone is usually playful, there's often a happy ending, and the happy ending happens *because* the characters triumphed over their problems. So romantic comedy is consistent with warm, positive resonant wit or resonant humor. On the other hand, in satiric comedy, the dramatic objective is to use humor to ridicule, there probably won't be a happy ending, but if there is, it happens *despite* the actions of the characters, not because of them.

Stern identifies an equally helpful difference between "ludicrous" and "ridiculous" comedy. Unlike Cho, who concludes that ludicrousness is disparagingly negative, Stern views ludicrous humor as playful and frivolous, enabling people to create and share bonds (what she calls "laughter without malice" and what you and I recognize as warm arousal-safety humor). On the other hand, ridiculous humor criticizes (look at the root word for ridiculous, after all), holds people up to scorn or contempt, and "uses laughter as a weapon to correct folly."[13] This falls into Freud's category of tendencious humor and is, of course, what you and I recognize as disparagement.

Catanescu and Tom used a device- or technique-oriented typology in their research consisting of comparison, personification, exaggeration, pun, sarcasm, silliness, and surprise.[14] Toncar used a similar typology consisting of pun, understatement, joke, ludicrousness, satire, and irony.[15] Neither of these typologies adds much, and as you can see in Table 3.1, the types can be easily categorized according to the three humor mechanisms.

Buijzen and Valkenburg developed the most recent typology of funny ads, and once again, the three classical humor theories and mechanisms are the foundation.[16] The goal of their study was to find out whether and how 41 humor techniques they identified in Dutch TV commercials would cluster into funny ad types. Their analysis produced a typology of seven types.

Since they note that three of them—slapstick, satire, and irony (which often involve outwitting and laughing at others)—all involve "relatively unfriendly and pungent humor,"[17] these are generated by disparagement. Incongruity theory explains the humorousness of their four less aggressive humor types (clownish humor, surprise, misunderstanding, and parody). In their typology, slapstick is explained by all three theories, since it includes "incongruities, malicious pleasure and aggressiveness"[18] (think Larry, Moe, and Curly here, and you've got the general idea).

In summary, advertising humor has been defined and described in a lot of ways and classified into many types. The importance and value of the three classical humor theories and mechanisms now seem especially obvious. All the humor types and techniques can be categorized quite easily according to the three humor mechanisms. What also seems clear is that typologies other than the HMT offer little in the way of improvement. The descriptions of humorous ads in each of the HMT's five types that follow also support this conclusion.

THE COMIC WIT AD

As you learned in Chapter 2, the source or stimulus for the incongruity mechanism is a deviation from expectations, causing surprise or uncertainty that triggers a tension, or need, to process and resolve the deviation. Resolving the incongruity relieves the tension, and we experience this relief as humor. As you also learned, Alden and several of his research colleagues have concluded that incongruity-resolution is by far the most common type of humor used in ads around the world. So it also shouldn't be a big surprise to discover that most of the humor types in Table 3.1 are at least partly generated by incongruity.

Humor generated by incongruity alone is used a lot in advertising, as it is in other forms of popular entertainment. Comic wit ads include jokes, ironic contrast, parody, double entendres, visual or verbal puns, comic reversal, comic exaggeration, comic understatement, humorous stereotypes (as long as they're not disparaging), or just plain silliness and absurdity. For example, note the in-

Figure 3.1   Comic wit for *The Econ-omist*: "E = IQ²." (Ad appears courtesy of *The Economist*.)

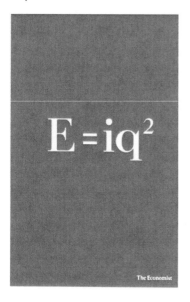

congruity-resolution in Figure 3.1 in an ad for *The Economist* magazine from an extremely successful 19-year (as of 2007) campaign called "White Out of Red." This visual parody of Einstein's famous equation generates cognitive uncertainty and then pleasure as we resolve the incongruity. By reading *The Economist*, we can square our own intelligence. Note the Raskin-type actual versus nonactual contrast. It is actually the case that this equation refers to what can happen to your intelligence if you read *The Economist*. It's not actually the case that it is Einstein's theoretical physics equation—it just looks like it.

The Findlay Market Horseradish Mustard ad in Figure 3.2 presents a comic exaggeration. What does that really hairy chest have to do with the product? Ah ha! We can

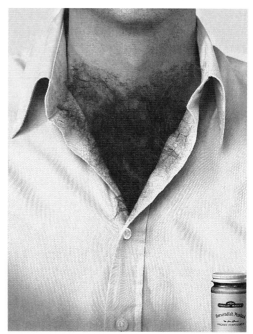

Figure 3.2   Comic wit for Findlay Market Mustard. (Ad appears courtesy of Mr. Gene Greens, "Mustard King.")

resolve this incongruity, and once again, it's in the form of a Raskin-type actual versus nonactual contrast. Findlay Market's Horseradish Mustard will "put hair on your chest," although we know it actually won't (at least we hope so).

The work of John Pattison and his colleagues for Hobart in Figure 3.3 presents a similar actual versus nonactual contrast. Hobart's Compact Undercounter equipment is so tough, if you ran into it in a dark alley, it would actually beat you up and steal your lunch money. Once again, this is comic exaggeration.

Four poster ads from an award-winning campaign for Weru AG, a manufacturer of windows and doors in Germany, are also excellent examples of comic wit (see Figures 3.4 through 3.7).

The incongruous contrasts in all four ads are also consistent with Raskin's actual versus nonactual contrast type. When we match the product name in the corner of each ad with the size of the tool in the visual, we have what we need to resolve the incongruity. These tools are *not actually* this small—they only sound as if they are because there's a Weru soundproof window between them and us. It's comic understatement.

Figure 3.3   Comic wit for Hobart. (Ad appears courtesy of Hobart, Troy, OH.)

Figure 3.4 Comic wit for
Weru AG: "Garbage Can."
(Ad appears courtesy of
Weru AG.)

Figure 3.5 Comic wit for
Weru AG: "Worker." (Ad
appears courtesy of
Weru AG.)

Figure 3.6 Comic wit for
Weru AG: "Gardener."
(Ad appears courtesy of
Weru AG.)

Figure 3.7 Comic wit for Weru AG: "Policeman." (Ad appears courtesy of Weru AG.)

In Figure 3.8, the incongruous contrast of the multiple-award-winning magazine ad for Leo Burnett, London, client H. J. Heinz is an example of Raskin's possible versus impossible contrast type. It differs from the normal versus non-normal contrast type because the contrast is fantasy based—it's simply impossible for a can of pasta to cling to the underside of the cupboard shelf all by itself (even if it is Spider-Man pasta). The resolution of the incongruity (why is that can hanging upside down in the cupboard?) and the surprise it produces make the ad both funny and an excellent example of comic wit.

Finally, the example in Figure 3.9, another award-winner from *The Economist*'s "White Out of Red" campaign, shows that comic wit can be successfully extended to promotional messages outside the traditional mass media. You can recognize this comic

Figure 3.8 Comic wit for H. J. Heinz: "Cupboard." (Ad appears courtesy of H. J. Heinz Company Limited.)

Figure 3.9 Comic wit for *The Economist*: "Brainy." (Ad appears courtesy of *The Economist*.)

exaggeration of the effects of reading *The Economist* as another great example of a possible versus impossible contrast (unless, of course, you think people's heads actually get bigger the more knowledge they stuff into them).

It's also clear the humor in all these ads is thematically related—reading *The Economist* will make you really smart, Findlay's Mustard is really spicy, Hobart food-service equipment is really tough, and Weru windows do a really great job of reducing noise. The humor in the Spider-Man pasta ad is also thematically related, or relevant, because it, like its namesake, can cling to things.

When to Use Comic Wit

First, it helps to recognize the differences between the more obvious types of comic wit. The intellectual (or cognitive) type (puns, riddles, and so on) probably isn't all that appealing to very young children. Buijzen and Valkenburg, who reviewed the small amount of academic literature on this topic, conclude that by the age of 4, "most children start to appreciate simple forms of verbal humor such as playing with the sounds of words or the incongruous labeling of objects and events."[19]

But research also suggests that during middle childhood (ages 8 to 11), kids begin to appreciate humor that's more complicated and abstract.[20] One team of researchers found a gender difference for this type of humor, with girls favoring the more cognitive and sophisticated puns and riddles.[21] Research conducted by Groch[22] and McGhee[23] also suggests that during early childhood, girls like "incongruous and surprising events, amusing behaviors, verbal forms of humor and animal antics more than boys do."[24]

Researchers have also found that as children get older they increasingly enjoy wordplay, and when they reach adolescence (ages 12 to 18), they like puns and irony but continue to enjoy slapstick and physical forms of humor.[25] When people reach adulthood, puns and other forms of wordplay are among the types of humor they enjoy most.[26] In the case of cognitively humorous ads in particular, Speck proposes they appeal to "the puzzle-solving skills of viewers who enjoy the excitement of a perceptual and cognitive challenge."[27]

Speck also concludes that comic wit has a weaker effect on comprehension than a nonhumorous ad, while the other four types seem to be more effective. Stern suggests that purely verbal wit is, or should be, used frequently in radio advertising because it's entirely verbal and can take advantage of radio's "theater of the mind."

Then there are the more physical and visual kinds of comic wit. This type of humor probably does work well with kids. Buijzen and Valkenburg propose this kind of humor—including funny faces, sudden visual surprises, unusual voices, and *anthropomorphism* and *personification* (animals and inanimate objects portrayed with human characteristics)—is especially appealing to children in early childhood because their orientation to the world is mostly visual. Citing both Groch and McGhee, they also note that girls favor incongruous humor and surprising events, "amusing physical behaviors, verbal forms of humor, and animal antics."[28] Around the age of 10, kids overall "begin to like social transformations as well as illogical behavior and situations."[29]

Once people reach adulthood, age differences are less important when it comes to explaining humor preferences, while demographic variables such as gender, culture, education, and socioeconomic status become better predictors.[30] In the case of comic wit, adult women tend to appreciate nonsensical and silly humor more than men do.[31] Finally, Stern also argues that physical comedy is good for attracting attention while not encouraging much cognitive processing.[32]

THE RESONANT WIT AD

When something incongruous (e.g., a pun, exaggeration, or understatement) is combined with arousal-safety humor, positively warm or negatively aggressive, we get a resonant wit ad. You'll recall that arousal-safety theory proposes that something seems funny when we initially experience a heightened feeling (or emotion) of anxiety or uncertainty for the well-being of ourselves or somebody else. If we can make a safety judgment that the object of the anxiety is safe or there aren't really any negative consequences (in other words, order will be restored), then the tension is relieved and we experience it as humor.

Resonant wit, such as the Singapore Cancer Society ad in Figure 3.10, is generated by a combination of arousal-safety (a thought-provoking suggestion about damage to people's lungs caused by cigarette smoking) and incongruity-resolution (what is the meaning of that lung-shaped ashtray?). You may also recognize Raskin's actual versus nonactual contrast in this ad. The ashtray symbolizes actual human lungs being damaged by a cigarette, except it's not actually lungs but an ashtray. The visual metaphor gets the point across pretty clearly, and the thematic relatedness of the humor is obvious.

The poster ad for the Mount Sinai Medical Center, shown in Figure 3.11, is a very similar example of resonant wit. And here again, we have a Raskin-type actual versus nonactual contrast in the visual pun created by the baseball's stitching. It fits nicely into Raskin's actual versus nonactual contrast statement: *It is the case* that the stitching represents minimally invasive surgery to repair a sports injury, *and it is not the case* that it is a real baseball's stitching. As far as the arousal-safety humor goes, there aren't many things that cause as much anxiety as thinking about surgery. The thematic relatedness of the humor in this ad is also obvious.

The ad created by HSR Business to Business for the Workshops of David T. Smith is another example of resonant wit (see Figure 3.12). The Workshops of David T. Smith makes reproductions of Shaker furniture, and, in the context of

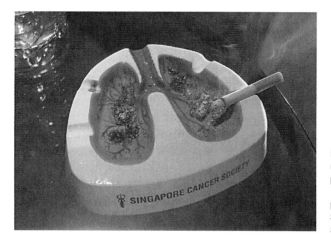

Figure 3.10 Resonant wit for Singapore Cancer Society: "Ashtray." (Ad appears courtesy of the Singapore Cancer Society.)

the ad, the copy suggests Mr. Smith and his artisans are just like the original Shakers. That is, up to a point. The second two lines of copy reveal the incongruity between two scripts (we're *actually* just like Shakers, we're *not actually* just like Shakers). There's mild arousal-safety humor in Mr. Smith's rejection of the Shakers' celibate lifestyle. See John Pattison's "Funny Business" piece in Box 3.2, where he offers some thoughts about advertising humor in general and the strategy behind this funny ad.

Another example of resonant wit, and one that's a little more aggressive in tone, is a TV spot titled "Surprise Dinner." This is one ad in a hugely

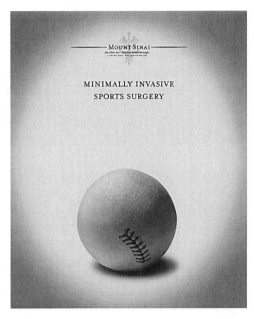

Figure 3.11 Resonant wit for Mount Sinai Medical Center: "Baseball." (Ad reprinted by permission of Mount Sinai Medical Center and DeVito/Verdi, New York, NY.)

successful campaign for Ameriquest Mortgage Company. You may remember seeing two other spots in this campaign in Super Bowl XL titled "Killed Him" and "Turbulence."

In "Surprise Dinner" (see Figure 3.13), we see a guy arriving at his girlfriend's apartment, and we watch as he prepares a surprise dinner of spaghetti. He checks his watch and adds spices to the sauce and flowers to the table—everything's under control. That is, up to the point when the girlfriend's especially white, fluffy cat knocks the pan of spaghetti sauce to the floor. Simultaneously, huge knife in one hand, he picks up the sauce-covered cat with the other as the girlfriend walks in the front door to witness what appears to be an especially gruesome cat murder. "Don't judge too quickly," Ameriquest advises. "We won't."

With its combination of *actual* (he didn't really kill the cat, it just looks like it) versus *nonactual* (he killed the cat) contrast and disastrous arousal-safety humor, this spot is a perfect example of resonant wit. And since the humor is used to make the point that Ameriquest won't rush to judgment about whether to give you a loan, it's clearly thematically related.

Figure 3.12   Resonant wit for the Workshops of David T. Smith: "Celibate." (Ad appears courtesy of the Workshops of David T. Smith.)

SHAKERS MADE
GREAT FURNITURE.

WE MAKE
GREAT FURNITURE.

SHAKERS WERE
CELIBATE.

WE MAKE
GREAT FURNITURE.

MOUNT LEBANON SHAKER CHEST
~ CIRCA 1800-1850 ~

Immodest? Perhaps. Unchaste? Never. Our fidelity to crafting early-American furniture the old-fashioned way is as incorruptible as the Shakers themselves. Just ask our kids. Or, better yet, call 888-353-9387 for a free catalog.

DAVID T. SMITH
& CO.
CABINET MAKERS
& GRAINERS
MORROW, OHIO

Funny Business

BOX 3.2. WHEN WE LAUGH, THE WALLS COME DOWN

When we laugh we feel better. We relax and are comfortable. Laughter is a natural part of life, one that we all have experienced, ever since we were young children. But what does laughter have to do with selling products? Everything.

Say, for example, we are selling a product to an intelligent, sophisticated woman who has an appreciation for the finer things in life. Or a 24-year-old guy who has an affinity for potty humor. By comparison, these two have very different taste levels when it comes to humor. However, with research, we can find out what makes each person tick. We can identify their respective funny bones. We then can couple this discovery with the unique selling proposition of what we're selling, to create a compelling, creative message that disarms your audience's skepticism and ultimately resonates.

A good example is an ad we did for the Workshops of David T. Smith (one in a series) [see Figure 3.12]. David T. Smith handcrafts high-end reproduction furniture. An original 1780 Shaker-style dresser, for instance, would cost hundreds of thousands of dollars. But a David T. Smith reproduction—indistinguishable from the original—would cost much less, around $7,000. Certainly a price not everybody can afford, but one his audience can.

David T. Smith, the man, embodies his brand, with his passion, sophisticated humor, and larger-than-life presence. His audience, on average, is 40 to 65 years old and financially well off. In addition to being intelligent, they have a deep respect for the history of early American furniture. They demand the best quality, and they are willing to pay for it. They also love solving problems. So we set the headline up like a riddle.

Shakers made great furniture.
We make great furniture.
Shakers were celibate.
We make great furniture.

The ad is designed in a very upscale, sophisticated fashion. Art direction deliberately emulates the craftsmanship of the furniture and contrasts nicely with the witty headline and copy, thus elevating the irony of the overall experience. The ad isn't funny for funny's sake. To the contrary, the ad is benefit rich, strategically focused, and purposeful.

Conclusion: When you allow your audience to discover your ad's surprise themselves (versus beating them over the head with it), the surprise is made all the more surprising. Take your readers by the hand, walk them up to the punch line, and let them discover it themselves. In the end, your audience will feel more rewarded and more endeared to the product or service you are trying to sell. This tactic draws your audience in and connects them emotionally to your product or service. It makes them feel good about it. It speaks their language. The language of laughter.

John Pattison, director-creative, HSR Business to Business, Cincinnati, OH

When to Use Resonant Wit

As far as the incongruity-resolution element of resonant wit is concerned, it seems likely that what we know about audience preferences for comic wit applies the same way. In general, appreciation for intellectual (or cognitive) wit probably increases with age. It's also likely that girls enjoy this type of advertising humor more than boys do—a difference that carries into adulthood. The physical and visual types of wit appeal to children earlier, and women probably appreciate nonsense and silliness in advertising more than men do. On the other hand, men probably favor the more aggressive types of resonant wit.

As for the arousal-safety element of resonant wit, we obviously need to distinguish between positive/warm resonant wit and aggressive resonant wit. Research on warmth as an emotional advertising appeal is somewhat limited, but a handful of researchers have found its effects on attitude toward an ad (an important variable measuring how much people say they like an ad) and purchase intention (how likely people are to say they plan to buy a certain product) are similar to those of

Figure 3.13   Resonant wit for Ameriquest Mortgage Company: "Surprise Dinner." (Ad appears courtesy of Ameriquest Mortgage Company Inc.)

humor in general.[33] More important, though, a study by Aaker and Stayman led them to conclude that women are more likely to respond positively to warm advertising than men are.[34] So it also seems likely that women respond more favorably to positive resonant wit than men do.

In terms of aggressive resonant wit, as children reach the end of early child-hood (ages 2 to 7), they begin to favor more gross, disgusting, and violent hu-mor. There's also an early gender difference, with boys favoring aggressive and violent humor more than girls do.[35] The enjoyment of this kind of humor, in-cluding sarcasm and irreverent behavior, increases into middle childhood, al-though children continue to enjoy slapstick, absurdity, disgusting and scatological humor, and humor based on the violation of taboos.[36]

The preference for gross types of humor, including scatological and dis-gusting humor, is greater among boys than girls in middle childhood—a trend that increases into adolescence.[37] Not surprisingly, this gender preference for more aggressive resonant wit also extends into adulthood. Although most adults appreciate slapstick and sexual humor, men more frequently enjoy ma-licious,[38] sick,[39] and sexual humor.[40]

THE RESONANT HUMOR AD

Resonant humor is generated entirely by the arousal-safety mechanism. It doesn't appear to be nearly as common as the other types. In fact, Speck found that, at only 12 percent, it was the least used type in U.S. television advertising. Comic wit was the most frequently used, at 31 percent.[41] Why is that? Proba-bly because, as we've seen throughout this book and in Table 3.1, incongruity is such an important part of humor generation.

For an ad to be purely resonant humor rather than resonant wit, the only stimulus must be arousal-safety in the form of (1) some kind of minor dis-aster experienced by someone; (2) a disruption to the social order; (3) some-thing even more aggressively taboo, shocking, or embarrassing; or (4) a warmly sentimental image. There can't be an incongruity. The Windsor Cana-dian ad in Figure 3.14 is a great example of warm, resonant humor. The stim-ulus of arousal is the dog's marginally tragic disruption to the cement layer's work, leading to mild anxiety and empathy. But the disaster facing our ce-ment layer is really not all that disastrous, and everything is going to be all right—especially after he gets home, relaxes, and enjoys a Windsor Canadian or two.

An ad for SCA Australasia's Sorbent Clean & Fresh (moistened, flushable toilet wipes), titled appropriately "Horse's Ass," is a perfect example of true "bathroom" humor (see Figure 3.15). Note the smile of satisfaction and contentment on the face of the, well, horse's ass. If you had to put your head where he does, you'd be happy your partner uses Clean & Fresh, too.

The 20-year-old "We'll leave the light on for you" radio campaign for Motel 6, created by the Richards Group and starring humorist Tom Bodett, offers a classic example of warmly resonant humor. This campaign has earned more than 150 individual creative awards and was ranked 91st on *Ad Age*'s list of Top 100 Advertising Campaigns of the 20th Century.[42] Although some of the campaign's more than 1,000 spots occasionally included wit and even mild disparagement of topically relevant people—ethically challenged business executives and striking professional baseball players, for example—the foundation for the entire campaign is warm arousal-safety humor. You can see from the spot in Figure 3.16 why this type of ad was originally called "sentimental humor."[43] Larry Oakner presents an entire chapter devoted to this campaign in his celebration of funny radio advertising, *And Now a Few Laughs from Our Sponsor*.[44]

Three poster ads for the Tate Britain Tour, winners of a Grand Prix for Corporate Image campaign at the 2006 Cannes International Advertising Festival, are perfect examples of mild arousal-safety

Figure 3.14   Resonant humor for Windsor Canadian. (Ad appears courtesy of Jim Beam Brands Co.)

Figure 3.15   Resonant humor for Sorbent Clean & Fresh: "Horse's Ass." (Ad appears courtesy of SCA Australasia.)

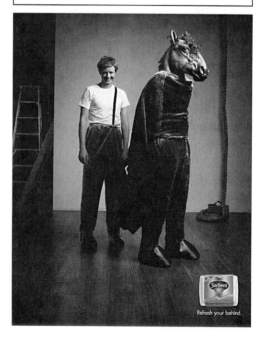

Figure 3.16   Resonant humor for Motel 6: "Tom's Mailbag." (Ad appears courtesy of Motel 6 and the Richards Group, Inc.)

CLIENT: MOTEL 6
JOB: :60 RADIO
TITLE: "TOM'S MAILBAG 2"
JOB#:   MTL-04-0005
DATE: 01/09/04

TOM: Hi, Tom Bodett for Motel 6. It's time once again to reach into Tom's Mailbag. Ronald in Atlanta writes, "Dear Tom, it's bad enough that we Americans get accused of being too fat, but now they're picking on our pets too. I have noticed that my own dog Sparky is getting a bit . . . husky. And when I throw a stick, he just uses it to stir up a batch of sloppy joes. Should I be concerned?" Well, Ronald, yes. But instead of subjecting Sparky the Large to a low-carb kibble diet or a little terrier treadmill, maybe he just needs to get out more. So take him on a road trip. Pets are always welcome at Motel 6, where you get a clean, comfortable room for the lowest price of any national chain. Because after a long day of running around and sniffing stuff, he'll need a good rest. I'm Tom Bodett for Motel 6, and we'll leave the light on for you and your "pleasantly plump" best friend. An Accor hotel.

humor, in which people experience some kind of tragedy, problem, or challenge, such as splitting up with a romantic partner, contemplating an important business meeting, or suffering from a hangover (see Figures 3.17 through 3.19). The Tate Britain, however, empathizes with the sufferers and encourages the rest of us to do so, too. The humor is thematically related to the campaign's message about the kinds of intellectual and emotional fulfillment that can be found at a world-class art museum.

When to Use Resonant Humor

Everything we discussed about preferences for the warm and sentimental (rather than the aggressive) arousal-safety elements of resonant wit ads applies to resonant humor, as well. It seems likely that, compared with men, women favor positive resonant humor—a difference that begins in childhood. Likewise, boys and men probably appreciate the more aggressive and shocking forms of resonant humor.

Speck also offers a few clues regarding the use of resonant humor and advertising outcomes. He proposes that resonant humor is probably best if the goal is to generate a positive attitude toward the ad or toward the brand (typically measured in terms of how good or bad or how likable or unlikable people say the brand is). He also found this type of humor encourages people to view the source as more trustworthy compared with nonhumorous ads or those of other humor types. This latter conclusion is especially important, since, as you'll learn in Chapter 4, there hasn't been much research on whether humor contributes much to source credibility.

Figure 3.17   Resonant humor for Tate Britain: "Split Up." **(Ad appears courtesy of Tate Britain.)**

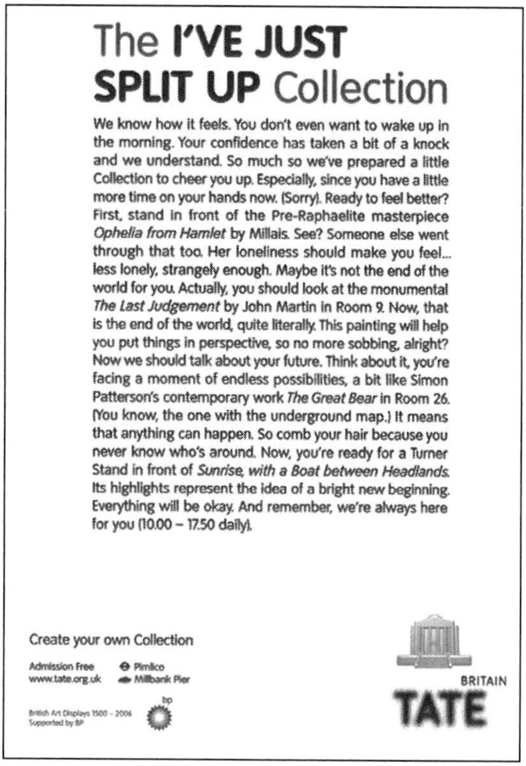

THE SATIRICAL AD

The disparagement and superiority theories we looked at in Chapter 2 propose that satire relates to the social context for humor and suggests we laugh when we're encouraged to feel superior to someone else. The arousal stimulus is the disparaging portrayal or playful victimization of a person, group, idea, practice, or, often in the case of advertising, competitor. The resulting tension is a mixture of pleasure and anxiety—pleasure from feeling superior and anxiety from feeling it's socially inappropriate to enjoy the ridicule or criticism of somebody else.

Although harsh disparagement is pretty rare in commercial advertising, it seems to be turning up more and more often in the form of satire and comparative advertising. For example, when Universal/Orlando Theme Park asks, "Fairy tales and pixie dust not quite your thing?" it's pretty obvious whom they're talking about. Satire is often used in comparative ads, although there aren't any hard numbers to confirm just how often.

The humor in satirical ads is generated by the disparagement and incongruity-resolution mechanisms. That's because, unlike the incongruity-resolution and arousal-safety mechanisms, disparagement doesn't work very well by itself in advertising or pretty much anywhere else. As one influential scholar notes, "Playfulness and wit are needed for disparagement to seem humorous."[45] Celebrated advertising satirist Stan Freberg also recognizes the problem—"outrage in its natural state is not too salable."[46]

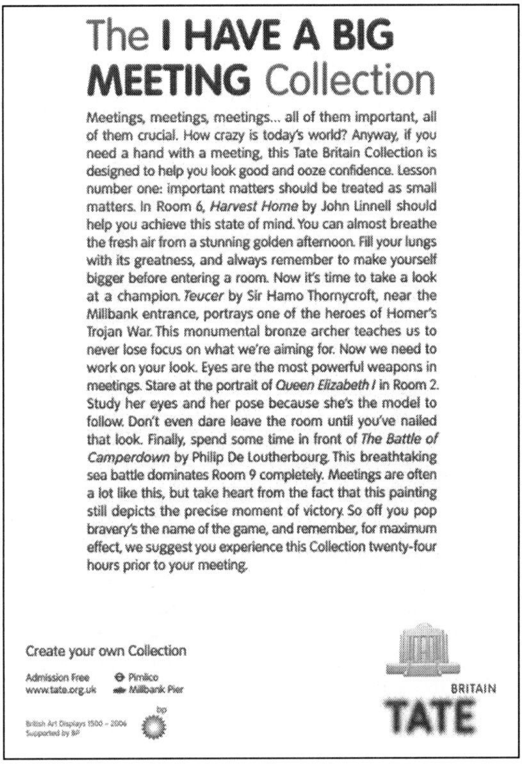

A terrific example of a satirical attack ad comes from a campaign for Juniper Networks, a marketer of information technology products and services (see Figure 3.20). Note the actual versus nonactual contrast. In the context of this ad, Juniper's larger competitor, Cisco, invented the

Figure 3.18   Resonant humor for Tate Britain: "Big Meeting." (Ad appears courtesy of Tate Britain.)

wheel. But we know this isn't actually true. This overly complex wheel is merely what it would look like if they had. The humor is thematically related because it refers directly to a proposed Cisco shortcoming. Don't miss the "Funny Business" piece in Box 3.3 by Tim Oden, a cocreative director (with colleague Bruce Parks) responsible for the Juniper Networks campaign.

The radio spot for the St. Michael's Majors hockey team in Figure 3.21 is another great example of a satirical attack ad. The disparagingly incongruous description of National Hockey League players using references to their contracts and endorsement deals ridicules them for being more interested in making money than playing the kind of hockey the real fan wants to see. Note here, again, the actual versus nonactual Raskin-type contrast. This is wordplay, where the various types of promotional deals made by big-league hockey players are actually referred to in the play-by-play rather than their real names.

Again, this humor is thematically related to a proposed shortcoming of major-league players.

A very unusual example of satire is a poster campaign for the 3rd Lair Skatepark in Golden Valley, Minnesota (see Figures 3.22 through 3.24). What's so unusual? While the target of some of the satire is, in fact, lawyers and landlords, the posters also ridicule not only 3rd Lair itself ("this dump") but also the target audience ("knee-scraped little blister pods"). In this case, the contrast is normal versus non-normal. While it's normal for ads to ask customers to buy products because they're a good value or offered at a good price, it's not normal for ads to say the products are overpriced but customers should buy them anyway for reasons completely unrelated to their value. The humor is thematically related to 3rd Lair's "boarder" image. See a description of the strategy behind these ads, written by one of its creators, Jeff Rabkin, in Box 3.4.

Figure 3.19   Resonant humor for Tate Britain: "I'm Hungover." (Ad appears courtesy of Tate Britain.)

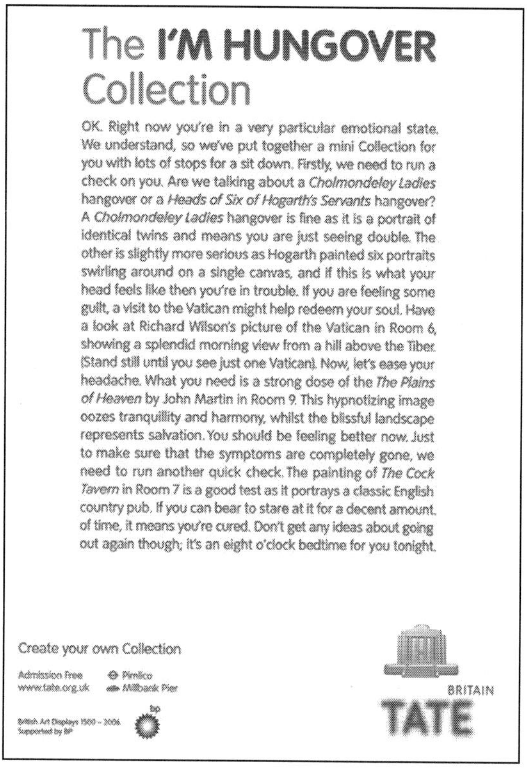

Figures 3.25 and 3.26 present two examples of satirical attack ads created for the nonprofit Center for Union Facts. Since the objective is more political in nature, as opposed to commercial, it's not surprising the satire is quite a bit more aggressive than the other ads we've looked at. The first one uses a riddle-like actual versus nonactual contrast—why is a union like a roach motel? The second ad uses cognitive wit to marginally soften the bite of the attack—a witty headline ("Male, Pale & Stale") condemns union leadership for consisting almost entirely of older white men. Without the clever headline, the ad would lack humor.

When to Use Satire

First of all, it seems fairly obvious that disparagement can seem excessively harsh and consequently not funny. This response is so common, in fact, people who study political advertising have a name for it—it's called *backlash*. This is probably why Cho, in the study described earlier, found that disparagement was negatively correlated with perceived humorousness. Speck also concludes that people often don't respond well to aggressive satire,[47] partly because most people are at least a little reluctant to enjoy other people's ridicule.

Although this topic hasn't been studied much, it's likely audience responses to satire differ based on the target of the

Figure 3.20 Satire for Juniper Networks: "If Cisco Had Invented the Wheel." (Ad appears courtesy of Juniper Networks.)

Figure 3.21 Satire for the St. Michael's Majors hockey club: "Pro Hockey Players." (Ad appears courtesy of St. Michael's Majors hockey club.)

ANNOUNCER: And we're down to the final seconds of this one. "Shaving Cream Endorsement" flips the puck through the air, knocked down by "Free Agent Next Year." "Free Agent" slides it over to "5 Million a Year." On the left side, "5 Million's" hit hard by "Spokesman for Athletic Equipment He Doesn't Even Use." And there's a penalty on the play. . . . Wanna see great hockey players before they hit the NHL? Then check out the St. Mike's Majors this Thursday when they take on the Oshawa Generals. St. Mike's Majors, hard-core hockey.

Funny Business

Box 3.3. **ATTACKING A GOLIATH COMPETITOR WITH SATIRE**

Some comments from a guy who's a humor skeptic for the 95 percent of us writers whose local/regional clients can't afford bad jokes. . . .

The ad biz attracts people who like to think they're clever. Many are. This should not be confused with humorous. Few people can construct humor. But if you can deploy one of those few people for your brand— successfully—now *that's* clever.

You asked for ads I think are humorous. To be true to my own rhetoric, I chose one I had to take responsibility for. It was the first of many in our *Wall Street Journal* campaign for Juniper Networks by the fabulously gifted cartoonist Kevin Pope. We mined humor because against competitor Cisco, we had to gain brand awareness fast on 1/100th the budget. In this campaign, I think humor is a real workhorse because of the following factors:

It draws the eye before the brain can say No.
It has the balls to name a goliath competitor.
It instantly puts Juniper in the router business.
It taps widespread anti-Cisco sentiment: They're too complex!

Most of the time, humor in ads is like lipstick, bleached teeth, and silicone implants. It's great if it attracts my attention, but unless it connects with fulfilling a need I have, it's just another pretty and exceedingly expensive face.

Think about Super Bowl spots. You have an audience unlike any other, one that actually *wants* to see your ad. So creatives deliver funny spots. Some are brilliant. Most are like open mic night at the comedy club. Quick: Name a spot and brand from the last Super Bowl. Even if you can, did you switch to that brand?

The best advertising makes clear, cogent connections between your need and my product. That alone is very difficult to do, even if I can find you amidst kaleidoscopic media choices.

So the burden's on the court jester to be serious about getting results with humor because the client is king.

Tim Oden, executive VP and creative director, Ackerman McQueen, Inc., Oklahoma City, OK

Figure 3.22   Satire for the 3rd Lair Skatepark: "Bone-Head Lawyers." (Ad appears courtesy of 3rd Lair Skatepark/Skateshop.)

```
✻✻✻✻✻✻✻✻✻✻✻✻✻✻✻✻✻✻✻✻✻✻✻✻✻✻✻✻✻
MAYBE THIS STUFF DOES COST TOO
MUCH. WHAT THE HELL? YOU'RE
ALREADY HERE AND IT'S YOUR
MOM'S MONEY ANYWAY. AND IF YOU
BUY YOUR CRAP HERE WE'LL MAKE
ENOUGH MONEY TO FIGHT OFF THE
BONE-HEAD LAWYERS AND LANDLORD
DOLTS WHO WANT TO SHUT US DOWN
AND OPEN A WALLPAPER STORE TO
SELL CHINTZ DRAPERIES AND DUCK
BORDERS. YOU WANT THAT TO HAP-
PEN? NO. WE DIDN'T THINK SO.
JUST BUY IT ALREADY.
✻✻✻✻✻✻✻✻✻✻✻✻✻✻✻✻✻✻✻✻✻✻✻✻✻✻✻✻✻

          THANK YOU

   3RD LAIR SKATEPARK - PROSHOP

✻✻✻✻✻✻✻✻✻✻✻✻✻✻✻✻✻✻✻✻✻✻✻✻✻✻✻✻✻
```

Figure 3.23   Satire for the 3rd Lair Skatepark: "High-Dollar Paraphernalia." (Ad appears courtesy of 3rd Lair Skatepark/Skateshop.)

```
############################
YEAH, WE KNOW, YOU COME HERE
TO SKATE NOT TO BUY A BUNCH OF
HIGH-DOLLAR PARAPHERNALIA. BUT
LOOK AROUND. YOU THINK WE KEEP
THIS PLACE HEATED ALL WINTER
ON PISS-ASS SKATE FEES? GET
SMART ALREADY. IF WE DON'T MOVE
MERCHANDISE, 3RD LAIR GOES
DINOSAUR AND YOU'RE BACK HUMP-
ING THE DRIVEWAY. GOT IT? SO
BUY A BEANIE. BUY A BOARD. BUY
A DAMN MAGAZINE IF THAT'S ALL
THE COIN YOU GOT.
############################

          THANK YOU

   3RD LAIR SKATEPARK - PROSHOP

############################
```

disparagement. Is it a competitor, the user of a competitor's product, a generic competitor, the advertiser, the target audience, or a generic type of person? Who the target is will impact the audience's likelihood of successful *misattribution*, which we talked about in Chapter 2. For example, if the target of the humor is the advertiser (which would be self-deprecating humor), then misattribution is easy, since you don't have to feel guilty when people are making fun of themselves.

On the other hand, if the target of the satire is another advertiser or a competitive brand user, then the principle we talked about in Chapter 2—that people are more likely to enjoy the ridicule of their enemies than they are

Figure 3.24   Satire for the 3rd Lair Skatepark: "Blister Pods." (Ad appears courtesy of 3rd Lair Skatepark/Skateshop.)

```
+++++++++++++++++++++++++
SO YOU THINK OUR CLOTHES ARE
TOO EXPENSIVE? WHY DON'T YOU
GO SHOP AT THE MALL WITH YOUR
SISTER THEN. WE'VE GOT TO MAKE
MONEY HERE. WHY ELSE WOULD WE
SIT IN THIS DUMP ALL DAY? YOU
THINK WE EVER GET TO SKATE?
THIS SHOP IS WHAT KEEPS THE
DOORS OPEN SO YOU KNEE-SCRAPED
LITTLE BLISTER PODS DON'T HAVE
TO BLEED IN THE STREETS. GO TO
THE MALL WITH YOUR SISTER -
HIT ON HER FRIENDS - BUT BUY
YOUR TROUSERS HERE.
+++++++++++++++++++++++++

          THANK YOU

   3RD LAIR SKATEPARK - PROSHOP

+++++++++++++++++++++++++
```

Funny Business

Box 3.4. GETTING BOARDERS TO READ WITH SATIRE

No features. No benefits. These ads just cut to the universal truth of capitalism: A business has to sell stuff or it dies. A 15-year-old skateboard brat can understand that. This audience can sniff out phony posers without effort. So we wrote the copy with a kid's attitude but from an adult's perspective, and we made up our own slang instead of mangling theirs. Most skateboard marketing, especially point-of-sale, uses strong visuals and very little copy. Everyone just assumes that these kids don't read. But we knew these posters would stand out in the store—get noticed—and that the kids would read them if they were funny.

Jeff Rabkin, copywriter, Wowza, Minneapolis, MN

---

of their friends—applies. This explains why some researchers suggest aggressive satire works very well to encourage group morale and cohesion. The disparagement of outgroups and their members reinforces the shared experience of group membership and boosts the perception that a group and its members are superior and unique.[48]

Who enjoys this type of humor? Research suggests appreciation of disparagement humor—such as malicious and irreverent humor—starts when children reach the end of early childhood, around the age of 7.[49] As they get older, they increasingly enjoy sarcasm and humor featuring violent and irreverent behavior.[50] These preferences appear to continue during adolescence (ages 12 to 18), with preferences for sarcastic, ironic, irreverent,[51] and absurd humor.[52]

There's also a lot of research on comparative advertising that suggests how peo-

Figure 3.25   Satire for the Center for Union Facts. (Ad appears courtesy of the Center for Union Facts.)

Why Is a Union Like a Roach Motel?

Because Getting in Is the Easy Part.

We have the story behind the new union scheme to force employees into unions without the right to vote.

**Trapping bugs is fine.
Trapping people isn't.**

UnionFacts.com
The 12.5 million facts they don't want you to know

ple are likely to respond when an advertiser satirically attacks a competitor. Advertising is called comparative when it indirectly or directly compares the sponsored brand with one or more competitors. One team of researchers, Dhruv Grewal and his colleagues, conducted a comprehensive *meta-analysis* of 22 years of research (nearly 80 published studies) directly comparing comparative advertising's effectiveness with noncomparative advertising.[53] Meta-analysis is a sophisticated research method used to analyze the findings of many studies on the same topic. What they, as well as other researchers, have learned about how comparative ads work suggests quite a bit about how and when advertisers should use satire to attack a competitor.

Preferences for disparagement humor by gender also emerge during childhood, with boys preferring disparagement humor that includes teasing and ridicule.[54] Again, during middle childhood, boys like hostile humor more than girls do, especially humor that makes fun of other people or shows kids behaving irreverently toward adults.[55] This preference continues into adolescence and adulthood, with men enjoying aggressive, malicious, and hostile types of humor more than women do.[56]

Research on comparative advertising suggests comparative ads gain more attention and enhance message awareness, brand-name awareness, and message processing.[57] Research on political advertising also shows that negative information attracts more attention and is more easily recalled.[58] Speck's conclusion that satire is the most effective type of humor for gaining recall and comprehension of an advertising message seems to be, then, more than just a coincidence.

Marketplace experience and research both suggest that if advertisers are going to attack their competitors, the best scenario is if they're seen as a "feisty little competitor"[59] and the other guy is, as Tim Oden put it in Box 3.3, a "Goliath." Examples of this scenario include the Pepsi Challenge (born in 1975 and partly credited with causing Coca-Cola's "New Coke" fiasco); Jack in the

Figure 3.26   Satire for the Center for Union Facts. (Ad appears courtesy of the Center for Union Facts.)

Box's attack on McDonald's and Subway; EarthLink's attack on America Online; and, of course, Apple's recent attack on the PC world.

If an advertiser decides to make fun of a competitor in an ad, what should he
or she make fun of and how aggressive should the attack be? Sorescu and Gelb
conclude that attacking a competitor's product in a comparative ad isn't nearly
as risky as attacking the company. In their study, a negative image ad attacking
Toyota's competitors for exporting jobs was rated lower on every measure—
approval of the message, fairness, believability, and informativeness—compared
with both a negative product feature and a positive comparative ad. This was
true even among people who drove a Toyota.[60]

The Grewal research team also provides some insight into this issue. They
found the effects of comparative ads on favorable attitudes toward the sponsored brand to be greater when the ads contain evaluative (more subjective)
messages instead of factual (more objective) ones.[61] As an example, the Juniper
Networks ad implying Cisco would have added a lot of useless bells and whis-
tles to their version of the wheel is an evaluative kind of comparison—it's
mainly subjective. On the other hand, criticizing union leadership for being
"male, pale, and stale," and showing a bunch of pictures to prove it, is a little
more factual in nature. So why might more subjective criticisms be associated
with more favorable attitudes? The Grewal team argues this happens because
comparative ads encourage affective, or emotional, responses rather than cognitive, or rational, ones.

Research on negative comparative advertising also offers a clue or two about
how aggressive the attack should be. Comparing high- and low-negativity comparative ads, Sorescu and Gelb found that the low-negativity ad scored significantly higher on not only measures of believability but also fairness of its
content, approval of its content, informativeness, and overall ad evaluation. It
also did significantly better than the positive comparative ad on measures of
believability, informativeness, and overall ad evaluation.[62] The message seems
clear—it's OK to make fun of a competitor, but advertisers should be careful
not to get too nasty about it.

Finally, what's the best target audience for comparative satire? Advertisers
should definitely forget the users of the brand they're satirizing. After all, a satirical attack ad is basically implying the target brand's users are stupid for using
the brand they do. The good news is that a comparative ad will have favorable
effects among the people an advertiser would most like to influence—people
who switch between the sponsored and compared brands and people who
don't use either one. In Sorescu and Gelb's study, they developed a test ad that
compared aspirin unfavorably with Tylenol. Both third-brand users and switch-

ers responded more favorably on approval and believability compared with aspirin users. On the other hand, aspirin users had significantly lower ratings of the message and lower ratings of Tylenol as a brand. In addition, both third-brand users and switchers rated the Tylenol brand higher than did aspirin users.[63]

THE FULL COMEDY AD

We get full comedy when a single ad uses all three humor mechanisms to generate humor. These types of ads include an incongruity, which is identifiable as an actual versus nonactual, normal versus non-normal, or possible versus impossible contrast. Unlike resonant wit or resonant humor ads, though, full comedy ads are aggressive in the sense that people are encouraged to negatively interpret someone or something in the ad. But unlike pure satire, the disparagement is either softened somewhat with warm arousal-safety or includes some other element of negative or aggressive arousal-safety humor.

The Miller Lite TV spot shown in Figure 3.27 (titled "Epidemic") is a great example of full comedy. The spot begins with a typical bar scene, with guys at the bar enjoying a beer, while the sounds of a ball game are heard in the background. Then one of the guys lowers his bottle of light beer, looks at it in puzzlement, and says, "I can't taste my beer." He looks at the other guys at the bar and, with a rising note of panic in his voice, says it again: "I can't taste my beer." Suddenly, everybody realizes they can't taste their beer, either. Pandemonium breaks out, and an epidemic of light-beer-related taste failure spreads throughout the city—running, screaming, weeping chaos in the bowling alleys and streets. The ad concludes with three guys sitting in a bar (wisely drinking Miller Lite) and watching the bedlam through a window. The voice-over delivers the punch line: "Next time, try the light beer that actually tastes like . . . beer."

What makes the Miller Lite spot full comedy? First, we have incongruity in the form of a Raskin-type actual versus nonactual contrast. In the context of this ad, there's an actual epidemic of taste failure caused by tasteless light beer. But there is, of course, no actual epidemic. This is comic exaggeration. We have arousal-safety humor in the disaster that occurs—the poor guy on his knees, arms outstretched to the sky, weeping and moaning seems to do a pretty good job of highlighting just how total this disaster is. And, of course, we have disparagement in the satirical attack on other brands of light beer for their lack of taste. Is the humor thematically related? Absolutely. How much more obviously could Miller Brewing make the point that you should drink Lite for the taste?

The newspaper ad for the Atlanta Ballet in Figure 3.28 (titled "Two Dancers Die") is another great example of full comedy. The contrast is between the normal versus non-normal. It's certainly non-normal and unexpected for the Atlanta Ballet to encourage people to come see Romeo and Juliet, not because they like the ballet, but because they dislike it enough to enjoy seeing some of the dancers die. This idea is, of course, fairly aggressive arousal-safety humor—death is probably the ultimate arousal-safety stimulus. Disparagement in the form of self-deprecation tells us the folks at the Atlanta Ballet don't take themselves too seriously—at least not as seriously as we're accustomed to thinking of serious ballet types. The humor is somewhat thematically related to the Atlanta Ballet's image.

Two radio spots (see Figures 3.29 and 3.30) from a multiple-award-winning campaign for the National Thoroughbred Racing Association are also great examples of full comedy. As you read the copy for the spots, imagine you're listening to the prototypical horse-racing commentator describing a race (although this is one of those situations where your imagination simply can't do justice to the actual performance).

Figure 3.27   Full comedy for Miller Lite: "Epidemic." (Ad appears courtesy of Miller Brewing Company.)

Both ads, structured identically, are consistent with Raskin's actual versus nonactual contrast type. These ads sound like actual horse races, but they're not. The horse-racing metaphor is simply being used as a vehicle to satirize types of people (e.g., sorority girls, bitter women, Japanese businessmen, and, of course, golfers), using many of their less-than-flattering characteristics in the place of the horses' names. Disparaged also are other recreational activities that fail to measure up to the enjoyment of thoroughbred racing. Thinking about the kinds of personal and public disasters that occur both in karaoke bars and on golf courses generates arousal-safety humor that is encouraged further by the commentator's rapid and breathless delivery. The humor is strongly thematically related, emphasizing repeatedly why listeners will have a much better time if they go to the track.

Another unique example of full comedy is the radio spot (titled "New Word") in Figure 3.31. This internationally award-winning commercial is part of an enforcement-focused marketing campaign, produced and funded by the Insurance Corporation of B.C., a government-owned auto insurer. The spot is a parody of a Sesame Street-like TV segment designed to teach little kids the

Figure 3.28 Full comedy for the Atlanta Ballet: "Two Dancers Die." (Ad appears courtesy of the Atlanta Ballet.)

Figure 3.29 Full comedy for the National Thoroughbred Racing Association: "Karaoke." (Ad appears courtesy of the National Thoroughbred Racing Association.)

COMMENTATOR: And they're off. Out of the gate it's Karaoke Bar with Watered-Down Drinks. Quickly moving to the front it's Newlyweds with I've Got You Babe. Next it's Sorority Girls with—I don't believe it—Like a Virgin. Now, coming on strong, it's Bitter Babes with I Will Survive. And here comes Throbbing Headache with Thumping and Pounding. Oh, no! Here comes Japanese Trio with Ruv Me Tender, You Right Up My Rife, and Rouie Rouie. And in the end, it's going to be Ringing Ears, Mother of All Migraines, and Six Hours You'll Never Get Back.

SFX: Ringing bell and crash of starting gate.

ANNOUNCER: For a better time, go to the track. National Thoroughbred Racing. We bet you love it.

Figure 3.30   Full comedy for the National Thoroughbred Racing Association: "Golf." (Ad appears courtesy of the National Thoroughbred Racing Association.)

COMMENTATOR: And they're off. Out of the gate is Day of Golf with Plaid Pants and Funny Hat. Now it's Hit the Ball, It's in the Woods, and Walk after It. And now it's Hit the Ball, It's in the Sand, and Walk after It. Now on the inside, it's Pull Yourself Together and Concentrate, with Knees Bent, Head Down, Arms Straight, Firm Grip, Easy Swing, Hit the Ball, and . . . no! . . . It's in the Pond. Out of nowhere comes Temper Tantrum with Cursing and Swearing, and Temper Tantrum isn't letting up. And in the end, it's Maniac Man, Thrown Clubs, and 17 More Holes of Hell.

SFX: Ringing bell and crash of starting gate.

ANNOUNCER: For a better time, go to the track. National Thoroughbred Racing. We bet you love it.

meaning of a new word—another actual versus nonactual contrast. The target of the disparagement is, of course, car thieves, and the reference to showering with lots of other guys evokes arousal-safety humor. To figure out whether or not it's thematically related, ask yourself whether you think a car thief might reconsider stealing a car after hearing it. The Insurance Corporation of B.C. has produced other equally aggressive and funny radio spots for its bait-car program. You can find out more about those and see actual videos of car thieves discovering they've stolen a bait car (talk about arousal-safety humor!) at www.baitcar.com.

Figure 3.31   Full comedy for the Auto Crime Police and the Insurance Corporation of B.C.: "New Word." (Ad appears courtesy of the Insurance Corporation of B.C.)

ANNOUNCER: Research tells us that car thieves aren't that smart. So for their benefit, let's keep this message simple.

MUSIC: Child's music box begins playing and continues throughout.

ANNOUNCER: Today, let's focus on some words that might be helpful to know if you're a car thief. Today's word is the word *right*. Let's try using it in a sentence. You have the *right* to remain silent. You have the *right* to an attorney. Prison food doesn't taste *right*. It don't feel *right* taking a shower *right* beside these other guys. Auto crime police enforcement is up. It's *right* to be worried if you're a car thief.

When to Use Full Comedy

The little available research directly comparing different funny ad types suggests full comedy is probably better than the others when it comes to getting attention and encouraging positive product-related attitudes and perceptions.[64] There's also the possibility that full comedy, like resonant wit and resonant humor, may not wear out as quickly—possibly because it relies only in part on incongruity for its humor.

In addition, when you consider how people respond differently to humor generated by the three mechanisms, it seems obvious that we should be able to apply these responses to full comedy as well. For example, as far as the incongruity and arousal-safety elements of a full comedy ad are concerned, we can expect that important differences by age and gender—such as preferences for verbal (or cognitive) versus physical comedy and for warm versus aggressive arousal-safety—probably apply in exactly the same way. Similarly, as far as the disparagement goes, we can probably also expect people to respond differently depending on who the advertiser is, the target of the disparagement, the aggressiveness or negativity of the disparagement, the age and gender of the target audience, and whether the attack is evaluative or factual.

More important, though, it also seems likely that full comedy may be the best type of ad to use for broad, general audiences. Buijzen and Valkenburg found that slapstick, which is full comedy in their typology, is the most frequently used type of TV ad (in the Netherlands, anyway) and that it's a type of humor enjoyed by people of all ages. They also specifically note that advertisers tend to use humor generated by all three mechanisms for general audiences.

CONCLUSIONS ABOUT HUMOROUS AD TYPES

One thing this chapter suggests is that the HMT holds up pretty well, if only because most of the time it's fairly easy to identify funny ads as one of the five types. That's probably the most important test of a good typology. Does it work? Is it useful?

This doesn't mean, though, that all the other humor typologies we talked about are worthless. The similarities of these other typologies and types to those in the HMT help make the differences among them even clearer. For example, even though no one's probably going to adopt Stern's typology, her application of drama theory helpfully reveals some very important differences between physical comedy, witty humor, romantic comedy, satire, and the ludicrous versus ridiculous.

Something else worth recognizing is the versatility of humor. As the ads in this chapter show, thanks to its roots in the three classical humor mechanisms, humor represents a rich source for the creation of compelling advertising messages—from cognitively engaging to warmly emotional and everything in between. This is probably another explanation for why humor is used so often. Another explanation for its varied use is something else we explored in this chapter—the wide difference in responses to humor among different types of people. And I suspect we still merely scratched the surface.

Finally, and as you'll also discover in Chapter 4, advertising professionals' use of humor often seems to match up pretty well with the conclusions of academic theorists and researchers. Although that wasn't my goal when I picked the examples in this chapter, they generally seem to be quite consistent with what theory and research suggest is the most effective use of humor. Among the more obvious examples are Juniper Network's satirical attack on a much larger "Goliath" competitor, 3rd Lair's tongue-in-cheek disparagement of itself and its own boarder target audience, and BK's "unintentional" and short-lived (but long enough to hit the "blogosphere") use of extremely racy double entendres.

NOTES

1. Tony Schwartz, *The Responsive Chord* (Garden City, NY: Anchor, 1973).

2. Paul S. Speck, "The Humorous Message Taxonomy: A Framework for the Study of Humorous Ads," in *Current Issues and Research in Advertising*, eds. James H. Leigh and Claude R. Martin Jr. (Ann Arbor: University of Michigan, 1991), 15.

3. Lynette S. Unger, "Observations: A Cross-Cultural Study on the Affect-Based Model of Humor in Advertising," *Journal of Advertising Research* 35, no. 1 (1995): 66–72.

4. Jeffrey H. Goldstein and Paul E. McGhee, *The Psychology of Humor: Theoretical Perspectives and Empirical Issues* (New York: Academic, 1972).

5. J. Patrick Kelly and Paul J. Solomon, "Humor in Television Advertising," *Journal of Advertising* 4, no. 3 (1975): 31–35.

6. Lynette S. McCullough and Ronald K. Taylor, "Humor in American, British, and German Ads," *Industrial Marketing Management* 22, no. 1 (1993): 17–29.

7. Hyongoh Cho, "Humor Mechanisms, Perceived Humor and Their Relationships to Various Executional Types in Advertising," *Advances in Consumer Research* 22 (1995): 191–197; Paul E. McGhee, *Humour: Its Origin and Development* (San Francisco: Freeman, 1979), 193.

8. Cho, "Humor Mechanisms," 193.

9. Cho, "Humor Mechanisms," 193.

10. Cho, "Humor Mechanisms," 193.

11. Barbara B. Stern, "Advertising Comedy in Electronic Drama," *European Journal of Marketing* 30, no. 9 (1996): 37–60.

12. Stern, "Advertising Comedy in Electronic Drama," 42.

13. Stern, "Advertising Comedy in Electronic Drama," 42.

14. Cordruta Catanescu and Gail Tom, "Types of Humor in Television and Magazine Advertising," *Review of Business* 22, no. 1/2 (2001): 92–96.

15. Mark F. Toncar, "The Use of Humour in Television Advertising: Revisiting the US-UK Comparison," *International Journal of Advertising* 20, no. 4 (2001): 521–540.

16. Moniek Buijzen and Patti M. Valkenburg, "Developing a Typology of Humor in Audiovisual Media," *Media Psychology* 6 (2004): 146–167.

17. Buijzen and Valkenburg, "Developing a Typology," 162.

18. Buijzen and Valkenburg, "Developing a Typology," 162.

19. Buijzen and Valkenburg, "Developing a Typology," 150.

20. McGhee, *Humour: Its Origin and Development.*

21. David M. Brodzinsky, Karen Barnet, and John R. Aiello, "Sex of Subject and Gender Identity as Factors in Humor Appreciation," *Sex Roles* 7 (1981): 561–573.

22. Alice Groch, "Generality of Response to Humor and Wit in Cartoons, Jokes, Stories, and Photographs," *Psychological Reports* 35 (1974): 935–938.

23. Paul E. McGhee, "Laughing Matter: A Symposium: Sex Differences in Children's Humor," *Journal of Communication* 26, no. 3 (1976): 176–189.

24. Buijzen and Valkenburg, "Developing a Typology," 151.

25. Dan S. Acuff and Robert H. Reiher, *What Kids Buy and Why* (New York: Free Press, 1997); McGhee, *Humour: Its Origin and Development.*

26. McGhee, *Humour: Its Origin and Development.*

27. Speck, "The Humorous Message Taxonomy," 12.

28. Buijzen and Valkenburg, "Developing a Typology," 151

29. Buijzen and Valkenburg, "Developing a Typology," 151.

30. Buijzen and Valkenburg, "Developing a Typology"; Marc G. Weinberger and Charles Gulas, "The Impact of Humor in Advertising: A Review," *Journal of Advertising* 21, no. 4 (1992): 35–59.

31. Brodzinsky et al., "Sex of Subject and Gender Identity"; Anne M. Johnson, "Language Ability and Sex Affect Humor Appreciation," *Perceptual and Motor Skills* 75 (1992): 571–581.

32. Stern, "Advertising Comedy in Electronic Drama."

33. David A. Aaker, Douglas M. Stayman, and Michael R. Hagerty, "Warmth in Advertising: Measurement, Impact and Sequence Effects," *Journal of Consumer Research* 12, no. 4 (1986): 365–381; David A. Aaker and Donald E. Bruzzone, "Viewer Perceptions of Prime-time Television Advertising," *Journal of Advertising Research* 211, no. 5 (1981): 15–23.

34. David A. Aaker and Douglas M. Stayman, "What Mediates the Emotional Response to Advertising? The Case of Warmth," in *Cognitive and Affective Reactions to Advertising*, eds. Patricia Cafferata and Alice Tybout (Lexington, MA: Lexington Books, 1989), 287–304.

35. Acuff and Reiher, *What Kids Buy*; McGhee, "Laughing Matter: A Symposium."

36. Acuff and Reiher, *What Kids Buy*; Patrice A. Oppliger and Dolf Zillman, "Disgust in Humor: Its Appeal to Adolescents," *Humor* 10 (1997): 421–437.

37. Oppliger and Zillman, "Disgust in Humor."

38. Lynette S. Unger, "The Potential for Using Humor in Global Advertising," *Humor* 9, no. 2 (1996): 133–168.

39. Thomas R. Herzog and Joseph A. Karafa, "Preferences for Sick versus Nonsick Humor," *Humor* 11 (1998): 291–312.

40. Groch, "Generality of Response to Humor"; James Hassett and John Houlihan, "Different Jokes for Different Folks," *Psychology Today* 12 (1979): 65–101.

41. Speck, "The Humorous Message Taxonomy."

42. "The Advertising Century," AdAge.com, http://www.adage.com/century/campaigns.html (accessed February 13, 2006).

43. Speck, "The Humorous Message Taxonomy."

44. Larry Oakner, *And Now a Few Laughs from Our Sponsor* (New York: Wiley, 2002).

45. Dolf Zillman, "Disparagement Humor," in *Handbook of Humor Research*, vol. 1, eds. Paul E. McGhee and Jeffrey H. Goldstein (New York: Springer-Verlag, 1983), 85–108.

46. Stan Freberg, *It Only Hurts When I Laugh* (New York: Times Books, 1988), 272.

47. Speck, "The Humorous Message Taxonomy."

48. Gary A. Fine, "Sociological Approaches to the Study of Humor," in *Handbook of Humor Research*, vol. 1, eds. Paul E. McGhee and Jeffrey H. Goldstein (New York: Springer-Verlag, 1983), 159–181; Jerry Suls, "Cognitive Processes in Humor Appreciation," in *Handbook of Humor Research*, vol. 1, eds. Paul E. McGhee and Jeffrey H. Goldstein (New York: Springer-Verlag, 1983), 39–57; Unger, "The Potential for Using Humor"; Avner Ziv, *National Styles of Humor* (Westport, CT: Greenwood Press, 1988).

49. Buijzen and Valkenburg, "Developing a Typology."

50. Acuff and Reiher, *What Kids Buy*.

51. Acuff and Reiher, *What Kids Buy*; Oppliger and Zillman, "Disgust in Humor."

52. McGhee, *Humour: Its Origin and Development*.

53. Dhruv Grewal, Sukumar Kavanoor, Edward F. Fern, Carolyn Costley, and James Barnes, "Comparative versus Noncomparative Advertising: A Meta-Analysis," *Journal of Marketing* 61, no. 4 (1997): 1–15.

54. McGhee, "Laughing Matter."

55. McGhee, "Laughing Matter."

56. Norbert Mundorf, Azna Bhatia, Dolf Zillman, Paul Lester, and Susan Robertson, "Gender Differences in Humor Appreciation," *Humor* 1 (1988): 231–243; Unger, "The Potential for Using Humor"; Thomas W. Whipple and Alice E. Courtney, "How to Portray Women in TV Commercials," *Journal of Advertising Research* 20 (1980): 53–59.

57. Grewal et al., "Comparative versus Noncomparative Advertising."

58. Alina B. Sorescu and Betsy D. Gelb, "Negative Comparative Advertising: Evidence Favoring Fine-Tuning," *Journal of Advertising* 29, no. 4 (2000): 25–40, 26.

59. Ted Sann, cited in Mallorre Dill, "When Advertisers Attack," *Adweek*, September 30, 2002, 23.

60. Sorescu and Gelb, "Negative Comparative Advertising."

61. Grewal et al., "Comparative versus Noncomparative Advertising."

62. Sorescu and Gelb, "Negative Comparative Advertising."

63. Sorescu and Gelb, "Negative Comparative Advertising."

64. Paul S. Speck, "On Humor and Humor in Advertising" (PhD diss., Texas Tech University, 1987), 494.

4

How Does Silly Sell?

IN Chapter 2, we explored the psychological and linguistic theory behind humor and how it works, focusing mainly on what people think is funny and why. In this chapter, you're going to read about a lot of theory and research again, but this time it's all about how both advertising researchers and professionals believe humor works to amuse, inform, and persuade in a variety of advertising situations and circumstances.

Earlier, I quoted an advertising professional who had observed there was "little research on the topic of humor in advertising." I also pointed out that a good response to that observation is "not exactly." Academic advertising researchers have conducted a lot of research on humor. So much, in fact, that some of them (including me) have stopped and summarized the growing body of literature at least three times.[1] These comprehensive literature reviews are done from time to time when there's been a lot of research on a topic and a summary of it is needed to help everybody figure out what's been done, what's been learned, and where to go next. The findings and conclusions from these three reviews are summarized in Box 4.1.

We also have two surveys conducted 20 years or so apart that show what advertising's creative gurus think about humor and how their views have changed. Tom Madden and Marc Weinberger first surveyed advertising creative and research executives in the early 1980s.[2] I partially replicated their study, sending an updated version of their questionnaire (thanks substantially to Dr. Weinberger, who resurrected a hard copy of his 23-year-old questionnaire!) to the top creative executives working for the 150 largest ad agencies in the United

Funny Business

Box 4.1. CONCLUSIONS FROM THREE REVIEWS OF THE ADVERTISING HUMOR RESEARCH LITERATURE

Sternthal and Craig (1973)

- Humor attracts attention.
- Humor may detrimentally affect comprehension.
- Humor may distract the audience, yielding a reduction in counterargumentation and an increase in persuasion.
- Humorous appeals appear to be persuasive, but the effect is at best no greater than serious appeals.
- Humor tends to enhance liking for sources and source credibility.
- Audience characteristics may confound the effect of humor.
- Humor should be relevant and perceived as funny.
- A humorous context may increase liking for the source and create a positive mood. This may increase the persuasive effect of the message.
- To the extent that a humorous context functions as a positive reinforcer, a persuasive communication placed in such a context may be more effective.

Weinberger and Gulas (1992)

- Humor attracts attention.
- Humor does not harm comprehension.
- Humor enhances liking of sources and ads but does not enhance source credibility.
- Humor does not appear to offer an advantage over nonhumor at increasing persuasion.
- Audience factors affect humor response.
- Related humor is superior to unrelated humor.
- The nature of the product affects the appropriateness of a humor treatment.

Beard (2004)

- Humor attracts attention to advertising with very few exceptions.
- People often transfer their liking of humor to the ad and the brand.

- Humor can enhance memory and comprehension in TV, radio, and magazine advertising, especially for expressive and low-risk or low-involvement products.
- In some situations, humor is more persuasive than a neutral appeal.
- Humor affects persuasion in the form of purchase intention, via attitude toward the ad and attitude toward the brand.
- Humor is generally processed peripherally, distracting audiences from processing claims and, consequently, reducing counterarguing.
- More intense levels of humor likely lead to more positive effects on ad-related outcomes, and moderate levels lead to more positive brand-related outcomes and purchase intention.
- Few, if any, positive effects will occur if attempted humor is not perceived as funny.
- There is an interaction between humor and warmth.
- Low-NFC individuals (people who have a low need for cognition) respond to humor with a stronger attitude toward the ad, attitude toward the brand, and purchase intention.
- High-NFC individuals (people who have a high need for cognition) respond positively to more intense humor, although they process the humor differently.
- Individuals who enjoy or appreciate humor respond more positively to it.
- Males enjoy humor on the average more than females do.
- Humor use is more prevalent in the broadcast media.
- Humor is used most for low-involvement or low-risk products.
- Incongruity-resolution is the dominant humor mechanism present in humorous advertising throughout the world.

States. Many of them sent me additional thoughts and even ads, some of which you have seen or will see in other chapters of this book.

These advertising professionals represent the top layer of creative leadership in advertising today, with many of them also serving as agency chairpersons, partners, and presidents. With an average of more than 22 years' experience, there's little doubt they are advertising's most informed and influential professionals when it comes to humor.

Should there be a big difference between advertising creatives today and those from 20 years ago? If you've seen many ads from the early 1980s, you can appreciate how much advertising has changed in both content and style. From our history in Chapter 1, you learned that professional thought about humor varied from period to period for many reasons. Perhaps most important, the use of humor changed dramatically in the late 1980s with the adoption of increasingly aggressive arousal-safety-type humor.

One important reason I combine and compare the findings of academic research with professionals' views is that, surprisingly, it's never really been done. Oddly enough, in some practice-oriented disciplines, such as advertising, the people who practice it and the academics who research and teach it often don't communicate as much as they could or probably should. For example, it's often pointed out that academic research on advertising rarely reaches professionals and that it seems to have minimal impact on what they do.[3] In addition, the value of typically *basic* academic research (versus *applied* research) is often questioned by advertising professionals (perhaps a little too gleefully on some occasions) and sometimes even other academics.[4]

Yet there are good reasons why academic researchers and advertising professionals should have similar beliefs about things such as humor and how it works. Most academics have quite a bit of full-time work experience in advertising, with a couple of surveys reporting an average of nearly 11 years.[5] In turn, many professionals participate in advertising education by teaching classes as part-time instructors, serving as advisers and guest speakers, and contributing to textbooks.

When I did a survey a few years ago, I found that many academics consider several practical and practice-oriented books about advertising to be among the most important, such as very influential books by Al Ries and Jack Trout[6] and advertising legend David Ogilvy.[7] On the other hand, not all that long ago, advertising professionals were frequent contributors to academic research themselves. Throughout the 1970s and 1980s, many of the articles published in advertising's academic journals focused on topics professionals were concerned about,[8] and many were even authored by them.[9]

In this chapter, we're going to explore what academic researchers and advertising professionals have concluded about humor. It represents the first time the findings of decades of academic advertising research have been directly compared with the views of advertising's top creative minds to produce what is likely the most definitive set of conclusions in existence regarding how advertising humor is used and when it will be effective. We'll finish up with some questions for future research on advertising humor.

ADVERTISING HUMOR AND COGNITIVE MESSAGE EFFECTS

Getting attention in advertising is very important, and it's one of the first and most important reasons why advertisers originally started using humor in their ads. Measuring whether an ad attracted attention typically starts with asking people if they can recall seeing it. The assumption is that ads can't accomplish anything unless they attract attention and get noticed.

Once people pay attention to an ad, it's generally hoped they'll absorb some information and be able to remember it later—in some cases, even if it's only the name of the product or brand. In both the study and practice of advertising, these hoped-for outcomes are called *awareness*, *recall*, and *comprehension*. They're measured by asking people who've seen an ad whether they can recall what the product or service was and what the ad was supposed to say about it. The idea that attention is related to comprehension is based on a cognitive (or thought-based) model of humor's effects. This model proposes that humor encourages people to process advertising messages by first getting their attention and then encouraging them to think about the messages.

The reviews of the academic research literature have almost overwhelmingly shown that humor does a great job of attracting attention, although there's some disagreement as to whether or not it helps or harms comprehension. Sternthal and Craig concluded humor probably has a negative effect on comprehension, although Weinberger and Gulas questioned that conclusion. When I did my update of the literature, I found studies suggesting humor can be positively related to recall and comprehension in TV, radio, and magazine advertising, especially for expressive products (those we typically buy because of the way they make us feel rather than for practical reasons) and low-risk or low-involvement products (routine purchases that don't cost much or that we don't worry about too much).[10]

If humor works well to attract attention to advertising, why might this have a negative effect on comprehension? In a nutshell, it's possible that humor could successfully attract attention to an ad but harm comprehension by redirecting people's attention away from the information, claims, or arguments in the ad. This is predicted by something called the *distraction hypothesis*, which we'll look at more closely a little later on. The consequences of this, though, could be good or bad depending on other factors, such as the type of product being advertised or the intended advertising goal. One of the most important of these other factors is something we've already talked about quite a bit—*relatedness*.

Sternthal and Craig simply concluded humor should be relevant. Weinberger and Gulas more specifically concluded humor works better when it's related in some way to the product or service being advertised. When I reviewed the literature, I found support for a tentative conclusion—based substantially on research conducted by Weinberger and his colleagues[11]—that the impact of humor on attention and comprehension for different types of products could, in fact, differ by two of the types of relatedness we looked at in Chapter 2—*intentional* and *thematic*.

You may recall from Chapter 2 that intentional relatedness has to do with whether the humor in an ad is dominant or the message is dominant. In humor-dominant ads, the message is subordinate to the humor. This means that if the humorous elements are removed, the advertising message can no longer be understood. On the other hand, in message-dominant ads, the humor is subordinate to the overall message. This means the humor is embedded in a message that is basically nonhumorous. Message-dominant ads can also have an image focus or an information focus. They have an image focus when humorous verbal or visual elements are used to reinforce the image or reputation of a product or advertiser. The humor has an information focus when the humor in the ad contains message arguments or claims.

In one study, Spotts and his team looked at intentional relatedness and attention. They found that humor-dominant magazine ads were associated positively with attention, but only for expressive low-risk products. Message-dominant, image-focused humor was positively associated with attention for functional high-risk products and for expressive low-risk products.[12]

Humor's effects also seem to vary by thematic relatedness in radio advertising. You may recall from Chapter 2 that thematic relatedness means the humor is directly related to the product and its uses, benefits, brand name, or typical users. Weinberger and his colleagues found that in magazine advertising, there was no difference for related versus unrelated humor and its effects on either attention or comprehension, regardless of the product type being advertised. But there were positive effects of thematically related humor in radio ads on attention and comprehension for expressive high-risk and expressive low-risk products.

It seems fairly clear why both types of relatedness should encourage comprehension, even if the effects by product type aren't all that clear. If humor is (1) related directly to something about the product in an ad (thematically related), (2) necessary for recognizing and understanding an ad's message (humor dominant), or (3) incidentally used to reinforce message elements (message dominant, information focused), then the humor should help encourage people to process at least some of the information in an ad. In fact, one recent study provided evidence to support exactly these kinds of conclusions. We'll talk about it a little later.

What Do the Pros Think?

The majority of advertising creative professionals today agree humor is effective at gaining attention, it is better at gaining attention than nonhumor, and it helps gain awareness if it's used in advertising for a new product (see the survey findings in Table 4.1). Advertising creatives in the early 1980s also agreed with all these things, but when you compare what they thought with creative executives today, it's clear that today's creatives are even more convinced that humor is better than nonhumor at gaining attention.

Thanks to our two surveys, we also know what creative professionals think about various aspects of the comprehension issue. The views of today's creatives about the relationship between humor and comprehension have changed just a little from those of the early 1980s. The majority view humor as (1) not

Table 4.1. Attention and Comprehension Objectives for Humor

OBJECTIVE		2005 (%)	1984 (%)
Better at gaining attention than nonhumor	*agree	72	54
	disagree	12	16
Effective at gaining attention	effective	90	96
	not effective	0	2
Helps gain awareness of new product	agree	91	83
	disagree	1	5
Harms comprehension more than nonhumor	agree	27	39
	*disagree	51	31
Effective at gaining comprehension	*effective	33	49
	*not effective	1	22
Harms recall more than nonhumor	*agree	11	29
	disagree	63	53
Effective as nonhumor for name registration	agree	69	68
	disagree	8	15
Effective as nonhumor for simple points	effective	67	71
	not effective	10	9
Effective as nonhumor for complex points	agree	36	33
	disagree	34	44
Humor works best when it is related	agree	91	88
	disagree	1	4
Effective as nonhumor for gaining retention	effective	70	78
	*not effective	1	28

Note: Scales calculated identically with Madden and Weinberger (1984). Agree = 1 and 2, disagree = 4 and 5 on a 5-point scale. Not effective = 1 and 2, effective = 6 and 7 on a 7-point scale. Comparisons are with Madden and Weinberger's creative respondents only ($N = 73$).
* Significant differences $p < .05$; all probabilities are two-tailed.

particularly effective at registering complex copy points; (2) no more harmful to comprehension and recall than nonhumor; and (3) as effective as nonhumor for gaining name registration, for gaining retention, and for registering (i.e., getting people to make note of and remember) simple copy points.

Three significant differences show that the views of today's creatives have grown much more favorable toward humor—more of them disagree that humor harms comprehension more than nonhumor, and fewer agree that humor harms recall more than nonhumor and that it is not effective for gaining retention. It's a little surprising to discover, though, that more of the current executives are less certain about whether humor is or is not effective at gaining comprehension in general.

How about relatedness? Almost 90 percent of the creatives in the 1980s agreed humor works best when it's related and relevant, and more than 90 percent of today's creatives also agree. And when they took the time to write additional comments about humor on the questionnaires I sent them, the importance of relatedness or relevance was one of the most frequent things they mentioned. A sampling of these open-ended comments, summarized in Box 4.2, offers additional insight into this prevalent belief.

Matchup: Academics and Pros

As we've seen, the creative leaders of both the 1980s and today agreed that humor is superior to nonhumor in gaining attention. As we've also seen, these views are a good match with the findings of academic research and what the reviews of it show—near-overwhelming support for the effectiveness of humor in attracting attention and creating awareness.

Professionals' views regarding comprehension are also somewhat consistent with the findings of academic research. For quite some time, research had suggested humor was harmful to comprehension (and you may recall from Chapter 1 this was a professional concern that lasted throughout the twentieth century). Studies conducted during the 1980s and 1990s, though, suggested the issue wasn't quite so clear cut. The most recent research supports the conclusion that humor might positively affect memory and comprehension in some media and for some product types. So it doesn't seem terribly surprising to find that the views of creatives are also a little mixed. They believe humor might be good for encouraging some kinds of comprehension (the weaker ones, it seems) and not so good for others (such as gaining retention for complex copy points). As we've also seen, they agree overwhelmingly that humor should be related.

Funny Business

Box 4.2. THE IMPORTANCE OF RELATEDNESS

"In advertising, humor is the means to an end, not the end itself." Bruce Fitzgerald, creative director, MARC USA Miami, Miami, FL

"Humor should not be the objective of a campaign. It works when it's relevant to the overall strategy." Laurence Klinger, VP and chief creative officer, Lapiz Integrated Hispanic Marketing, Chicago, IL

"There is nothing more effective in TV advertising than great humor that hinges on a product truth or insight. And few things more elusive." Dennis Ryan, chief creative officer, Element 79 Partners, Chicago, IL

"[Humor] *must* be tied to the product. . . . if it has no relevance consumers will only remember the joke, not the product." Jeff Morris, VP and cocreative director, Kupper Parker Communications, Inc., Saint Louis, MO

"The humor must be inherent to the product (and its use), not an adjunct to it." Kevin Hawley, executive VP and creative director, Fahlgren Benito, Tampa, FL

"To be effective in advertising, [humor] has to be relevant to the brand's position in the marketplace." Ron Luscinski, creative director, the Ballpark Advertising Agency, Santa Monica, CA

"Stay on message, make sure there is an immediate connection between the funny scenario and product or service. Trust your instincts as to what is and is not funny." Bruce Waters, VP-creative, Al Paul Lefton Co., Philadelphia, PA

"Humor needs to propel the point of the message, not drown it." Larry Postaer, executive VP and creative services director, RPA, Santa Monica, CA

"[Humor] should always be relevant to the product, service, or audience specifically, never gratuitous." Gary Backaus, chief creative officer, Archer-Malmo, Memphis, TN

"[Humor is] extremely effective and persuasive *when it's based* in the product's USP. When done for humor's sake (e.g., Bud Light), it's simply an awareness driver." Jim Myers, VP and creative director, Rhea & Kaiser Marketing Communications, Naperville, IL

AUDIENCE PERCEPTIONS OF THE HUMOR'S SOURCE

At the time of the earliest review of the research literature, there hadn't been any studies of how funny advertising might affect perceptions of the advertiser or brand. Persuasion studies Sternthal and Craig found, though, suggest humor enhances liking for sources and *might* enhance their credibility. Weinberger and Gulas later concluded that research had consistently confirmed humor enhances liking of both sources and advertisements, but they questioned whether humor might enhance source credibility (i.e., whether a source is viewed as knowledgeable or trustworthy).

When I reviewed the literature, it seemed obvious that academic researchers had established nearly beyond question that *successful* humor not only enhances liking for message sources and ads themselves but also transfers that liking to the brand or product. Unfortunately, there hadn't been any new research on the issue of advertising humor's effects on source credibility beyond an early study conducted by Paul Speck.

Speck found that nonhumorous ads encouraged people to view the source as more knowledgeable compared with humorous ads. However, he also found the use of "sentimental humor" (what I call "resonant humor" in Chapter 2) encourages people to view the source as more trustworthy compared with nonhumorous ads or those of other humor types.[13]

What Do the Pros Think?

My survey showed that creative executives definitely believe successful humor puts people in a positive mood. Since it seems likely that a positive mood could only be a consequence of enjoyment and liking, then this belief seems entirely consistent with the findings of academic research. But creatives in the 1980s were skeptical regarding whether humor has a positive effect on source credibility, and their twenty-first-century peers agree. As we've also seen, there's not much research available to establish whether funny ads affect source credibility or not.

HUMOR AND PERSUASION

The issue of humor's effects on persuasion picks up where concerns about attention, awareness, comprehension, and liking of sources leave off. No matter how you define persuasion, it can't happen unless an ad attracts attention and unless audience members process some kind of information from it. And it's pretty obvious that people are more likely to be persuaded by someone they like than someone they don't.

The first two reviews of the research literature led to a conclusion that the effects of humor on persuasion probably aren't any greater than the effects of a serious or nonhumorous ad.[14] When I reviewed the literature, though, I found that the most recent research suggests humor might be more persuasive in some situations. *Persuasion* generally means people have developed a positive attitude toward the brand, although it's also often defined as *purchase intention*.

Humor and Liking

First, if persuasion is defined as purchase intention (as a rule measured in terms of how likely people say they are to buy a product), then humor seems to affect it by first causing people to like the ad itself (an important variable called *attitude toward the ad*) and this liking, in turn, causes people to like the brand (another important advertising variable called *attitude toward the brand*). Attitude toward the ad has been hugely important ever since some groundbreaking studies reported that how much people like an ad is one of the strongest predictors of an ad's sales success and that it has a direct and substantial effect on attitude toward the brand.[15] Attitude toward the brand is typically measured in terms of how good or bad or how likable or unlikable people say the brand is. The model in Figure 4.1 shows the relationships among these variables.

So when people see a funny ad they enjoy and like, this encourages them to like the brand being advertised, and this brand liking encourages them to think, "The next time I need one of those, I'm going to buy that brand." This finding is predicted by something called the *affect-transfer hypothesis* of humor's effects.[16] This affective model represents another theoretical explanation for how humor affects persuasion and, ultimately, a purchase decision.

The transfer of affect (liking as well as other emotional responses) from an ad to a brand is based on classical conditioning—this is what Russian physiologist Ivan Pavlov did to his dog. Classical conditioning means taking two things that are already connected (e.g., humor and liking) and then adding something else (such as the insurance company AFLAC). In the language of classical conditioning, humor is an unconditioned stimulus and liking is an unconditioned response. They are connected by an unconditioned, or naturally occurring,

Figure 4.1 Humor's direct and indirect effects on purchase intention.

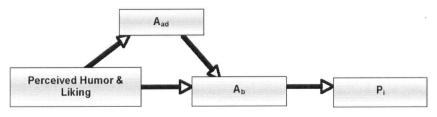

relationship. When a new or conditioned stimulus (such as AFLAC) is repeatedly delivered at the same time as the original stimulus (humor), we wind up with a conditioned relationship between the new stimulus (AFLAC) and the old response (liking).

The consequences? Much like Pavlov's hungry dog salivated when it heard the sound of a bell, when people think of AFLAC, they associate amusement and liking with it. The bottom line of all this, though, is that the more people like an ad, the more they will like the brand. And the more they like the brand, the more likely they are to buy it.

Distraction Can Be Good

A second theoretical explanation for how humor affects persuasion has to do with how people process the information in a funny ad. This is based on the cognitive model of humor's effects we talked about earlier, rather than the affective model. Theoretically, humor can distract people from processing the claims (or arguments) in an ad and, consequently, make the ad more persuasive. This conclusion is mainly based on another important idea about how humor works to affect persuasion: the *distraction hypothesis*. Research supports the likelihood that humor can affect persuasion by getting in the way of cognitive processing and the development of *counterarguments*.[17]

The distraction hypothesis predicts that an ad with a message that contradicts what people already believe will be more persuasive if they're distracted from thinking about the arguments in the message. Why? Because when people know someone is trying to persuade them and the persuasive arguments are something they don't agree with, then they have a tendency to think of the reasons they disagree (this is called the generation and rehearsing of counterarguments). This situation happens fairly often in advertising, such as when people see or hear an ad for a new product that's inconsistent with their existing attitudes or beliefs. So, in these kinds of situations, the humor in an ad can distract people, encouraging them to accept the message in the ad and be persuaded by it.

The distraction hypothesis helps explain the success of the classic and funny "Tastes Great, Less Filling" campaign for Miller Lite beer, launched in the early 1970s. This campaign placed eighth on *Ad Age*'s list of the Top 100 Advertising Campaigns of the 20th Century.[18] The humor in the ads probably distracted men from the widespread belief that light beer was "diet" beer, at least long enough to persuade them to try it. Associating a bunch of masculine athletes with what was perceived as a feminine product (at the time, mostly women worried about diets and calories) probably didn't hurt much either.

A recent study supports the distraction hypothesis and its likely effects. The researchers were looking at the relationship between humor and argument strength and how they affect attitude toward the ad and attitude toward the brand.[19] They found that people who perceived an ad as more humorous were, in fact, less sensitive to the strength of the claims in the ad compared with people who perceived the ad as less humorous. Not only that, although perceptions of humorousness tended to increase both attitude toward the ad and attitude toward the brand, this happened only in the case of weak ad claims. In other words, when humor was low, subjects based their responses to the ad, at least in part, on claim strength rather than on humor. One important thing to keep in mind about this study, though, is that the humor in the test ad was incidental and not related.

Another even more recent study produced similar findings.[20] An experiment using two versions of a print ad for a low-risk convenience product (a fictitious brand called Awesum Bubble Gum) showed that college students responded with more favorable attitude toward the ad and attitude toward the brand when the funny version of the ad (again, incidental humor) was combined with weak arguments. On the other hand, it appeared that the ad with the stronger arguments but no humor also had a favorable effect on attitudes.

Why might that be? The researchers proposed it was because of the distraction hypothesis. The incidental humor distracted the research subjects, reduced counterarguing, and enhanced persuasion—but only when the ad contained weak arguments. When the funny ad contained strong arguments, the subjects weren't distracted from them, so they counterargued, and that made the funny ad less persuasive. On the other hand, when the ad contained strong arguments and no humor, the subjects weren't distracted from the persuasive arguments, and the results were more persuasive.

Finally, it's important to point out how consistent these explanations for humor's effects on persuasion are with advertising's most important theory, the *elaboration likelihood model* (ELM).[21] The ELM argues there are two routes to persuasion—one *central* and one *peripheral*. The central route predicts that when people are *motivated* to think about a message (e.g., they are highly involved or the message is especially relevant) and *able* to think about it (e.g., the message is fairly easy to understand), then they'll cognitively elaborate on the claims in the ad (basically, think about them) and be persuaded by issue-relevant arguments.

The ELM's peripheral route, on the other hand, predicts that people may still be persuaded even if they are unmotivated or unable to process arguments. Message elements unrelated to the product (called *peripheral cues*), and which a person already has positive attitudes about, can be used to associate those positive attitudes with the product or brand, leading to a weaker and temporary kind of persuasion. What are common peripheral cues in advertising? Celebrities, attractive models, enjoyable music, pleasing visuals, and, that's right, humor. As predicted by the distraction hypothesis, humor can encourage lower levels of elaboration (especially when combined with weak rather than strong arguments, as you've already learned), leading to reduced perceptual defenses and, in turn, persuasion.

What Do the Pros Think?

Today's creative leaders and those from the 1980s similarly agreed and disagreed about the various ways advertising humor might affect persuasion (see the survey findings in Table 4.2). Few of them agreed that humor is especially effective at getting people to yield to message arguments (at 33 percent and 40 percent), at increasing intention to purchase (at 29 percent and 43 percent), or at increasing persuasion more than nonhumor (at 37 percent and

Table 4.2.   Persuasion Objectives for Humor

OBJECTIVE		2005 (%)	1984 (%)
Increases persuasion more than nonhumor	agree	37	27
	disagree	20	28
Gaining yielding to message arguments	effective	33	40
	*not effective	2	23
Gaining intention to purchase	effective	29	43
	*not effective	7	24
Persuading to switch brands	agree	63	52
	disagree	8	12
Enhances positive mood	*agree	60	44
	disagree	18	18
Mood aids persuasion	agree	73	80
	disagree	11	6
Creates greater sales effect than nonhumor	agree	32	28
	disagree	17	25
Gaining actual purchase	*effective	23	40
	*not effective	9	27

Note: Scales calculated identically with Madden and Weinberger (1984). Agree = 1 and 2, disagree = 4 and 5 on a 5-point scale. Not effective = 1 and 2, effective = 6 and 7 on a 7-point scale. Comparisons are with Madden and Weinberger's creative respondents only (N = 73).
* Significant differences $p < .05$; all probabilities are two-tailed.

27 percent). The majority generally agreed, though, that humor can persuade people to switch brands. They also agreed, as I already mentioned, that humor can enhance positive mood and that a positive mood enhances persuasion. Current creative executives differ in three areas from those of the 1980s, all of which indicate more favorable views toward humor. Significantly fewer of them believe humor is not effective at gaining yielding or gaining intention to purchase and significantly more of them agree humor enhances a positive mood.

A final part of the relationship between humor and persuasion is whether it directly causes a sale. There isn't any academic research on this issue, but we do know what creative professionals think. Creatives in the early 1980s were skeptical that humor has a direct effect on sales. And most of their twenty-first-century cohorts agree. Overall, not very many agreed that humor creates a greater sales effect than nonhumor or that humor is an effective tactic for gaining actual purchase. It's also interesting to note, though, that significantly fewer of today's creatives report believing that humor is both effective or ineffective at gaining actual purchase, suggesting more of them aren't quite certain either way about this outcome.

Matchup: Academics and Pros

Professionals' views are mainly consistent with the findings of academic research. However, though the lack of strong agreement that humor can increase persuasion more than nonhumor or that it's effective at gaining purchase intention is consistent with the reviews of Sternthal and Craig and Weinberger and Gulas, there's growing support for the conclusion that humor can affect persuasion in the form of purchase intention and does so via effects on attitude toward the ad and attitude toward the brand. But it's also important to note that when the creatives were surveyed, they weren't asked whether they thought humor affects persuasion directly or through some other variable such as attitude toward the ad or attitude toward the brand, so the belief that humor doesn't affect persuasion is not inconsistent, since the research shows it has its effects through other variables.

HUMOR EFFECTS AND AUDIENCE CHARACTERISTICS

Few studies had looked at the effects of audience characteristics at the time of Sternthal and Craig's review, so they merely concluded different types of audiences probably respond differently to humor. Weinberger and Gulas found research supporting the conclusion humor is more persuasive and appealing to men. The most recent academic literature suggests researchers have made quite a bit of progress exploring the effects of audience characteristics.

Do Smart People Like Funny Ads Less?

People who have a high *need for cognition* (NFC)—defined as the enjoyment people get out of thinking or actively processing information[22]—don't seem to respond quite as well to humorous ads as low-NFC people do. Why should we care? The fact is, advertisers don't think that much about whether their audiences are high- or low-NFC. Theoretically, though, it's important because it helps us understand better how humorous ads work and because NFC is related to other audience characteristics that are more useful.

Research suggests NFC is positively correlated with intelligence, education, the need to evaluate, objectivism, and openness to experience, and it is negatively correlated with dogmatism and the tendency to become bored.[23] Research also suggests people low or high in NFC are attracted to different kinds of media content. High-NFC people generally watch less TV and like to get their news and information from magazines and newspapers. They're also more likely to watch public TV instead of commercial TV, and they prefer news and current affairs programs to game shows.[24]

Related to advertising, high-NFC people respond better to factual appeals instead of emotional ones and to high-quality or strong arguments, and they're more likely to follow the ELM's central rather than peripheral route to persuasion. Since they enjoy thinking about things, they're more likely to form their attitudes about a brand based on the relevance and strength of the information in an ad. On the other hand, low-NFC people respond better to peripheral cues, among them, of course, humor. So they're predicted to base their attitudes toward a product and brand based on peripheral cues.[25]

A recent study found that humor in print ads was, as predicted, more strongly associated with attitude toward the ad, attitude toward the brand, and purchase intention for low-NFC subjects versus high. As we might expect, and based on the distraction hypothesis, the researcher also found that fewer "unfavorable thoughts" were generated among the low-NFC subjects.[26]

But this doesn't mean high-NFC people won't respond to humor. Another recent study found that humor led to increased interest and attitude toward the ad among low-NFC subjects as expected, but it also found more intense levels of humor led to favorable attitude toward the ad in high-NFC subjects.[27] Patrick De Pelsmacker and Maggie Geuens, two frequent contributors to the academic literature on advertising humor, concluded these results are in line with the expectations of the ELM and with the results of other research showing that low-NFC individuals are more susceptible to peripheral cues. But they also concluded the findings support what they called a *combined-influence hypothesis* in the sense that high-NFC people can be influenced by both central and peripheral routes, but the peripheral cues may need to be more intense to get their attention. All of a sudden, the award-winning and cognitively humorous advertising for *The Economist* magazine, such as the example in Figure 4.2, seems as if it's probably right on target.

Sense of Humor

Surprise! People who like humor respond more positively to funny ads. A researcher named Thomas Cline and his colleagues were the first to explore the effects of an audience characteristic they call *need for humor* (NFH).[28] Their NFH variable—defined as a person's tendency to generate or seek out humor—has two parts. The first is *internal humor*, which is the need people have to experience humor internally (i.e., generate it themselves). The second part is *external humor*, which is the need to seek out amusement, wit, and nonsense from external sources.

Cline and his colleagues proposed that if they could confirm high-NFH people respond more favorably to funny ads, we would not only learn more about how humor works, but we'd also have a better idea about when it will work well. The findings of one of their studies did, in fact, show that a funny ad had a stronger effect on attitude toward the ad for high-NFH subjects and that they even formed more negative attitudes toward a low-humor ad.

What good is this finding? The researchers point out that NFH could be a useful segmentation variable. Although they admit it would be impractical to administer NFH questionnaires to people on a broad scale, it does seem fairly

Figure 4.2 Cognitively humorous ad for *The Economist*: "Optimist." (Ad appears courtesy of *The Economist*.)

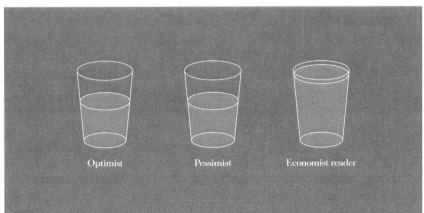

obvious that high-NFH people should be identifiable by the media content they choose to watch and read, in the same sense that high-NFC people are. They also note that if attitude change is the advertising goal, humor probably works best with high-NFH audiences.

Do Guys Like Humor More?

Quite a bit of research seems to suggest men enjoy humor on the average more than women do, or at least certain types of humor. Weinberger and Gulas found research suggesting men prefer aggressive and sexual humor, while women seem to like nonsensical humor more. A recent study confirmed these differences and that they seem to apply to the advertising of services. The researchers found that, on the average, college students don't believe humor is appropriate in advertising for all services, and especially professional services. Men, though, responded more favorably to humor when it was used for the types of services generally viewed to be inappropriate for the use of humor, including professional services.[29] The Buijzen and Valkenburg study, which you read about in Chapter 3, also offers an excellent overview of how different audience types, including men and women, are likely to respond to different types of humor.[30]

Make It Funny . . . or Else

After reviewing the literature, Sternthal and Craig simply concluded that advertising humor should be perceived as funny. A recent study shows just how important this is.[31] The researchers found that, as expected, funny radio ads had a stronger effect on attitude toward the ad and attitude toward the brand than a nonhumorous ad. They also found that incongruity-resolution humor was more likely to be perceived as humorous than incongruity alone. But here's the most important finding. These effects were completely overwhelmed by the effects of perceived humor. In other words, the study suggests there will be no positive effect on attitude toward the ad or attitude toward the brand for any type of humor unless it's perceived as funny. The study also highlighted the risks associated with not being funny. People who didn't think the test ad was funny viewed it as annoying and not entertaining, and they felt the brand was neither good nor novel.

What Do the Pros Think?

Current creative leaders have similar views regarding the audiences best suited for humorous advertising compared with creatives from the early 1980s (see

Table 4.3. Audiences Best and Least Suited to Humor

	2005		1984	
Audience Segments	Best Suited (%)	Least Suited (%)	Best Suited (%)	Least Suited (%)
Male	88.9	3.3	*52.2	7.5
Female	48.9	36.7	*30.0	*30.0
Upscale	48.9	36.7	58.2	*10.4
Downscale	60.0	24.4	*23.1	36.6
Younger	90.0	2.2	*70.9	*0.7
Older	17.8	70.0	12.7	*49.3
Better educated	72.2	15.6	*61.2	*6.7
Less educated	50.0	30.0	*21.6	38.8
Professional	62.2	20.0	*47.8	18.7
Nonprofessional	58.9	22.2	*32.8	24.6

Note: Percentage mentioned ($N = 90$). Comparisons are with Madden and Weinberger's creative and re-search executive respondents ($N = 141$).
* Significant differences $p < .05$; all probabilities are two-tailed.

the survey findings in Table 4.3). Younger and better-educated audiences accounted for some of the highest proportions of "best suited" responses in both samples. However, there are significant differences, and some of these changes in views regarding audiences (e.g., males, females, downscale consumers, less educated, professional, and nonprofessional) are pretty big. Once again, it's obvious that today's advertising creatives are more favorable toward the use of humor than those from the 1980s since a majority of them view all but one audience segment as "best suited" for humor—the older segment.

The professionals also overwhelmingly agree that a funny ad had better be funny. Some of their observations, summarized in Box 4.3, show just how important they think this is.

Matchup: Academics and Pros

The current belief that men respond more positively to funny advertising is a perfect match with the findings of academic research. Although there isn't much research available on the other types of audiences, it's interesting to note that creatives believe better-educated consumers are also especially well-suited targets for humor. This belief is somewhat inconsistent with research findings that suggest low-NFC people respond better to humor. On the other hand, it's not entirely inconsistent, since other recent research findings suggest high-NFC people will respond to humor if it's intense enough. It's also clear that advertising creatives recognize how critical it is for their funny ads to actually be funny, which is also consistent with recent research.

┌───┐
│   **Funny Business**   │
│   │
│   BOX 4.3. **THE IMPORTANCE OF BEING FUNNY**   │
└───┘

- "Humor done badly is the worst offense. If you are going for humor, you better make it funny." Neil Markey, senior VP and executive director-creative, Duncan & Associates, Los Angeles, CA
- "Make sure the humor or joke is funny or it will probably backfire on you and work against the product or service being advertised." Mike McCabe, VP and creative director, Bader Rutter & Associates, Inc., Brookfield, WI
- "If you're not funny, don't try to create humorous ads." Michael Robertson, senior VP and director of creative, Heil-Brice Retail Advertising, Inc., Newport Beach, CA
- "Humor done well can work brilliantly. Humor done badly can be very detrimental." Erich Funke, Newport Beach, CA
- "Execution is everything. Your intention to make something funny means nothing if it isn't funny. Also, different people find humor in differing things." Kirk Ruhnke, senior VP and creative director, Laughlin/Constable, Inc., Milwaukee, WI
- "Humor is a lot like art. It's subjective. It's not always universally appreciated. And, most of all, it's harder to do than you'd think." Jim Spruell, executive vice president and executive creative director, Fitzgerald & Company, Atlanta, GA

RESPONSES TO HUMOR BY MEDIA AND MEDIA CONTEXT

Noting the absence of research on media context, Sternthal and Craig simply observed that placing funny spots in humorous programs might be more effective because humor could work as a "positive reinforcer." This idea is consistent with the classical conditioning explanation for humor's effects we talked about earlier. It suggests that positive contextual (or peripheral) cues could become associated with the message and brand, leading to liking and favorable attitude change.

Weinberger and Gulas similarly conclude that little research supported a conclusion regarding an interaction effect between TV program environment and humor. There are really two issues here. The first has to do with whether a humorous ad will work better if it's delivered in a funny versus serious TV show or a funny versus serious magazine. The second is whether humor works better in some media than others (e.g., television as compared with magazines).

When I reviewed the research literature, I found there weren't enough studies available to support any conclusions regarding humor and media context, but I found some evidence that humor's effects on attention and comprehension might vary somewhat based on medium. Those were the studies by Marc Weinberger and his colleagues mentioned earlier.

The only recent study on this topic looked at levels of humor in TV programs and ads.[32] Men were more likely to use or recommend a product after seeing a high-humor ad embedded in a high-humor program. On the other hand, women responded more favorably to a high-humor ad embedded in a low-humor program. The researchers also found that, after seeing ads in a more humorous program, men were better able to recall the commercial and viewed the products less negatively. However, they also found that a high-humor program decreased their ability to recall brand names, so they concluded that ads placed in more humorous programs may not attract attention as well as those placed in less humorous programs.

The important study by Marc Weinberger and his colleagues that we've already discussed is one of the few to compare directly the effects of humor in different media. They concluded that humor generally enhanced attention in radio ads, although it appeared to hinder comprehension for some products in both radio and magazine advertising.

What Do the Pros Think?

According to the two surveys, few of today's creatives or those from the 1980s agreed humor works best in either a serious or humorous context. Between the two context variables, although there is no clear consensus, today's creatives seem to favor marginally the possibility that humor works best in a humorous context, as did those of 20 years ago, since smaller proportions of both groups disagreed with this statement, compared with the serious context, and slightly larger proportions agreed.

Similar majorities of today's creative executives and those from the 1980s believe the broadcast media and print media are best and least suited for humor, respectively (see the survey findings in Table 4.4). In addition, there are no significant differences among the media on the "best suited" scores, and a rank ordering of the scores between the two produces an almost identical list, with TV and radio best suited, followed by outdoor, magazine, newspaper, and direct mail.

Table 4.4.   Media Best and Least Suited to Humor

Medium	2005		1984	
	Best Suited (%)	Least Suited (%)	Best Suited (%)	Least Suited (%)
Magazine	41	2	39	*33
Newspaper	35	3	29	*45
Radio	81	0	88	2
Television	90	0	84	*3
Outdoor	51	2	40	*30
Direct mail	26	9	22	*64
Online	47	6	NA	NA

Note: Percentage based on a scale of 1–7, rounded to the nearest whole number. Comparisons are with Madden and Weinberger's creative and research executive respondents ($N = 141$).
* Significant differences $p < .05$; all probabilities are two-tailed.

There are some significant differences between the two groups, though, based on differences between the "least suited" proportions. Significantly smaller proportions of current creative professionals report that magazines, newspapers, TV, outdoor, and direct mail are least suited to the use of humor, compared with those from the early 1980s. Again, it seems obvious that current creatives are more favorable overall toward the use of humor, with many of them agreeing that any medium is "best suited" for a funny ad.

Matchup: Academics and Pros

Similarly small proportions of both groups of creatives agreed humor works best in either a serious or humorous context, and these views remained virtually unchanged during the past 20 years, with little clear consensus. Professionals seem well justified in their uncertainty. As we've seen, reviews of the academic literature have found little research devoted to examining the relationship between media context and humor effects.

In addition, although academic researchers have consistently found that the ways advertisers use humor in different media are consistent with these views (i.e., humor is used in broadcast advertising more often than in print advertising), none of the reviews found a sufficient amount of research upon which to base any firm conclusions as to whether humor is more effective in some media.

HUMOR EFFECTS BY HUMOR TYPE AND PRODUCT TYPE

Sternthal and Craig didn't have anything to conclude about how the effects of humor might differ based on different types of humor or whether it was used for different kinds of products. After they reviewed the academic research literature, Weinberger and Gulas concluded the use of humor isn't viewed as equally appropriate for all types of products. They also cited a study by Speck, who found that comic wit had less of an effect on comprehension than did a nonhumorous ad, while the other four types were more effective.[33] Speck also found that another of the funny ad types, full comedy, had the strongest effect on overall attention and that sentimental humor was associated with liking, while the more aggressive satire wasn't.

When I reviewed the research literature, it seemed fairly obvious that incongruity-resolution is the most frequently used type of humor. Researchers had also established that humor is used most often for expressive and low-risk or low-involvement products, and it seems to work most effectively for them as well.

Incongruity Humor Rules
Research conducted during the last 15 years or so leaves little doubt that incongruity-resolution is the dominant humor mechanism and type used in advertising throughout the world. This shouldn't be a big surprise since, as we found in Chapters 2 and 3, most humor has an element of incongruity.[34] Alden and his colleagues also concluded that funny ads in several countries—including the United States, Thailand, Korea, Japan, and Germany—depend most of the time on two of the Raskin-type contrasts we talked about in Chapter 2, normal versus non-normal and possible versus impossible contrasts. On the other hand, their research has shown that humor is used a little less often in Asian countries than in Western ones, possibly because it may be viewed as less appropriate due to greater concern about bringing "shame" to the advertiser.

But Raskin-type contrasts and Speck's HMT aren't the only ways researchers have studied the use and effects of funny ads. A handful of other researchers, whom you read about in Chapter 3, used an earlier typology of humor *devices* (e.g., pun, irony, and ludicrousness).[35] Research suggests funny ads in most countries tend to be *ludicrous*, which includes slapstick and exaggerated visual humor, such as when Sprint Nextel computer geeks practice their hip-hop dancing in the office (an extremely funny ad featured in Chapter 3), or verbal humor, such as when AFLAC's duck speaks in a human voice. In fact, one study found that 60 percent of the intentionally funny ads in Japan were ludicrous.[36]

Moderate versus More Intense Humor
Several recent and related research findings seem to suggest it might be better for an ad to be only moderately funny rather than shooting for extremely funny. One study reported, not unexpectedly, that incongruity humor was positively related to attitude toward the ad, attitude toward the brand, and purchase intention among viewers of Singaporean TV ads.[37] But the researchers also concluded

these effects were stronger for moderate rather than extreme incongruity and that moderate incongruity was perceived as even funnier. These findings are similar to those reported by Alden and his colleagues, who found that, on the average, Americans rate normal versus non-normal contrasts funnier than possible versus impossible ones[38] and that reality-based contrasts are funnier than unreal, fantasy-based ones.[39]

Surprise and Playfulness

If you recall some of the humor theory we covered in Chapter 2, it also shouldn't be surprising to learn that researchers have recently confirmed that surprise and playfulness are important predictors of whether or not people will perceive an intentionally humorous ad as funny. You may recall that surprise is a natural response to both incongruity and its resolution. You also learned in Chapter 2 that people are more likely to recognize humor or someone trying to be funny if there's a play cue. Recent research by Alden and his colleagues identified a strong relationship between surprise and perceived humor, that surprise moderated the effects of other predictors of perceived humor, and that perceived humor had a strong positive effect on attitude toward the ad.

A later study conducted by Alden and his colleagues of funny TV spots found that incongruity resulted in stronger surprise when viewers were more familiar with the situation in the ad (i.e., the ad presented a familiar schema).[40] For instance, an example of a familiar schema, as they note, is "shopping in a supermarket," whereas a generally less familiar schema is the "military staff meeting." The idea, though, is that if an ad shows something incongruous happening in a familiar schema, it should be more surprising than it would be if something incongruous were shown in an unfamiliar schema. They also found, as predicted, that playfulness, ease of incongruity resolution, and warmth all significantly moderated the effect of surprise on perceived humor.

Humor Use and Effects by Product Type

As we've already discussed quite a bit, research has consistently shown that humor is used most often for low-involvement or low-risk products, and it also seems to be more effective for them. Products are considered low involvement when people don't spend much time shopping for them or comparing different brands. They're low risk if there's not much risk involved in making a bad choice. Alden and his colleagues found that this pattern of use holds not just in the United States but in Korea as well and that humor was used more often in advertising for pleasure-oriented versus functional products in all but one of the five countries they studied.[41] Functional products are consumed for practical reasons, whereas pleasure-oriented products are consumed for pleasure or sensory-gratification reasons.

Another study of U.S. and U.K. advertising revealed that humor was used most often to promote low-involvement feeling products in both countries and least often for high-involvement feeling products.[42] *Feeling* is another name for pleasure-oriented products, which are also called "expressive," "emotional," or "transformational."

As we've already discussed, research conducted by Weinberger and his colleagues has shown humor is rarely used for expressive high-risk products (such as jewelry) and functional high-risk products (such as refrigerators) in U.S. radio, TV, and magazine advertising.[43] Humor is used most extensively in all three media for expressive low-risk goods and functional low-risk goods. Another study we've already talked about found that humor in magazine ads enhanced attention and recall for expressive low-risk products (e.g., snack foods) and enhanced initial attention for functional high-risk products (e.g., appliances, insurance). Its effects on these outcomes for other types of products were minimal, and in some cases, negative.[44]

Why is this? Generally, and based on the ELM, it's believed that peripheral cues such as humor should work better for low-involvement and low-risk products and not as well for high-risk and more durable, functional products. The reason is fairly obvious. The more risk involved in making a bad decision when buying a product, the more likely it is that people will want specific information about product features and benefits. Consequently, they'll also be more inclined to rely on the central route to persuasion.

What Do the Pros Think?

Neither of our surveys asked advertising creatives what they think about different types of humor. But we do know what types of products they think humor is most compatible with (see the survey findings in Table 4.5). Consumer nondurables continue to be viewed as the products best suited for humorous advertising, with corporate advertising as least suited. Compared with research and creative professionals from the early 1980s, a significantly larger proportion of today's professionals report that all the product and service categories are best suited for humorous advertising. In two categories, consumer durables and industrial or business products, significantly smaller proportions indicated the categories are least suited.

Once again, significant differences between creatives from the 1980s and today's creatives reveal more favorable views toward the use of humor for all types of products and services. These beliefs are also mainly consistent with

Table 4.5. Products and Services Best and Least Suited to Humor

	2005		1984	
Product or Service	Best Suited (%)	Least Suited (%)	Best Suited (%)	Least Suited (%)
Consumer nondurable	90	4	*70	8
Consumer durable	77	16	*37	*30
Industrial/Business product	58	31	*24	*48
Business service	63	28	*47	22
Corporate advertising	32	63	*13	65
Retail advertising	71	22	*36	32

Note: Percentage mentioned. Proportions rounded to nearest whole number. Comparisons are with Madden and Weinberger's creative and research executive respondents (*N* = 141). The *N* for the present sample ranges from 80 to 86, due to missing responses.
* Significant differences $p < .05$; all probabilities are two-tailed.

the findings of academic research, which suggests humor is most effective for expressive and low-risk or low-involvement products, most of which are consumer nondurables.

OTHER FACTORS

Both of the surveys asked advertising professionals about the creation of advertising humor, its structural characteristics, and other factors related to its effective use. Current creatives and those from the 1980s share similar views toward these other factors (see Table 4.6). Fewer creatives agree it's more important to pretest humor than other types of advertising or that there's a greater risk of a negative effect, which is a little odd when you consider that more professionals also agree humor is harder to create.

A significantly larger number of current creatives agree humor can be as powerful as a unique selling proposition (USP), compared with creatives from the 1980s. As I mentioned in Chapter 1, in the 1950s legendary adman Rosser Reeves originally advocated the USP concept, which proposes that a single (mainly rational) product feature, promise, or benefit should be at the heart of every advertising message strategy. Significantly fewer of today's creatives agree that humor wears out more quickly. One notable exception to this pattern of differences is the significantly smaller number agreeing that humor creates more good feelings toward a brand. Regarding the structure of humorous ads, larger proportions of today's creatives, compared with those from the 1980s, agree both a humorous start or a humorous end to otherwise serious commercials makes them work better.

Weinberger and Gulas did find a few older studies on the topic of repetition and wear-out, although the findings were mixed and seemed to suggest

Table 4.6. Other Factors

FACTOR		2005 (%)	1984 (%)
Humor can be as powerful as a USP	agree	67	*46
	disagree	24	*36
Humor is harder to create	agree	63	73
	disagree	18	14
Greater risk of negative effect	agree	28	*42
	disagree	49	*27
Wears out more quickly	agree	23	*50
	disagree	58	*25
More important to pretest	agree	9	*27
	disagree	70	*44
Humorous start of serious commercial helps	agree	51	*15
	disagree	9	*29
Humorous end of serious commercial helps	agree	37	*17
	disagree	15	*32
Creates more good feelings toward the brand	agree	47	*98
	disagree	21	NA

Note: Comparisons are with Madden and Weinberger's creative and research executive respondents (N = 141).
* Significant differences $p < .05$; all probabilities are two-tailed.

that it probably depends on what type of funny ad it is. And only one recent study offers any evidence that humor may or may not wear out faster. An item measuring whether subjects had previously seen the ads they studied led the researchers to tentatively conclude that appreciation for the humorous and neutral ads and the brands they advertise seemed to improve with increasing exposure to them, compared with the erotic and warm ads they studied.[45]

In summary, significant differences between today's creatives and those Madden and Weinberger surveyed back in the early 1980s demonstrate more favorable current views toward humor. Unfortunately, there's little academic research in these areas to compare these findings against. Likewise, while some research is available on the issue of wear-out, it seems to have mainly just scratched the surface in terms of when or why.

QUESTIONS FOR ANOTHER DAY

Comparing the findings of some four decades of academic research on advertising humor with the beliefs of top advertising creatives tells us a great deal about how, when, and why funny advertising works. Combining the cumulative findings of years of academic research with the many years of experience of the top creative minds in the United States produces the following definitive list.

You can hardly go wrong using humor in advertising if . . .

- your most important goal is to attract attention
- your goal is to generate awareness and recall of a relatively simple message (think AFLAC)
- your humor is thematically related
- your goal is to get the audience to like you or your brand
- you want to persuade an audience that you expect to disagree initially with the main points in your argument
- your target audience is men, especially young ones
- your audience has a low need for cognition, a high need for humor, or even better, both
- you have very good reasons for wanting to use the broadcast media
- you're advertising a low-involvement or low-risk product or service
- the humor you have is really funny, but possibly not too funny

But there's another side of this coin and one that's nearly as valuable. The many comparisons we've made in this chapter also tell us what we don't know about how humor works. Here are some questions it would be nice to have answers to in the future.

What else would be good to know about humor's effects on attention and comprehension? Since creative professionals hold several favorable views of humor and its effects on attention and comprehension, and several studies seem to confirm them, future research should continue to explore these effects. It would be helpful for academic researchers to extend these prior findings (1) to media other than radio, TV, and magazines (e.g., outdoors); (2) for product types other than nondurables (especially services); (3) for different types of relatedness; (4) for different media vehicles and contextual variables (e.g., magazine genres, such as humor versus news; radio formats, such as country versus talk radio; or program types, such as comedy versus sports); and (5) for dependent variables such as name registration and retention of specific copy points.

The value of research on these topics is especially obvious when we consider that (1) creative executives view any medium as well suited for humor, (2) they view virtually any product or service as well suited for humor, and (3) there remains little consensus regarding whether humor works best in a serious or a humorous context. In fact, as I mentioned in Chapter 1, there's been very little research on either the use or effects of humor in outdoor advertising, despite the fact that a short drive down a well-traveled highway in any major city shows humor is used a great deal in the outdoors.

How intense should humor be? There's funny and there's *funny*! Research suggesting humor intensity can have different effects on most message outcomes[46] helps explain a much earlier research finding that the use of low levels of humor had about the same effects on persuasion as no humor at all, while extensive use of humor had a negative effect on persuasion.[47] Alden and his colleagues' consistent findings that humor perception differs by type of contrast and strength of contrast also support the importance of further research on levels of humor intensity and persuasion,[48] as does another research finding that moderate incongruity was perceived as more humorous.[49]

Does humor affect source credibility? The effect of humor on source credibility is also an important topic for future research. One useful thing to know would be whether humor has an effect on the credibility of celebrity endorsers and advertised services. This is especially important since creatives clearly agree humor can be effective for the advertising of intangible services, which often relies on communicating elements of credibility, such as trustworthiness and expertise.

Why do some audiences respond differently to humor, and how do their responses differ? Researchers interested in extending research on NFC could examine the proposition that high-NFC people might respond more positively to cognitive (or witty) humor.[50] The variables to examine could include argument strength, humor relevance, and measures of perceived humor to see how high-NFC people might be different.[51]

What about the effects of humor other than incongruity? A great deal of research confirms the importance of incongruity-resolution as a mechanism for the generation of advertising humor. Researchers have also looked at the effects of different types of contrasts and important moderators, such as surprise, playfulness, and warmth. But we don't know much about the perceived humor and message effects of the other humor mechanisms—arousal-safety and disparagement. It would be interesting and helpful to extend the study of humor types to measures of effects, including attention, comprehension, recall, attitude toward the ad, attitude toward the brand, and purchase intention.[52]

What about repetition? Finally, only one recent study offers any insight into the effects of repetition and the extent to which funny ads may wear out faster than others. This may be the single most important question to answer, especially when you consider that the smaller audiences for most TV programs today, and the higher costs of producing TV ads, means advertisers are repeating their spots more than ever. It's interesting to note that, although Sternthal and Craig observed in 1973 that advertisers assumed humor wears out faster, today's creatives seem fairly convinced that's not the case.

The small handful of available studies suggests some useful directions for investigating this important problem. Most obviously, it seems likely that incongruity humor depending on surprise probably wears out faster. On the other hand, other humor types—such as satire, or humor combined with warm, arousal-safety stimuli—may lead to appreciation and liking with repeated viewing. It would also be useful to know how the effects of repetition on humor perception vary by audience characteristics (such as NFC, sex, and NFH) as well as by medium.

NOTES

1. Fred Beard, "Humor in Advertising: A Review of the Research Literature, 1993–2003," in *Proceedings of the 9th International Conference on Corporate and Marketing Communications (CMC)*, ed. T. C. Melewar (Coventry, U.K.: University of Warwick, 2004), 42–56; Brian Sternthal and Samuel C. Craig, "Humor in Advertising," *Journal of Marketing* 37, no. 4 (1973): 12–18; Marc G. Weinberger and Charles Gulas, "The Impact of Humor in Advertising: A Review," *Journal of Advertising* 21, no. 4 (1992): 35–59.

2. Tom Madden and Marc G. Weinberger, "Humor in Advertising: A Practitioner View," *Journal of Advertising* 24, no. 4 (1984): 23–29.

3. Fred Beard and David Tarpenning, "What's So Funny? A Conceptual/Instructional Model of Humorous Advertising Message Factors," *Southwestern Mass Communication Journal* 17, no. 2 (2002): 14–29; Lawrence C. Soley, "Advertising Research: Is It Socially Superfluous?" in *Proceedings of the 1994 Conference of the American Academy of Advertising*, ed. Karen W. King (Athens, GA: American Academy of Advertising, 1994), 45–59.

4. Johan Arndt, "What's Wrong with Advertising Research?" *Journal of Advertising Research* 16 (June–July 1976): 9–16; Ivan L. Preston, "The Developing Detachment of Advertising Research from the Study of Advertisers' Goals," *Current Issues and Research in Advertising* 8 (1985): 1–15; William Weilbacher, "Dilemmas in Advertising Research," *Journal of Advertising* 10, no. 3 (1981): 14–18.

5. Beard and Tarpenning, "What's So Funny?"; Kent M. Lancaster, Helen E. Katz, and J. Cho, "Advertising Faculty Describes Theory v. Practice Debate," *Journalism Educator* 45, no. 1 (1990): 9–21.

6. Al Ries and Jack Trout, *Positioning: The Battle for Your Mind* (New York: McGraw-Hill, 1981).

7. David Ogilvy, *Confessions of an Advertising Man* (New York: Atheneum, 1964); David Ogilvy, *Ogilvy on Advertising* (New York: Vintage, 1985).

8. Laura Yale and Mary C. Gilly, "Trends in Advertising Research: A Look at the Content of Marketing-Oriented Journals from 1976 to 1985," *Journal of Advertising* 17, no. 1 (1988): 12–22.

9. Thomas E. Barry, "Publication Productivity in Three Leading U.S. Advertising Journals: Inaugural Issues through 1988," *Journal of Advertising* 19, no. 1 (1990): 52–60; James A. Muncy,

"The *Journal of Advertising*: A Twenty-Year Appraisal," *Journal of Advertising* 20, no. 4 (1991): 1–11.

10. Harlan E. Spotts, Marc G. Weinberger, and A. L. Parsons, "Assessing the Use and Impact of Humor on Advertising Effectiveness: A Contingency Approach," *Journal of Advertising* 26, no. 3 (1997): 17–32; Marc G. Weinberger, Harlan Spotts, Leland Campbell, and Amy L. Parsons, "The Use and Effect of Humor in Different Advertising Media," *Journal of Advertising Research* 35, no. 3 (1995): 44–56.

11. Spotts et al., "Assessing the Use"; Weinberger et al., "The Use and Effect."

12. Spotts et al., "Assessing the Use."

13. Paul S. Speck, "On Humor and Humor in Advertising" (PhD diss., Texas Tech University, 1987).

14. Sternthal and Craig, "Humor in Advertising"; Weinberger and Gulas, "The Impact of Humor."

15. Andrew A. Mitchell and Jerry C. Olsen, "Are Product Attribute Beliefs the Only Mediator of Advertising Effects on Brand Attitude?" *Journal of Consumer Research* 18 (August 1981): 318–332; Russell I. Haley and Allan L. Baldinger, "The ARF Copy Research Validity Project," *Journal of Advertising Research* 31 (April–May 1991): 11–31.

16. David A. Aaker, Douglas M. Stayman, and Michael R. Hagerty, "Warmth in Advertising," *Journal of Consumer Research* 12 (March 1986): 365–380.

17. Leon Festinger and N. Macoby, "On Resistance to Persuasive Communication," *Journal of Abnormal and Social Psychology* 68 (1964): 359–366.

18. "The Advertising Century," AdAge.com, http://www.adage.com/century/campaigns.html (accessed February 13, 2006).

19. Stephen M. Smith, "Does Humor in Advertising Enhance Systematic Processing?" *Advances in Consumer Research* 20, no. 1 (1993): 155–159.

20. Thomas W. Cline and James J. Kellaris, "The Joint Impact of Humor and Argument Strength in a Print Advertising Context: A Case for Weaker Arguments," *Psychology and Marketing* 16, no. 1 (1999): 69–87.

21. Richard E. Petty and John T. Cacioppo, *The Elaboration Likelihood Model of Persuasion* (New York: Springer-Verlag, 1986).

22. Yong Zhang, "Responses to Humorous Advertising: The Moderating Effect of Need for Cognition," *Journal of Advertising* 25, no. 1 (1996): 15–33; Richard E. Petty and John T. Cacioppo, "The Elaboration Likelihood Model of Persuasion," *Advances in Experimental Social Psychology* 19 (1986): 123–205.

23. John T. Cacioppo, Richard E. Petty, J. A. Feinstein, W. Blair, and G. Jarvis, "Dispositional Differences in Cognitive Motivation: The Life and Times of Individuals Varying in Need for Cognition," *Psychological Bulletin* 119, no. 2 (1996): 197–253.

24. Maggie Geuens and Patrick De Pelsmacker, "Affect Intensity, Need for Cognition and Television Viewing Behavior and Preferences," in *Society for Consumer Psychology Winter Conference Proceedings* (Austin, TX, 1998), 51–54.

25. Zhang, "Responses to Humorous Advertising."

26. Yong Zhang, "The Effect of Humor in Advertising: An Individual-Difference Perspective," *Psychology and Marketing* 13, no. 6 (1996): 531–546, 532.

27. Maggie Geuens and Patrick De Pelsmacker, "Need for Cognition and the Moderating Role of the Intensity of Warm and Humorous Advertising Appeals," *Asia Pacific Advances in Consumer Research* 3 (1998): 74–80.

28. Thomas W. Cline, Moses B. Altsech, and James J. Kellaris, "When Does Humor Enhance or Inhibit Ad Responses? The Moderating Role of the Need for Humor," *Journal of Advertising* 32, no. 3 (2003): 31–45; Cline and Kellaris, "The Joint Impact."

29. Douglas L. Fugate, Jerry B. Gotlieb, and Dawn Bolton, "Humorous Services Advertising: What Are the Roles of Sex, Appreciation of Humor, and Appropriateness of Humor?" *Journal of Professional Services Marketing* 21, no. 1 (2000): 9–23.

30. Moniek Buijzen and Patti M. Valkenburg, "Developing a Typology of Humor in Audiovisual Media," *Media Psychology* 6 (2004): 146–167.

31. Karen Flaherty, Marc G. Weinberger, and Charles S. Gulas, "The Impact of Perceived Humor, Product Type, and Humor Style in Radio Advertising," *Journal of Current Issues and Research in Advertising* 26, no. 1 (2004): 25–36.

32. Stephen D. Perry, Stefan A. Jenzowsky, Cynthia M. King, Huiuk Yi, Joe B. Hester, and J. Garrenschlaeger, "Using Humorous Programs as a Vehicle for Humorous Commercials," *Journal of Communication* 47, no. 1 (1997): 20–40.

33. Speck, "On Humor."

34. Dana L. Alden, Wayne D. Hoyer, and Choi Lee, "Identifying Global and Culture-Specific Dimensions of Humor in Advertising: A Multinational Analysis," *Journal of Marketing* 57, no. 2 (1993): 64–75; Dana L. Alden and Drew Martin, "Global and Cultural Characteristics of Humor in Advertising: The Case of Japan," *Journal of Global Marketing* 9, no. 1/2 (1995): 121–143.

35. Marc G. Weinberger and Harlan E. Spotts, "Humor in U.S. versus U.K. TV Advertising," *Journal of Advertising* 18, no. 2 (1989): 39–44; Dana L. Alden, Wayne D. Hoyer, Choi Lee, and G. Wechasara, "The Use of Humor in Asian and Western Television Advertising: A Four Country Comparison," *Journal of Asia-Pacific Business* 1, no. 2 (1995): 2–23.

36. Alden and Martin, "Global and Cultural Characteristics of Humor."

37. Chanthika Pornpitakpan and Tze Ke Jason Tan, "The Influence of Incongruity on the Effectiveness of Humorous Advertisements: The Case of Singaporeans," *Journal of International Consumer Marketing* 12, no. 1 (2000): 27–46.

38. Alden et al., "The Use of Humor in Asian and Western Television Advertising."

39. Dana L. Alden, A. Mukherjee, and Wayne D. Hoyer, "Extending a Contrast Resolution Model of Humor in Television Advertising: The Role of Surprise," *Humor* 13, no. 2 (2000): 193–217.

40. Dana L. Alden, A. Mukherjee, and Wayne D. Hoyer, "The Effects of Incongruity, Surprise and Positive Moderators on Perceived Humor in Television Advertising," *Journal of Advertising* 29, no. 2 (2000): 1–16.

41. Alden et al., "Identifying Global and Culture-Specific Dimensions of Humor in Advertising"; Alden et al., "The Use of Humor in Asian and Western Television Advertising."

42. Mark F. Toncar, "The Use of Humour in Television Advertising: Revisiting the US-UK Comparison," *International Journal of Advertising* 20, no. 4 (2001): 521–540.

43. Weinberger et al., "The Use and Effect."

44. Spotts et al., "Assessing the Use."

45. Patrick De Pelsmacker and Maggie Geuens, "The Communication Effects of Warmth, Eroticism and Humour in Alcohol Advertisements," *Journal of Marketing Communications* 2, no. 4 (1996): 247–262, 256.

46. Patrick De Pelsmacker and Maggie Geuens, "The Advertising Effectiveness of Different Levels of Intensity of Humour and Warmth and the Moderating Role of Top of Mind Awareness and Degree of Product Use," *Journal of Marketing Communications* 5, no. 3 (1999): 113–129.

47. Jennings Bryant, Dan Brown, Alan R. Silverberg, and Scott M. Elliott, "Effects of Humorous Illustrations in College Textbooks," *Human Communication Research* 8, no. 1 (1981): 43–57.

48. Dana L. Alden and Wayne D. Hoyer, "An Examination of Cognitive Factors Related to Humorousness in Television Advertising," *Journal of Advertising* 22, no. 2 (1993): 29–37; Alden et al., "Extending a Contrast Resolution Model"; Alden et al., "The Effects of Incongruity."

49. Pornpitakpan and Tan, "The Influence of Incongruity."

50. Geuens and De Pelsmacker, "Need for Cognition."

51. Thomas W. Cline, Moses B. Altsech, and James J. Kellaris, "When Does Humor Enhance or Inhibit Ad Responses? The Moderating Role of the Need for Humor," *Journal of Advertising* 32, no. 3 (2003): 31–45.

52. Pornpitakpan and Tan, "The Influence of Incongruity."

5

When Humorous
Ads Aren't Funny

A DVERTISERS have been offending audiences for a long time, and humor (or at least an attempt at it) is often the culprit. As you know from the history of advertising humor presented in Chapter 1, advertisers at the turn of the last century often presented racist, sexist, and other potentially offensive themes. But, and as we'll see a little later in this chapter, present-day examples of offensive ads, including humorous ones, aren't very hard to find either.

The relationship between humor and negative audience responses, such as offense, raises several interesting questions. For example, why would an advertiser want to offend people? Most advertisers today, as one pair of scholars observe, "presumably do *not* intend to offend or 'gross out' consumers."[1] It also seems fairly likely that some of the advertising-related offense going on might happen by accident. For example (and I do really hate to keep picking on them), even though executives at shoe marketer Just for Feet were concerned about how audiences might respond to their "tongue-in-cheek" Super Bowl XLI "bag 'em and tag 'em" spot, they still gave in when agency Saatchi & Saatchi argued audiences would love it.

But there's at least one legitimate reason for an advertiser to intentionally create an offensive ad. As one researcher notes, advertisers often use controversial advertising "as a way to attract public attention and obtain extra publicity. Controversy can, therefore, result in a very successful overall campaign."[2] Observing that the use of "shocking" content in advertising is on the rise, the authors of a recent study of "shockvertising" found that it did, in fact, significantly increase attention, enhance memory, and positively influence behavior among a sample of college students.[3]

Advertising critic Bob Garfield, who credits (or blames, really) fashion mogul Calvin Klein for creating the shockvertising genre, similarly notes that it works "(a) by provoking widespread outrage, inevitably reported in the press, creating a level of buzz typically outstripping by orders of magnitude the reach of the actual media buy, which buzz (b) bemuses the relatively small target audience. Offend the many, in other words, to impress the few."[4]

Another question: Why might funny advertising, in particular, be shocking or offensive? As we've already seen, humor is often used very aggressively in advertising, and both academics and advertising professionals agree humor can be risky. From Just for Feet's Super Bowl mishap to the Unilever Bestfood brand Pot Noodle's recent and sexually aggressive "Slag of All Snacks" campaign in the U.K. (which you'll read more about in Chapter 6), the fact is, advertising's history includes many, many examples of either inadvert or intentional humor-related offense.

In this chapter, we'll look for answers to these questions and a few others, including (1) What kinds of things in general offend people about advertising? and (2) Do humorous ads offend people, and if so, what kind of humor is it, and is humor actually the culprit? Finally, we'll tackle this question: Ethically speaking, why should advertisers care if people are offended by an ad, intentionally funny or not?

ADVERTISING THAT OFFENDS

There's a wide variety of products, services, ideas, and themes that often seem to cause audience reactions of distaste, disgust, anger, outrage, or other types of offense. First, and high on the list of products and services people don't want to see ads for, are personal and feminine hygiene products, underwear, alcohol, contraceptives and pregnancy tests, and drugs for terminal illness.[5] One researcher found that inherently offensive services include abortion, sterilization, VD treatment, mental illness, palliative care (i.e., care and treatment for the terminally ill), funeral homes, and artificial insemination. He also found that college students were most offended by ads for "racially extremist groups."[6]

Then there are the inherently offensive themes. Topping this list are ads that present sexual practices, racial or religious prejudice, terrorism, and just about any kind of behavior that might be considered antisocial.[7] Like humor appreciation, offense seems to differ by gender, too. One researcher found that women are more likely to be offended by indecent language, nudity, sexism, racism, and antisocial behavior than men are. More important, though, this same researcher concluded that his subjects were more likely to be offended by themes than by the advertised products, services, or ideas.

More than a few people have noticed that collections of offensive ads seem to have more than their share of often irrelevant sexual imagery or innuendo (remember Burger King's "Coq Roq" from Chapter 3?).[8] Two scholars studying the "everyday meaning of disgust in an advertising context" (yes, I was a little surprised to discover it happens that often, too) confirmed the inherently offensive nature of sexual themes.[9] Their research showed that the second most often mentioned category of disgusting advertising by a sample of college students was "indecent, sexually oriented, sexist, and sexually objectifying portrayals."

The U.K.'s Advertising Standards Authority (ASA), an advertising watchdog organization, found that people are most offended by the portrayal of children in a sexual way. Other inherently offensive themes and portrayals include, in the following order, (1) women in sexually degrading situations, (2) images or words unsuitable for children, (3) women in other demeaning situations, (4) portrayal of violence, (5) men in sexually degrading situations, (6) men in other demeaning situations, (7) swearing or bad language, (8) portrayal of mentally ill people, and (9) stereotyping of people. Once again, women are significantly more likely than men to be offended by all these themes and portrayals.[10]

The relationship between offense and media type hasn't attracted much attention, although at least one early study confirmed that ads on television and radio are considered more offensive and annoying, on the average, than print ads.[11] Research on attitudes in general toward advertising also confirms that people's attitudes are much more negative toward advertising in the broadcast media than in the print media.[12]

The ASA, which, until recently, regulated only nonbroadcast advertising, similarly found that U.K. residents are more likely to report being offended by advertising in what they call "push" media (in their purview, outdoor advertising, direct mail, and newspapers) rather than "pull" media—less intrusive media that people have more control over, including magazines, some types of Internet advertising, and cinema. Perhaps the ASA's most important finding related to media type and advertising context is that 96 percent of the survey respondents think advertisers should avoid potentially offensive ads if it's likely children will see them.

WHY SHOULD FUNNY ADVERTISING OFFEND PEOPLE?

The idea that humor and offensive products and themes might often appear together in advertising shouldn't be too surprising. Advertisers started using potentially offensive themes for the same reason they originally began using humor—to cut through the clutter and get attention. And as we've already discussed elsewhere in this book, advertising professionals and researchers agree that humor effectively attracts attention, and attention and awareness are the objectives best achieved by humor. Controversial or offensive themes and aggressive humor represent what advertising historian Michael Schudson calls the "visibility school of advertising," the main task of which is "to get the public's attention—through humor, bizarre visuals, anything that will grab."[13]

As we've also discussed, people enjoy humor and their enjoyment is linked to increased liking for both ads and brands. Most advertisers today believe this to be the case, although the belief that humor would likely cause offense was prevalent at the turn of the last century. As you also learned in Chapter 1, new potential for humor to offend occurred with the emergence of increasingly aggressive humor in the late 1980s.

Humor and Potentially Offensive Products, Services, Ideas, and Themes

It seems likely that humor may cause offense when it's used for inappropriate products and services or combined with themes that are, themselves, offensive. But no one had previously checked to see if this was actually the case prior to the study you'll read about a little later. For example, and as you learned in Chapter 4, humor is least appropriate for products and services that are serious and intimate or that require high involvement. On the other hand, humor is most appropriate for low-involvement and low-risk products and services.

But humor might actually work well in advertising for some undesirable and potentially offensive services, or for advertising dealing with uncomfortable topics, by distracting consumers and reducing perceptual defenses.[14] One survey of U.K. consumers found that humor might even reduce an ad's potential for causing offense, especially for men and younger people in general.[15] The ASA-U.K. also found that three-quarters of their respondents agreed it would be OK for government and charity advertisers to use shocking advertising to make an important point or to be thought provoking. Only 34 percent of them, though, agreed such a tactic was appropriate for commercial advertisers.

Humor Type and Audience Offense

As we've already discussed, the three classical humor mechanisms or processes—incongruity-resolution, arousal-safety, and humorous disparagement—generate five humorous advertisement types: comic wit, resonant humor, satire, resonant wit, and full comedy.

Very little research has looked at whether or not there might be a relationship between humor type and offense. As you learned in Chapter 3, people seem to respond less positively to aggressive satire and disparagement[16] and more favorably to resonant humor. Based on what you've learned in other chapters, it's also likely that arousal-safety humor might lead to offense more often than humor generated by the other mechanisms. Research on arousal-safety or disparagement humor in advertising, though, is rare.

Humor Relatedness

As you discovered in both Chapters 2 and 4, there's also research on three types of advertising humor relatedness—intentional, structural, and thematic. Most studies have examined intentional relatedness. The problem is, when advertising practitioners have referred over the years to the importance of humor being relevant or related, they were generally referring to thematic relatedness. Whether or not thematically unrelated humor leads to irritation and offense has never been studied.

Humor and Media Type

Although it seems obvious that people are more likely to be offended by advertising in intrusive media, there's no research to suggest whether offensive humor happens more often in some media than others. The surveys we looked at in Chapter 4 confirmed that advertising's creative gurus believe radio and television are the media best suited for humor, and direct mail and newspapers are the least suited. Estimates of the use of humor show its use is greatest in the broadcast media and less frequent in the print media, although we have almost no estimates of the use of humor in outdoor and newspaper advertising.

EXAMPLES OF OFFENSIVE HUMOR

As I mentioned earlier, you don't have to look hard to find examples of intentionally funny advertising that offended people. Here are some I thought you might enjoy.

Cam's Exam

Creating awareness of the importance for women to self-examine their breasts seems like an unlikely job for a funny ad. But the Breast Cancer Society of Canada took the risk and offered up its controversial "Cam's Breast Exam" spot. The ad, which first ran in October of 2000, was created by Elspeth Lynn and Lorraine Tao of the Toronto-based Zig ad agency.

The public service announcement, made to look like a direct-response TV spot, stars smooth-talking "Cam," who asks, "Are you too busy to do your monthly breast self-exam? Unsure of the right technique? My name's Cam, and I'd like to help. Let me examine your breasts for you, absolutely free." Super-imposed copy encourages viewers to "Call Toll Free: 1-866-RING-CAM." Cam assures viewers he is "highly trained and highly motivated," as a Barry White soundalike croons seductively in the background. Viewers are informed that a team of call takers (three of Cam's friends sitting on a couch) is standing by. "So put your breasts in my hands," says Cam. "Let Cam do your breast exam." Of course, the Breast Cancer Society doesn't really want women to put their breasts in Cam's hands. They were just reminding them of how important it is they examine their own.

In a *Marketing* magazine article, a writer describes some of the responses to Cam. "In a letter to the editor published in the *National Post*, one woman de-scribed being 'appalled' and 'offended' by the ad." "Of all organizations dealing with women's health, the Breast Cancer Society should know better," the critic said. Another woman, in a letter to the *Calgary Herald*, wrote that, having been "diagnosed with breast cancer two years ago at age 42, I find the proposed ad to be extremely poor taste."[17] Executives at the Breast Cancer Society were suf-ficiently concerned about responses to the ad to tell a business reporter they wouldn't provide a copy of it to be shown on a local business program until everyone agreed Cam and the spot "weren't going to be slagged." The Society's executive director also politely declined my request to reproduce still frames from the ad in this book, although as of October 2006, the spot could be found in several places on the Web, including at AskMen.com.

However, there was no shortage of praise for "Cam" from other advertisers. The spot received a Merit Award in the Public Service/Political category from the One Show competition in 2002. The spot also won two other awards: an International ANDY Award, 2001 (Distinction) for Television, and a Cannes Lion International Advertising Festival award, 2001 (Shortlist) for Public Health and Safety.

The U.K.'s Most Offensive Ad of All Time

And, yes, it was clearly intended to be funny. A TV spot for KFC's Zinger Crunch Salad was not only the most complained-about ad ever for the ASA-U.K., they even credited it with "turning good table manners, or the lack of them, into a national debate." The ASA received 1,671 complaints about the KFC TV spot, created by ad agency Bartle Bogle Hegarty, London. In the ad, three women working in a telephone call center are singing about how great the salad is. Unfortunately, it's impossible to understand them because their mouths are full of the salad—really full. At the end of the spot, one of the women answers the phone, singing, "Hello, emergency helpline." The ad's offense? Actually, there were several. The majority complained it encouraged bad table manners, defeating parents' efforts to teach kids not to speak (or sing, apparently) with a mouthful of food. Forty-one of the complainants said their kids had actually copied the ad. Almost all the complainants said the ad was just plain unpleasant to watch.

Sixty-three people said the ad encouraged dangerous behavior because it could lead to choking. More than 100 believed the ad reflected negatively on the emergency services organization. Twenty-seven thought the commercial was making fun of people with speech impediments or hearing difficulties. Twelve even thought the commercial encouraged overeating. Despite the number of complaints, the ASA didn't uphold any of them. Why did the ad fall short of being seriously offensive? The ASA pointed out that viewers couldn't actually see the food in the actors' mouths.[18]

Trivializing Suicide with a Tater

Hundreds of Canadians were offended when a TV spot for Imperial margarine portrayed a brokenhearted baked potato ending it all by throwing itself (himself? herself?) from a microwave onto a fork because of an empty Imperial margarine tub, while Air Supply's "All Out of Love" played in the background. The reason for the offense? Complainers claimed it trivialized suicide. A VP of brand development for Imperial parent Unilever Canada said the company pulled the ad because of the complaints, although he also observed: "Unless you're prepared to produce Milquetoast, you're going to elicit some reaction."[19]

Offending America's Truckers

Advertising humorists collided with America's truckers twice during the last few years. First, Internet job-matching service Monster ran a spot in Super Bowl XXXVII in which a driverless 18-wheeler careened out of control as the voice-over observed: "Somewhere a trucking company needs a driver. Somewhere a driver needs a job." Although nearly 50 percent of the respondents to an eTrucker.com poll thought the ad was funny, the American Trucking Association, along with several other trucking industry associations, didn't. They complained the ad communicated a negative image of American truck drivers, apparently missing the fact the truck had no driver.[20]

America's truckers also failed to appreciate Coca-Cola's Full Throttle energy drink spot in Super Bowl XL. Truckers started complaining even before the ad ran, organizing a letter-writing campaign demanding Coke either change the ad or pull it entirely. The problem with "Auto Melee," created by New York–based agency Mother, wasn't that the truck was lacking a driver. The problem was that the truck's driver dangerously tailgated a much smaller truck (carrying a giant rival Red Bull can), filled the smaller truck's rearview mirror with a menacing close-up of his mammoth Peterbilt grill, blared his horn, and ultimately ran the Red Bull truck off the road. Even though the last part of the 60-second spot lasted only 3 or 4 seconds, truckers were still not amused. "Every year somebody in Madison Avenue gets lazy and does the old scary truck cliché. This year it was Coca-Cola," complained a vice president of public affairs for the American Trucking Association.[21] Possibly the most amusing part of the whole episode is that, ironically, truckers have helped make energy drinks the fastest-growing segment of the nonalcoholic beverage market. Coke didn't pull or change the ad.

Proclaiming Jihad on the Automotive Market!

For the president of a Mitsubishi dealership in Columbus, Ohio, dressing sales representatives in burqas (the traditional head-to-toe dress warn by Islamic women) and promising free rubber swords for the kids on "Fatwa Friday" apparently seemed like a good idea. The plan was to poke a little fun at radical Islamic extremists with promises that the dealership's "prices are lower than the evildoers' every day [i.e., low prices versus low people, get it?]. Just ask the Pope." and that they have vehicles that can carry "12 jihadists in the back."[22] But the Columbus chapter of the Council on American-Islamic Relations didn't get the joke, and neither did the radio stations that refused to run the ad. "Using this kind of thing as a promotional pitch when so many people are dying from the criminal activity of suicide bombers, that's not funny," the chapter's president told a reporter. Despite initial promises the jihad-themed campaign would go forward as planned, the dealer eventually relented and sent an apology to the Council.

But ads aren't the only form of commercial communication where humor can go seriously wrong.

Big Tobacco Offends with a Jingle

People calling a toll-free telephone number printed on packages of Lucky Strike filter cigarettes heard a male chorus (described by a *New York Times* columnist as "a cross between an Irish Spring commercial and Monty Python's Lumberjack Song") singing the following jingle.[23]

Oooh, the tobacco plant is a lovely plant,
Its leaves so broad and green.
But you shouldn't think about the tobacco plant,

If you're still a teen.
Cause tobacco is a big person's plant,
And that's the way it should be.
So, if you're under 21 go and climb a tree.
Oh, the tobacco plant is a lovely plant,
And that, my friends, is no yarn.
We let it ripen in the field,
Then hang it in a barn.

As the chorus hummed along in the background, a voice-over acknowledged the song wasn't very good and told listeners, "Write a better song about the tobacco plant, and we'll use it. Now press 1 to find select stores in your area. Or press 2 for any other company information." The recording was part of a campaign for Brown & Williamson in Louisville, Kentucky, a subsidiary of British American Tobacco. They started using the funny messages at about the same time the tobacco industry was saying it had not directly targeted children with ads for cigarettes, and it never would. Earlier callers to the number heard this message: "Brown & Williamson Tobacco is in love. We're a giant corporation, and you make us feel like a little kitten. Thank you, lover. By the way, the other tobacco companies hate you and think you are ugly. They told us so."

A company spokesman for Brown & Williamson told a *Times* columnist that the messages were intended to show that "we don't take ourselves too seriously, that we're not too stuffy. . . . It's designed to put a smile on peoples' faces when they call our '800' numbers."[24] It didn't, however, put smiles on the faces of antismoking advocates. The president of the Campaign for Tobacco-Free Kids noted: "It's an extraordinarily clever way to seek to undermine the gravity of the health concerns of tobacco and the public's low respect for them as a company."[25]

Another antismoking executive noted the tobacco industry has a long history of using humor. He said humorous tobacco advertising includes "the not-so-subtle cracks at tobacco opponents in the 'antismoking' ads financed in part by Philip Morris that often portray antismoking advocates as intrusive busybodies while sending the appealing message that smoking is what adults do."[26]

Scary Direct Mail in the U.K.

Imagine you're sorting through your mail and you find a crime scene dossier. Included in the authentic-looking dossier are pictures of murder victims (including a man's neck with rope burns on it), a coroner's report, and a plastic bag labeled "Evidence" containing pieces of what look like bloodstained fabric.

The dossier also contains a wanted poster of an alleged serial killer named "the Carbon Copy Killer." And, uh-oh, all the murder victims have the same name as you (remember Arnold Schwarzenegger looking for "Sarah Connor" in *The Terminator*? That's the general idea). Newspaper clippings describing the murders of three people, all with your name, strongly suggest the next knock on your door might be Mr. Carbon Copy. OK? Now imagine this. It wasn't mailed to you—it was mailed to your kid.

Almost 200 people complained to the ASA-U.K. about Channel Five's elaborate mailer, designed to promote their broadcast of *CSI: NY*. Most of them complained the mailing was "offensive and distressing" and that Channel Five failed to make it clear enough that it was a phony. Even though Channel Five pointed out that the mailing displayed their logo on the envelope and cover of the file, and that the name of the show was mentioned throughout, the ASA ruled the ad violated their code. As they observed, the "disturbing nature of the programme and contents of the mailing would seriously offend those who had not specifically requested information about the *CSI* series."[27]

FINDING OUT WHEN HUMOR IS OFFENSIVE

So say we agree humor in advertising might be related to offending people. When, where, and how might it happen? Might different types of humor be more or less likely to cause offense? Does relatedness have anything to do with it? Are people more or less likely to be offended by funny ads in some media compared with others? Rephrasing these issues as formal research questions and then looking for answers might help us figure out how or when humor may or may not be related to audience offense.

The next research challenge would be finding a collection of ads that people complained about and then studying the complaints using content analysis. To conduct a content analysis, it would be helpful for the complaints to be in a standard format. It would also be nice if the complaints included why people complained about the ads and, even better, if the collection of complaints included all or most of the mass media and not just one or two.

Fortunately, the Advertising Standards Authority of New Zealand maintains such a collection. And they even make it available on the Web. Although several advertising self-regulation organizations exist in the English-speaking world, up until just recently, the ASA-N.Z. was the only one to publish complete reports, for all media, in a standardized format and for a long period of time. The adjudicated complaint reports are very thorough, often including multiple descriptions of the ads; verbatim statements by complainants; deliberations of ASA-N.Z. board members; and in many cases, statements from ad agency executives, advertisers, and media representatives. In addition, since research has shown that attitudes toward controversial products and services and reasons for offense are based more on religious and historical factors, rather than geographic ones, findings for offense in New Zealand advertising should be similar to what we'd expect to find in other Western societies.[28]

To answer our research questions, I downloaded 308 adjudicated ad complaint reports published on the Web by the ASA-N.Z. The reports represent all the ads New Zealanders complained about for the years 2001 to 2004 and which the ASA chairman identified as possibly violating Rule 5, among others, of the ASA-N.Z. code of ethics. Rule 5 states, "Advertisements should not contain anything which in the light of generally prevailing community standards is likely to cause serious or widespread offence taking into account the context, medium, audience and product (including services)."[29]

Two research assistants coded the complaints to see if the ads included any of the potentially offensive products, services, ideas, and themes we talked about earlier. The themes (e.g., an ad portraying women in sexually degrading situations) were coded from the point of view of the people who complained, relying only on their comments or summaries of them. Instead of coding the ads as funny or not, coders identified whether they thought the advertisers intended the ads to be funny. This is how we avoid the problem of relying only on subjective perceptions of whether an ad was actually funny.

For ads judged to be intentionally humorous, the complaints were then coded for whether the humor was generated by one or more of the three humor mechanisms—incongruity-resolution, arousal-safety, and disparagement. They were also coded for whether the humor appeared to be thematically related and in which medium the ads appeared.

In content analysis, reliability statistics are used to find out whether the coding was done reliably (see Table 5.1)—the higher the reliability coefficient for a category, the more confidence we can have in the validity, or accuracy, of the findings. Only two categories had low coefficients—thematic relatedness and product/service/idea type. Although these relatively high reliability coefficients don't guarantee the validity of the research findings, they do suggest we had good operational definitions, categories, and coders.

Answering the Research Questions

Sixteen of the complaint reports were thrown out because the ASA-N.Z. couldn't confirm the ads existed or if they were actually ads. My favorite is a complaint about a railway station's radio promotion during which a radio DJ allegedly invited volunteers to win CDs or concert tickets by "peeing in their

Table 5.1. Categories and Reliabilities

	Percent Agreement	Cohen's Kappa
Code of ethics principles	.906	.817
Basic ethics rules (there are 12)	1.00	*NA
Intentional humor (was the advertiser's intent to be humorous?)	.906	.808
Product/Service/Idea type	.938	.646
Theme/Appeal	.844	.785
Humor type: incongruity-resolution	.906	.815
Humor type: arousal-safety	.875	.758
Humor type: disparagement	.938	.873
Thematic relatedness	.719	.507
Medium in which the ad appeared	.875	.818

* The reliability software returns a Cohen's *kappa* of zero when percent agreement for a category is 100 percent.

pants." About 41 percent of the remaining 292 offensive ad complaints were possible violations of only Rule 5 of the ASA-N.Z. code. However, some also represented possible violations of other ethics principles and rules—not surprisingly, mainly those having to do with "social responsibility" and "decency."

Do ads people think are offensive also frequently include intentional humor? As we suspected, intentional humor and offense do in fact often go together in advertising. Slightly more than 40 percent (117) of the ads New Zealanders complained about for reasons of offense were also judged to be intentionally funny.

Do intentionally funny ads that offend people often present products, services, or ideas that are, themselves, inherently offensive? The answer is not all that often. Only about 14 percent of the offensive and intentionally funny ads people complained about included one of the inherently offensive products, services, or ideas (e.g., feminine hygiene products or contraceptives). Not only that, but this percentage is not significantly different from the nonhumorous offensive ads. What this suggests is that people don't complain about either intentionally humorous or nonhumorous ads all that often because they're for inherently offensive products, services, or ideas.

How often do offensive and intentionally humorous ads present themes (e.g., words or images inappropriate for children, sexually degrading portrayals, violence) that are, themselves, inherently offensive? Now the results start to get pretty interesting. Almost 70 percent of the intentionally funny ads New Zealanders complained about included one of the inherently offensive themes. This finding strongly suggests that a funny ad is much more likely to offend people when it includes a theme that also offends people. Again, though, this finding was not significantly different from nonhumorous ad complaints, at 67.4 percent. The importance of this will become clear a little later on.

Since some of the complaints included more than one offensive theme in a single ad, the frequencies for all of them were counted and analyzed. Among the 292 ad complaints, the complaint reports mentioned a total of 249 from our list of inherently offensive themes. The 12 theme categories were combined into the 6 shown in Table 5.2. The table shows that both the intentionally humorous and nonhumorous ads New Zealanders complained about presented images and words unsuitable for children and bad language far more often than any of the other offensive themes. But more important, although there are some notable differences between intentionally humorous and nonhumorous ads, they're not significant. What this means is that people seem to complain about both intentionally humorous and nonhumorous ads for about the same reasons.

Are ads that are both offensive and intentionally funny more likely to be one of the five humor types than the others? They certainly are. Of the 117 offensive and intentionally funny ad complaints, the coding scheme successfully coded all but 2 into one of the five funny ad types. Ninety-nine (86 percent) of the 115 correctly coded ad complaints were resonant wit ads. Comic wit and resonant humor ads accounted for only 6 each, followed by full comedy, with 4. A little surprising was the discovery that none of the complained-about ads consisted of satire.

Do ads that are both offensive and intentionally funny present unrelated humor more often than related humor? Not really. Of the 117 humorous and offensive ads audience members complained about, the humor was related in 97 (82.9 percent). The finding is consistent with the belief that advertisers don't use thematically unrelated humor very often.

Do ads that are both offensive and intentionally humorous appear more frequently in certain media? Based on what we learned earlier, it's no surprise to

Table 5.2. Crosstabulation: Intentional-Humor Complaints versus Offensive-Only Complaints by Potentially Offensive Themes

	Humor (%)	Nonhumor (%)
Sexual themes and nudity	17.0	14.8
Images or words unsuitable for children	31.0	43.0
Gender-related demeaning or degrading situations	11.0	6.7
Portrayed or strongly implied violence	9.0	10.0
Bad language	28.0	24.8
Other (e.g., stereotyping, prejudice)	4.0	0.7
	N = 100	N = 149

Note: Differences between humor and nonhumor are not statistically significant: $X^2 = 11.04$, $df = 5$, $.05 < p < .10$.

find that more than half (52.1 percent) of the offensive and intentionally funny ads were on TV, followed by radio (19.7 percent), outdoor advertising (14.5 percent), newspapers (6 percent), and magazines (3.4 percent). Other print media, including mail, account for the remaining 4.3 percent. As Table 5.3 shows, these frequencies differed somewhat from the nonhumorous ads, with offensive and intentionally humorous ads appearing more often on TV and radio and less often in newspapers. The differences, though, were not quite statistically significant.

So how should we interpret these findings? First, and just as you might expect, humor is often present in ads that offend people, but it seems unlikely that intentional humor itself significantly contributes to offense. Although more than 40 percent of the offensive ads were attempts to be funny, estimates of humor use suggest that 40 percent of the ads in a population such as this would not be unexpected, if intentional humor had nothing to do with causing offense. So these findings strongly suggest intentional humor is neither more nor less likely to cause offense than nonhumorous ads.

Other findings also support a conclusion that the likelihood an intentionally funny ad will offend somebody differs little from a nonhumorous one. The study's findings show both intentionally humorous and nonhumorous offensive ads mostly present themes that are themselves inherently offensive. If the use of humor had contributed something unique to audience offense, then there would have been a significantly larger percentage of nonoffensive themes among the intentionally humorous complaints, compared with nonhumorous offensive ads. This finding supports the conclusion that people are offended most often by inherently offensive themes, and whether or not intentional humor is used in the ad doesn't seem to make much difference.

The findings support a second conclusion, and one that is consistent with the first. When an intentionally humorous ad is also offensive, it's almost always a resonant wit ad—a product of the incongruity-resolution and arousal-safety humor mechanisms. Early research by Paul Speck showed that the most

Table 5.3. **Crosstabulation: Intentional Humor by Media Type**

Media	Humor (%)	Nonhumor (%)
Newspapers	6.0	13.1
Television	52.1	43.4
Radio	19.7	13.7
Outdoor advertising	14.5	17.1
Other (magazines, cinema, mail, online)	7.7	12.6

Note: Differences between humor and nonhumor are not statistically significant: $X^2 = 8.04$, $df = 4$, $p = .09$.

frequent type of humor in U.S. television advertising is comic wit (31 percent), and the least used is sentimental (or resonant) humor (12 percent).[30] So at 86 percent, it seems obvious there are many more resonant wit ads in this study's population of offensive ads than would be expected by chance. This second finding, moreover, is consistent with the first in that prior research and humor theory also strongly suggest that offense has less to do with intentional humor than with the humor's use of inherently offensive themes.

The tension generated by the intentional violation of social standards, norms, and taboos is an aggressive type of arousal-safety stimulus most likely to include an inherently offensive theme. In fact, words and images inappropriate for children and bad language were two complaints that accounted for more than 60 percent of the resonant wit ad complaints. It's also important to recognize how consistent this finding is with research on "shocking" advertising. You may recognize that Dahl and his colleagues' definition of shocking advertising— content that "attempts to surprise an audience by deliberately violating social norms for societal values and personal ideals"—is nearly identical to a negatively aggressive resonant wit ad.[31] In addition, as you may recall from Chapters 2 and 4, surprise is typically the result of incongruity-resolution humor, and the violation of social norms often happens with aggressive arousal-safety ads.

The findings of the study also show that, as suspected, people are more likely to be offended by ads that are delivered in the more intrusive media. TV, radio, and outdoor advertising are, by far, the most intrusive and difficult-to-avoid media, and they accounted for almost 90 percent of the offensive ads.

Finally, it's unlikely there's a relationship between humor relatedness and offense. Descriptively, previous research suggests thematically unrelated humor is rare in advertising. The study's findings support this, although the percentage of unrelated humor was somewhat lower than in Speck's content analysis of U.S. television ads. He found that more than 94 percent of the ads used humor that was thematically related or relevant.[32]

THE ETHICALITY OF AUDIENCE OFFENSE

Although it now seems likely that humor itself may not be all that offensive, it's also clear that advertisers often combine humor with themes and appeals that are. This may be just a reflection of the fact that humor is used as often as it is in advertising overall, or despite the research we just looked at, there may be something else going on. Still, given that humor and offense do happen together quite a bit, it seems worthwhile to finish up this chapter with the following question: Why should advertisers care if they offend people?

As we've discussed, advertisers are very worried about breaking through the cluttered media marketplace and getting noticed. The authors of a recent book on advertising ethics explain the problem well, noting that advertising agency creatives are under tremendous pressure to produce advertising that works. "At its best, this pressure for survival can be the birthplace of exhilarating creativity and ingenuity. At its worst, it can lead to advertising campaigns that not only push the boundaries of societal acceptance but also go beyond acceptable norms, thus creating ethical problems and dilemmas."[33]

Growing interest in advertising ethics is related to a variety of issues and complaints about advertising, as well as ethical problems in business in general. The following list summarizes these frequent criticisms about advertising:

- The promotion of consumption values and negative contributions to consumer culture
- Advertising aimed at kids
- Stereotypical portrayals of women; minorities; and balding, middle-aged white men (OK, the last one is my personal opinion)
- Political advertising (most recently, MoveOn.org and SwiftVets.com)
- Sex in advertising
- The promotion of unhealthy and addictive products (e.g., cigarettes, alcohol, and fast food)
- New and emerging "stealth" techniques
- The old standard—deception in advertising

Most important for our purposes, though, are continuing, if not growing, concerns about taste and decency in advertising, as well as the mass media overall. And this is where the problem of offensiveness falls.

Two Good Reasons for Being Ethical

Back to our question: Ethically speaking, why should advertisers care if people are offended by an ad, funny or not? According to Spence and his colleagues, ethics is defined as "a set of prescriptive rules, principles, values, and virtues of character that inform and guide *interpersonal* and *intrapersonal* conduct: that is, the conduct of people toward each other and the conduct of people toward themselves."[34] This definition is related directly to what John Merrill, a prominent expert on mass media ethics, points out—there are at least two good reasons why it's reasonable to expect that advertisers, like other media professionals, will want to be ethical.[35]

First, advertisers should be concerned about ethics because society in general is concerned about it. And people want and, arguably, deserve advertising that is, among other things, truthful and not excessively offensive. Ethicists define what society wants as "universal public morality." According to Spence and his colleagues, universal public morality specifies that everyone is worthy of moral respect and has rights to freedom and well-being (in other words, happiness). If the practices of a particular discipline, such as advertising, harm other people by violating their rights to moral respect, freedom, and well-being, then they contradict public morality and are probably unethical.

Even though there is no standard advertising ethical code used around the world, most of the more prominent ones recognize this commitment to universal public morality. Spence and his colleagues point out the core commonalities among the major ethical codes, including the Australian Advertiser Code of Ethics, the British Codes of Advertising and Sales Promotion, the U.S. Better Business Bureau (BBB) Code of Advertising, and the Canadian Code of Advertising Standards. These commonalities are listed here.

- A sense of responsibility to consumers, community concerns, and society
- Decency, honesty, and truth
- Avoidance of misrepresentation and deception
- A sense of fair competition
- The protection and promotion of the reputation of the advertising industry

The existence of these codes and commonalities shows that at least some advertisers throughout the world recognize ethical principles and try to self-regulate their practice in ways that are consistent with universal public morality.

There is a second reason why it's reasonable to expect that advertisers want to be ethical. As Merrill points out, people who work in the mass media should be ethical because it leads to self-respect and the sense of satisfaction that comes with doing the right thing. In other words, advertisers are probably like anyone else—they want to feel good about what they do. And for most people, it's difficult to feel good about what you do when lots of people find it objectionable. In addition, it's also worth recalling what the early advertisers we talked about in Chapter 1 felt about public esteem and their desire for professional status. Generally, it's understood that one of the hallmarks of a true profession is that its practitioners recognize some kind of ethical standards.

To a lot of people, the idea that people's behavior is directed by their own inner desire to be ethical sounds like an idealistic fantasy. But people who study and write about ethics practically guarantee that most people reach a state of moral development where they at least minimally recognize the importance of universal public morality. Moreover, there's a long history of philosophical thought that supports the belief that advertisers, like anyone else, will want to behave morally and ethically. Spence and his colleagues summarize these views, noting that "since everyone wants to be happy, for who wouldn't want to be happy, and since moral behavior and a moral character are a necessary condition for happiness, it is clearly in one's self-interest to be ethical and moral."[36]

What's Unethical and Why?

So, if there are reasons why society has a right to expect advertisers to be ethical, and many, if not most, advertisers themselves want to be ethical, how can we figure out what is in fact unethical in the practice of advertising? The fact is, few people either inside or outside the advertising industry would argue that an ad for a controversial product or the presentation of a potentially offensive image or idea is always unethical. When, and under what conditions, then, might this reasonably be considered unethical by either society or advertisers themselves?

Philosophers and ethicists use the terms *deontological* and *consequentialist* (or *utilitarian*) to refer to two different sets of arguments or theories they use to produce principles that support or refute the morality of behaviors or actions. Deontological arguments—such as Kant's categorical imperative, Aristotle's golden mean, Gewirth's principle of generic consistency, and Judeo-Christian ethics—propose that an action (such as lying, stealing, or punching people in the nose) is inherently wrong regardless of how much harm it causes.

On the other hand, the consequentialist argument proposes reasons or principles that something is morally wrong because of the amount of harm it causes. Consequentialist reasons are based primarily on Mill's utilitarianism, which proposes that an action becomes unethical when it can be shown to cause more harm than happiness, utility, value, or benefit for the majority of the affected people. The highest principle of utilitarianism—which Mill called, appropriately, the principle of utility—is best stated in his own words: "Actions are right in proportion as they tend to promote happiness; wrong as they tend to produce the reverse of happiness."[37]

In what ways might intentionally offending people with an ad be inherently wrong (i.e., violate a deontological ethical principle)? While we could use any of the deontological arguments to establish that causing widespread audience offense with advertising is inherently immoral, Bob Garfield has argued very persuasively that the "golden rule" is an especially useful approach to thinking about the problem. The golden rule is summarized in this Bible verse: "And as ye would that men should do to you, do ye also to them likewise."[38] We'll focus on this approach because, as many ethicists believe, the basic principle underlying the golden rule—treating others in a decent manner—is a near-global principle. It's also a belief shared by the followers of 21 of the world's religions.[39]

Deriving a deontological ethical principle based on the golden rule is fairly easy—all we need to do is imagine ourselves in exactly the same position as the person on the receiving end of something we're thinking about doing. If we act in a given way toward this other person, but are unwilling to be treated the same way in the same situation, then we've violated the golden rule and acted in an inherently unethical or immoral way. I like the way Garfield puts it: "What is complicated or ambiguous or debatable about the proposition that it is rude, selfish, boorish, obnoxious, sometimes cruel, and always fundamentally mean to barge into people's homes with material bound to upset them?"[40]

Advertisers and their agencies offer several explanations and justifications for creating ads they know will probably offend people. Ad agencies have a responsibility to create effective advertising for their clients, who, in addition, pay a lot of money for that advertising. They need to attract attention among the constantly growing number of other ads in our increasingly cluttered media. Their target audiences enjoy the humor and shockvertising that others find offensive. They are forced to create advertising in an increasingly politically correct world, where people are too thin-skinned and way too easily offended. And, they argue, if people don't want to see offensive ads, they can always avoid them by turning off their TVs or by simply choosing not to look at them.

These arguments and the acts they rationalize don't contradict the golden rule for any individual advertiser as long as he or she is willing to have someone else apply the same argument to advertising that offends him or her. For example, if advertisers agree they themselves would not resent being told they should turn off their TVs or take different routes to work if they are offended by a TV spot or billboard, then creating advertising that forces someone else to do the same thing doesn't result in an inherently immoral or unethical act. On the other hand, and as another example, if an advertiser doesn't agree that it's OK for someone else to place objectionable ads where his or her children will see them, then if he or she does the same thing, it violates the golden rule.

Harm to the Individual, Society, or the Advertising Industry

In what ways might offending people with an ad cause harm (i.e., violate a consequentialist ethical principle)? Seriously, how much harm could an ad really cause? The fact is, and partly because there's so much advertising, ads can conceivably cause some harm. For instance, if a lot of advertisers resort to the "scary trucker" scenario we talked about earlier, the image of truckers would, in fact, suffer some harm, and so would the truckers themselves. The main reason we worry about negative stereotypes in advertising is that they can lead to prejudice and discrimination, which harm both individuals and society overall.

Another example? If Big Tobacco conspires to use humor to make anti-smoking advocates look stupid and smoking look cool, then more young people may start smoking, and that, too, will lead to harm. In fact, when we look at what people say when they complain about an offensive ad, most of the time it's pretty clear the main reason they're offended is they believe the ad will cause harm to someone, usually their own or someone else's kids.

According to Spence and his colleagues, the "suspension of discontent" argument proposes people are, in fact, quite willing to waive their rights to not have to view, listen, watch, or read ads in the ad-supported media that may be offensive.[41] But they only do this as long as they believe there's some benefit for themselves, or if not themselves, society overall. These benefits may include free programming or media access, lower prices for products and services, information that helps them make better purchase decisions, or even the enjoyment they receive from clever and funny ads.

While most people seem willing to accept the notion that advertising overall contributes something of value, most advertisers probably have to admit that, individually, their ads don't benefit society very much, and, even then, only for the people in the target audience. So knowingly offending large numbers of people to impress just a few, for example, would seem to be unethical since the harm caused by the offense far outweighs the benefit. Garfield makes the point well: "Sometimes in advertising it is justified to offend the few to impress the many. It is never justified to offend the many to impress the few."[42]

It's also obvious that a consequentialist view is built into the advertising codes, where the principles governing offensive advertising, as in Rule 5 of the ASA-N.Z. code, typically require the offense to be either "serious" or "widespread," both of which are direct measures of how much harm an ad has caused or could cause. For example, although the volume of complaints about the KFC Zinger Crunch Salad TV spot I described earlier showed that offense was widespread, it was insufficient to establish that the offense was serious. The result was that the ASA-U.K. did not require KFC to stop running the ad.

Moreover, advertisements that lead to harm for advertising as an industry—a decline in positive views toward advertising as a contributor of something useful and valuable to individuals and society—would also be unethical based on a consequentialist argument. In the 2005 version of Gallup's annual occupational honesty and ethics poll, advertisers placed third from the bottom on a list of 21 occupations, with only 11 percent of a national sample of 1,002 adults giving them "very high" or "high" ratings for honesty. The good news is they did manage to beat out telemarketers and car salesmen.[43] The advertising professional's annual placement near the bottom of this poll clearly demonstrates that (1) advertising has a problem, and (2) it would appear to be unethical to encourage additional public contempt. This notion is well captured in a quotation attributed to one of modern advertising's most influential contemporary practitioners, John O'Toole: "When executing advertising, it's best to think of yourself as an uninvited guest in the living room of a prospect who has the magical power to make you disappear instantly."[44]

In addition, as I noted earlier, advertisers' obligation to protect and promote the reputation of the advertising industry is one of the core commonalities found in advertising codes of ethics around the world. To the extent that offensive advertising causes harm to advertising or the advertising industry, it should be considered unethical.

CONCLUSIONS ABOUT HUMOR AND OFFENSE

One thing seems fairly certain—offensive advertising is here to stay. As the marketing world becomes more and more competitive, and the media more and more cluttered with competing messages, attempts to get noticed by pushing the envelope of taste and propriety can only increase. Especially since it seems to work, at least for attracting attention and encouraging positive impressions among certain types of audiences.

There is good news, though, when it comes to advertising humor. Practically speaking, it seems as though advertisers' historic concerns about the risks associated with humor and its potential for causing offense should be limited almost entirely to aggressive arousal-safety humor. The other types of humorous ads—positive resonant humor, positive resonant wit, comic wit, full comedy, and even satire—may often fail to amuse, but they don't seem to lead to serious offense.

Ethically speaking, what should advertisers do to safely walk the fine line between provocative, compelling, breakthrough advertising and advertising that is unethically offensive? First, advertisers should take special care when using the intrusive media, in particular, TV, radio, and outdoor advertising. Second, and related to this, advertisers should target audiences with media vehicles carefully. These two suggestions combined would minimize the exposure of potentially offensive ads to audiences most likely to be offended by them. It would also curtail exposure to kids, which, as we've learned, is one of the main complaints people have about advertising.

Third, advertisers should take special care when presenting a potentially offensive theme. As the study described earlier revealed, 70 percent of the ads people found offensive included at least one sensitive subject. Any kind of sexual theme, for example, has a potential for being an especially big problem. Other themes, such as physical or mental illness or antisocial behaviors, also have a built-in potential for causing offense, mainly because people are sufficiently sensitive about them to really resent their use in attempts at humor (e.g., "Cam's Breast Exam" and "Tater Depression").

Fourth, and finally, advertisers should be especially careful when using aggressive arousal-safety humor. Nearly 90 percent of the intentionally funny ads that offended New Zealanders were arousal-safety-based resonant wit ads. There is clearly a place for this kind of humor in advertising, and it really appeals to some audiences, especially young men. But when advertisers use this type of humor, they should attempt to reach that target audience and as few others as possible. Critic Bob Garfield probably states the problem as well or better than anyone else—advertising is a shotgun, not a rifle.

NOTES

1. Terrence A. Shimp and Elnora W. Stuart, "The Role of Disgust as an Emotional Mediator of Advertising Effects," *Journal of Advertising* 33, no. 1 (2004): 43–54, 51.

2. David S. Waller, "Attitudes toward Offensive Advertising: An Australian Study," *Journal of Consumer Marketing* 16, no. 3 (1999): 288–294, 289.

3. Darren W. Dahl, Kristina D. Frankenberger, and Rajesh V. Manchanda, "Does It Pay to Shock? Reactions to Shocking and Nonshocking Advertising Content among University Students," *Journal of Advertising Research* 43, no. 3 (2003): 268–281.

4. Bob Garfield, *And Now a Few Words from Me: Advertising's Leading Critic Lays Down the Law, Once and for All* (New York: McGraw-Hill, 2003), 112.

5. Sharaf N. Rehman and John R. Brooks, "Attitudes toward Television Advertising for Controversial Products," *Journal of Healthcare Marketing* 7 (1987): 78–83; Aubrey Wilson and Christopher West, "The Marketing of 'Unmentionables,'" *Harvard Business Review* (January–February 1981): 91–102.

6. Waller, "Attitudes toward Offensive Advertising."

7. Waller, "Attitudes toward Offensive Advertising"; Wilson and West, "The Marketing of 'Unmentionables.'"

8. Herbert Rotfeld, "Your Flaming Arrows Might Hit the Wrong Target," *Marketing News* 33, no. 4 (1999): 6–8.

9. Shimp and Stuart, "The Role of Disgust," 50.

10. Advertising Standards Authority, "Serious Offence in Non-Broadcast Advertising," http://www.asa.org.uk/asa/research (accessed January 23, 2005).

11. Thomas F. Haller, "What Students Think of Advertising," *Journal of Advertising Research* 14, no. 1 (1974): 33–38.

12. Banwari Mittal, "Public Assessment of TV Advertising: Faint Praise and Harsh Criticism," *Journal of Advertising Research* 34, no. 1 (1994): 35–53.

13. Michael Schudson, *Advertising: The Uneasy Persuasion* (New York: Basic, 1984), 74.

14. Douglas L. Fugate, "The Advertising of Services: What Is an Appropriate Role for Humor?" *Journal of Services Marketing* 12, no. 6 (1998): 453–472; Lynette S. McCullough and Ronald K. Taylor, "Humor in American, British, and German Ads," *Industrial Marketing Management* 22, no. 1 (1993): 17–29.

15. Advertising Standards Authority, "Serious Offence in Non-Broadcast Advertising."

16. Paul S. Speck, "The Humorous Message Taxonomy: A Framework for the Study of Humorous Ads," in *Current Issues and Research in Advertising*, eds. James H. Leigh and Claude R. Martin Jr. (Ann Arbor: University of Michigan, 1991), 1–44; Hyongoh Cho, "Humor Mechanisms, Perceived Humor and Their Relationships to Various Executional Types in Advertising," *Advances in Consumer Research* 22 (1995): 191–197.

17. Lara Mills, "The Cam Effect," *Marketing Magazine*, November 6, 2000, 10.

18. Advertising Standards Authority, "Broadcast Advertising Adjudications: 1 June 2005," http://www.asa.org.uk/asa/adjudications/broadcast (accessed August 23, 2005).

19. Tim Nudd and Rebecca Flass, "Stick a Fork in It," *Adweek Southwest Edition*, March 26, 2001, 30.

20. Linda Longton, "Lost: A Sense of Humor," *Overdrive* (May 2003): 7.

21. Kate MacArthur, "Truckers Demand Withdrawal of Coke Super Bowl Ad," AdAge.com, http://www.adage.com, February 1, 2006.

22. All Headline News, "Ohio Car Dealer Blasted for 'Jihad' Radio Campaign," http://www.all-headlinenews.com (accessed September 24, 2006).

23. Michael Pollak, "Advertising: A Tobacco Company Comes Up with a Funny Little Jingle, but Antismoking Forces Are Not Amused," *New York Times*, April 26, 2000, C2.

24. Pollak, "Advertising: A Tobacco Company."

25. Matthew L. Myers, cited in Pollak, "Advertising: A Tobacco Company."

26. John F. Banzhaf III, cited in Pollak, "Advertising: A Tobacco Company."

27. "Five Slammed over 'Offensive' CSI Mail," Scotsman.com, http://business.scotsman.com (accessed March 21, 2006).

28. David S. Waller, Kim Shyan Fam, and B. Zafer Erdogan, "Advertising of Controversial Products: A Cross-Cultural Study," *Journal of Consumer Marketing* 22, no. 1 (2005): 6–13.

29. Advertising Standards Authority. "Advertising Code of Ethics," http://www.asa.co.nz/codes/codes.htm (accessed May 20, 2005).

30. Paul S. Speck, "On Humor and Humor in Advertising" (PhD diss., Texas Tech University, 1987), 494.

31. Dahl et al., "Does It Pay to Shock?"

32. Speck, "On Humor."

33. Edward Spence, Brett Van Heekeren, and Michael Boylan, *Advertising Ethics* (Upper Saddle River, NJ: Prentice Hall, 2004), 17.

34. Spence et al., *Advertising Ethics*, 2.

35. John C. Merrill, *Journalism Ethics: Philosophical Foundations for News Media* (New York: St. Martin's, 1997).

36. Spence et al., *Advertising Ethics*, 3.

37. John Stuart Mill, *Utilitarianism* (London: Parker, Son and Bourn, 1863).

38. The Holy Bible, Luke 6:31 (Cambridge: University Press).

39. Ontario Consultants on Religious Tolerance, "Shared Belief in the Golden Rule," http://www.religioustolerance.org/reciproc.htm (accessed April 1, 2006).

40. Garfield, *And Now a Few Words*, 124.

41. Spence et al., *Advertising Ethics*.

42. Garfield, *And Now a Few Words*, 118.

43. *Science Daily,* "Nurses Again Top Honesty-Ethics Poll," December 5, 2005, http://www.sciencedaily.com (accessed May 3, 2006).

44. John O'Toole, "John O'Toole Quotes," Thinkexist.com, http://en.thinkexist.com (accessed May 1, 2006).

Campaigns That Made Audiences Laugh . . . and Buy

IN this final chapter, we're going to explore in depth some explanations for the success of three hugely successful funny advertising campaigns. Our goal is to see how well the many theories, principles, and professional guidelines we've explored throughout this book can help us understand why these campaigns were so successful—and possibly predict when other ones will be, too. We're going to do this by looking at the findings of a qualitative multiple case study of the three campaigns.

Why a qualitative case study? As you've probably noticed by now, almost all the available research on advertising humor is quantitative. Quantitative research methods are great for measuring variables and relationships with precision and validity. Good examples are the survey you read about in Chapter 4 and the content analysis you read about in Chapter 5. But one big problem with quantitative research is that it's difficult to simultaneously account for the many factors that can impact whether a funny ad campaign will succeed—such as target audience, humor type, product type, and humor relatedness. Practice-oriented professions such as medicine, law, and business often depend on case studies in both research and teaching for exactly this reason.

To accomplish the goal of this chapter, we're going to focus on this question: How thoroughly do the existing theories, empirical studies, and professional guidelines about humor we've explored explain the success of actual humorous advertising campaigns?

WHAT'S A CASE STUDY?

The case study research method is a good match with what we're trying to accomplish with this chapter. When researchers study something like humor, they're generally trying to find out whether the findings or conclusions from earlier studies will hold up in different settings. For example, the positive effects of humor on attention that we've talked about throughout this book should also take place when we look for it in advertising for different types of products, in different media, or for different target audiences. This is called a *generalization*.

Often, the findings from previous studies are collected and tested in the form of a theory. You read about several theories pertaining to humor, persuasion, and advertising in Chapters 2 and 4. Each time predictions (or hypotheses) based on a theory are found to hold up in a new or different setting, researchers claim they have *replication*. Case study research relies on the same *replication logic* that experimental research does, which makes it possible for researchers to generalize their findings from one experiment to the next.[1]

Each time a hypothesis based on a theory is supported, belief in the validity of the theory is strengthened. But if a hypothesis is falsified, then the theory is changed to account for it, and this new version of the theory becomes the means, or vehicle, for generalizing research findings and conclusions to new settings or new cases. In case study research, this is called an *analytic generalization* or *theory-carried generalization*.[2] The many research findings and theories about how humor works in advertising we've explored in other chapters of this book provide the generalizations for our multiple case study.

There aren't many formulas to guide the analysis of case study data, and much of it depends "on an investigator's own style of rigorous thinking, along with the sufficient presentation of evidence and careful consideration of alternative interpretations."[3] But most case studies, including the one in this chapter, rely on a method of analysis called *pattern matching*. This means a pattern of data from a case is compared with a predicted pattern based on generalizations from previous research findings or theory. If the patterns match, then this strengthens inferences from the case to the theory.

To achieve the purposes of this chapter and study, we needed cases that could be considered "successful humorous advertising campaigns." I chose three that met all these criteria: (1) The advertising was clearly intended to be funny, (2) there was solid evidence the campaigns were effective (e.g., they encouraged attention, awareness, comprehension, recall, persuasiveness, source credibility, sales increases, or increases in other consumer behaviors), (3) there was evidence the funny ads struck a chord or resonated with audiences, and (4) the campaigns or their creators were recognized with industry awards.

CDW CORPORATION: "EMPATHETIC" HUMOR

Early in 2001, CDW Corporation, a business-to-business distributor of computer hardware and software, and ad agency DWP//Bates Technology (recently renamed simply JWT) launched the company's first multimillion-dollar advertising campaign. CDW was founded by chairman emeritus Michael Krasny, a former car salesman who got his start selling used computer equipment out of his home.[4] I previously wrote about this campaign in an article published in a scholarly journal.[5]

TV was the primary medium for CDW's "Empathy" campaign, with funny TV spots airing on cable networks CNN Headline News, ESPN, the Comedy Channel, Bloomberg, the Discovery Channel, and others. Magazine, radio, and online advertising supported the TV spots, with magazine ads appearing in business publications, such as *Business Week, Forbes, Time, PC World, Fortune,* and *PC Magazine.* Online banner ads appeared on CNET, USA Today.com, and CBS Marketwatch.com. The target audience for CDW consists of information technology (IT) managers at small and midsize businesses. The "Empathy" campaign ended in May 2003, when CDW began their thematically different, although also funny, "Passion" campaign.

The Advertising: Goals, Theme, Humor Type, and Relatedness

Early in the planning stages for the campaign, CDW's agency discovered that customers would probably respond very positively to themes of empathy and humor.[6] As a result, the strategy behind the resulting campaign and its tagline— "The Right Technology. Right Away."—was to inform customers that CDW understands and empathizes with their problems. CDW was one of the first in its industry to use advertising to build a brand image and, especially, to use humor to do it.

The star of the "Empathy" campaign is "Fred," an IT manager. We never actually saw Fred in the spots, as his technologically challenged, "Dilbert-esque" coworkers[7] came to his office to make their unreasonable requests and report their bizarre problems. As the second wave of spots broke in 2002, Fred remained invisible, but as we followed him down hallways and past offices, he met the same computer illiterates who now seemed determined to cause technological disasters of truly ridiculous proportions. "Dealing with technology is hard," says the voice-over in one of the spots. "That's why CDW makes buying it as simple as possible, with a personal account manager who understands what you need and gets back to you quickly."

According to former CDW VP-marketing Joe Kremer: "Through our depiction of Fred's world, we show how CDW understands what people responsible

for workplace technology face every day."[8] See the "Funny Business" piece in
Box 6.1 for a look inside the campaign by one of its principal creators at JWT,
Roy Trimble.

Funny Business

Box 6.1. AT CDW, EMPATHY IS SOMETHING TO LAUGH ABOUT

There is always some truth in humor. And some humor can always be
found in the truths of everyday life. CDW is a unique company. They focus on getting IT professionals the technology products they need. Simple and complex. Their dedicated account managers get to know their
customers and their technology needs. They also offer a deep and rich
understanding of the products people need, so in some ways, they become an extension of a company's IT department. And they do it in an
exceedingly responsive manner.

We know IT people as well as anyone. And we know they walk in the
door in the morning only to have a target slapped on their backs, and
they're running the rest of the day. All their well thought out plans to
work on the server, archive old files, update software, and everything else
is out the window. Everyone has a problem. An issue. A gripe.

We created a character. An unseen character named Fred (after our
own head of IT, Fred Gauker). From Fred's point of view, we move
through the office, and everyone has a crazy problem they need help
with. ("Hey, Fred, my laptop crashed. . . . Well, after I dropped it." "Three
o'clock, Fred, time to fry another hard drive." "Fred, I think I just crashed
the Internet.") And the sad thing is, they could all be true. And some actually are. Taken from true stories passed on to CDW from real customers.

For the IT guy, the truth hurts, but it can also make him smile. This is
really his day. This is an exaggerated version of what they all face. And
CDW is the company that understands them. CDW is the company that
is showing the world exactly what all those poor guys have to go through
every day. That empathy, that understanding goes a long way to communicate how they understand their problems. How well they get them.
How well they can serve them as a result.

Presented straight it would have been mean spirited. It would have
been boring. But IT guys have a slightly twisted sense of humor. They are,

after all, much smarter than all of us. They know it, and they don't miss a chance to make sure you know it. So we were able to give it a humorous, fun spin. For someone to do business with you, they have to like you. Who wouldn't like a company that gets you and your problems and then provides help to make your day a little easier?

The key here is humor grounded in reality. In truths. It's often funnier and more effective than humor for humor's sake. It pays off in awareness, sales, being named the top *B to B* campaign of the year, and a Gold EFFIE. It's always good to tell the truth.

Roy Trimble, executive creative director, JWT, Atlanta, GA

The full comedy in the CDW spots is generated by all three of the classical humor mechanisms. As you may recall from Chapter 2, a humorous response can occur when a single stimulus or text is consistent with two contrasting interpretations or scripts—one expected and the other unexpected. And according to Raskin's semantic script theory of humor, all such expected versus unexpected contrasts fall into one of three categories: actual versus nonactual, normal versus non-normal and possible versus impossible contrasts.[9]

The incongruity humor in the CDW spots is a good fit with Raskin's normal versus non-normal contrast type. The first expected script, given the workplace context, consists of office workers presenting their IT manager with various problems or requests. The second is an unexpected, non-normal, and contrasting script where the problems are actually caused by the exaggerated incompetence of Fred's coworkers. For example, in the TV spot shown in Figures 6.1 and 6.2 (titled "Custom Config"), Fred's coworkers present him with several dilemmas, such as "Fred, I don't know how many Notebooks we need, but they have to be here by tomorrow."

In the second TV spot, shown in Figures 6.3 and 6.4 (titled "Responsiveness"), Fred receives several similarly incongruous problems and challenges, such as "Great news, Fred! That incompatible software is a go."

The humor in the "Empathy" TV spots is also generated by the arousal-safety mechanism. As you already know from Chapter 2, a full arousal-safety sequence of events happens when a stimulus of arousal causes anxiety or uncertainty about our safety or well-being or that of someone else, often in the form of a near or actual disaster. If we can make a safety judgment that the consequences

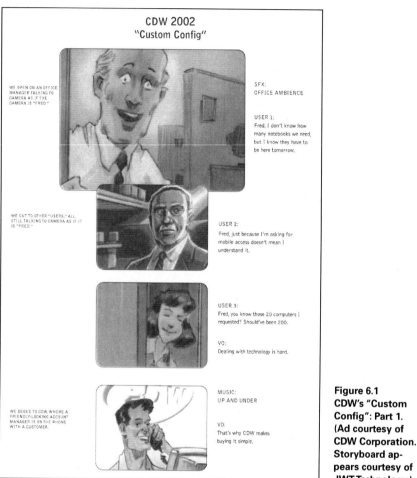

Figure 6.1 CDW's "Custom Config": Part 1. (Ad courtesy of CDW Corporation. Storyboard appears courtesy of JWT Technology.)

aren't too serious, the tension is relieved and the result will be affective pleasure, feelings of goodwill, or empathetic bonding with the victim. And this is exactly what happens over and over to Fred, as his coworkers present him with nothing less than a continuous stream of technological disasters.

Third, you may also recognize the mild disparagement-generated satire in the CDW campaign. In addition to making fun of corporate "techno nitwits"[10]—such as the second spot's conflicted server decision maker ("Fred, the sooner you order that server, the sooner I can change my mind about it")— the spots also disparage, in exaggerated, stereotypical fashion, the technologically incompetent office worker.

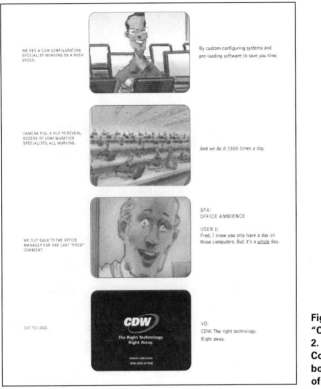

Figure 6.2 CDW's "Custom Config": Part 2. (Ad courtesy of CDW Corporation. Storyboard appears courtesy of JWT Technology.)

Is the humor in the CDW TV spots related? You may also recall from Chapter 2 that there are three types of relatedness: intentional, structural, and thematic. In terms of intentional relatedness, the CDW spots are message dominant and image focused. In message-dominant ads, humorous elements are embedded within a mainly nonhumorous message. We can tell the CDW spots are message dominant because it's clear the humor could be removed and the message still understood.[11] If we removed the parts about Fred's coworkers actually causing the problems, as well as the mild ridicule of people like them, the CDW ads would be fairly straightforward brand-image messages emphasizing the company's ability to help IT managers with their problems. The spots are image focused because the humor is used to reinforce CDW's image and reputation.

In message-dominant ads, like the CDW spots, structural relatedness refers to where the humor elements are located compared with the message elements. Like many other funny TV spots, there's humor at the beginning, and then the

Figure 6.3
CDW's "Respon-
siveness": Part 1.
(Ad courtesy of
CDW Corporation.
Storyboard ap-
pears courtesy of
JWT Technology.)

spots conclude with humorous tags toward the end. Most important, though, the humor in the CDW spots is thematically related. The humor emphasizes the brand-related theme of empathy—that CDW understands the problems faced by the target audience and can be counted on to help solve them.

Effectiveness

One of the main things we've learned about humor is that it's very effective for attracting attention and creating awareness. According to CDW executives, that's exactly what the "Empathy" campaign did.[12] In addition, the number of active CDW customers grew from about 300,000 in 2001 to 360,000 in 2002 alone—during a period when sales for most of CDW's competitors were going down.[13] According to the DWP//Bates Technology Web site: "During 2002, the

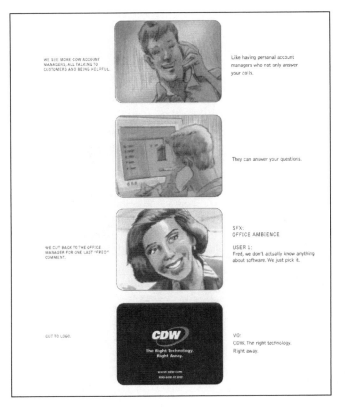

Figure 6.4 CDW's "Responsiveness": Part 2. (Ad courtesy of CDW Corporation. Storyboard appears courtesy of JWT Technology.)

worst downturn in the industry's history, CDW grew 8 percent, surpassing Gateway as the second largest direct marketer of PC products and making them the only clear threat to Dell—which outspent CDW 28:1 on marketing."

There's also a lot of evidence the "Empathy" campaign resonated with CDW's IT manager target audience. According to one industry observer, Fred "achieved an almost cult following among IT professionals who could relate to his troubles."[14] As one e-mail from a Fred admirer puts it: "I bust a gut every time I see them. And then I sob softly into my pillow."[15] The company even created space at CDW.com called "Fred's Corner," where contributors could post their own "most over-the-top, wackiest stories" of clueless business executives making unreasonable demands.[16] In fact, CDW received so many "Fred stories" (e.g., "Does a laptop get heavier when you load more software onto it?"), it published them in a book, titled *Welcome to I.T.* Finally, CDW responded to more than 10,000 requests for CDs containing the ads from the campaign.

Both CDW peers and industry observers recognized the "Empathy" campaign's success. The campaign earned CDW and its advertising agency *B to B Magazine*'s Integrated Campaign of the Year award in 2002. The campaign also won a Gold EFFIE from the American Marketing Association and a Silver ICON Award for excellence in technology marketing from *Adweek's Technology Marketing* magazine. The EFFIE is among the most prestigious advertising awards because it recognizes creative achievement in meeting and exceeding measurable advertising objectives. Finally, CDW VP-marketing Kremer received *B to B Magazine*'s Marketer of the Year in 2001, and VP-advertising Don Gordon received the same award in 2002.

Did It Have Legs?

"Fred" returned in CDW advertising in 2006 in the "Confidence" campaign. In this campaign, Fred has gained enough confidence to have a little fun with his coworkers by frequently pretending to have the near-supernatural ability to fix problems that great IT people seem to have. Why is Fred so confident? Because as he knows, and as CDW's Web site promises, "CDW has his back."

HOLIDAY INN EXPRESS: "SMART" HUMOR

Holiday Inn Express (HIE), a unit of InterContinental Hotels Group, grew from a plan in 1991 to 1,000 properties and $1 billion in sales in 1999—two years earlier than expected. Much of the credit for this success went to HIE's first major advertising campaign, in which it used funny brand-image TV advertising and the STAY SMART® theme to position itself as a smart choice for travelers.

HIE partnered with Fallon Minneapolis, a unit of France's Publicis Group, to launch the campaign in 1998. The chain targeted value-conscious 25- to 54-year-old male business travelers, many of whom don't receive full reimbursement for their travel expenses.[17] The TV advertising was delivered via cable networks such as ESPN, CNN, MSNBC, the Weather Channel, the Discovery Channel, and the History Channel.

The Advertising: Goals, Theme, Humor Type, and Relatedness

An HIE news release states that the campaign was "designed to differentiate and generate awareness for the Holiday Inn Express brand and help contribute to its success as a category leader in the limited-service segment."[18] The campaign's theme was "It won't make you smarter, but you'll feel smarter." See the "Funny Business" piece in Box 6.2, written by Ryan Peck, with Fallon Worldwide, for his insights into the campaign and why they chose humor.

Funny Business

Box 6.2. **HOLIDAY INN EXPRESS**

Let's be honest. Most people out there don't like commercials. Hate is not too strong a word.

Why? Two reasons. One, most commercials are awful. Crass. Stupid. Boring. And two, they are constantly interrupting the shows people are watching. No one wants to hear about the latest nail fungus remedy when they're dying to see if Matlock saves the world.

The one exception, of course, is when the commercial turns out to be as entertaining as the program itself. Wow the audience and all is forgiven. Make them laugh, and, heaven forbid, they might even end up liking you.

In the case of Holiday Inn Express, we've used the humor of the "Stay Smart" campaign in two general ways. The first is to communicate, in a fun and memorable way, that people who stay at the hotel save money without sacrificing service or comfort—and they feel smarter for doing so. Second, and more important, we've used the work to build a personality for the brand. One that has allowed people to see what the company is all about and made it possible for them to think, "Hey, I like Express. Let's stay there." Like it or not, you are your spots. If they're lame, you're lame. If they're fun, you're fun. Simple.

So, knowing that, why don't more companies make more interesting or entertaining spots? Well, it's complicated, but the big culprit is fear. It takes courage for a client to do something new, different, and surprising. In most hotel advertising, you see a montage that shows off the rooms and lobby while a voice-over talks about the fantastic amenities and friendly staff. Very safe. Holiday Inn Express shows an average Joe preventing a nuclear meltdown, four guys pretending to be KISS, and a 35-year-old underachiever winning on *Jeopardy!* Risky. And what does HIE get for it? Heads in beds and people all over America running around using "No, but I did stay at a Holiday Inn Express last night" as their own personal punch line.

Funny, isn't it?

Ryan Peck, copywriter, Fallon Worldwide, Minneapolis, MN

The spots don't show lobbies, cheerful desk clerks, rooms, or beds. What they show are everyday people who are empowered to perform extraordinary feats of exceptional scientific, technical, or practical knowledge because they stayed at HIE. The campaign's theme and slogan emphasize that guests not only make a smart choice in picking HIE,[19] they'll even feel and act smarter because they stayed there. You saw one of my favorite spots from this campaign (titled "Snakebite") in Chapter 2.

The HIE TV spots consist of the resonant wit ad type, with their humor generated by a combination of the incongruity-resolution and arousal-safety mechanisms. The TV spots shown in Figure 6.5 ("Ebola") and Figure 6.6 ("Not the Pilot") are two more of my favorite spots from the campaign. In "Ebola"—which was included in the CBS television special "World's Greatest Commercials"—an apparent scientist in full body suit and mask explains to his colleagues that they're studying a "very rare strain of the Ebola virus." When the tiny vial containing the virus falls to the floor

Figure 6.5   HIE's "Ebola." (STAY SMART® ad appears courtesy of InterContinental Hotels Group.)

and shatters, he assures the team there's no call for alarm since it's not an airborne strain. Asked how long he's been studying the virus, he admits he's not actually a scientist. He then delivers the punch line for the joke: "But I did stay at a Holiday Inn Express last night."

Similarly, "Not the Pilot" opens on a ski slope, where a helicopter waits to transport a group of excited snowboarders to the top of the mountain for a day of free-riding. "Let's rock, dude," one of them says to the pilot, and he responds with an authoritative "10-4." But as they start to lift off, one of the boarders sees a guy on the ground frantically waving his arms at them. "Hey, dude, I think that dude wants you," he tells the pilot. "Oh, that's just the pilot," the dude at the controls says. That's right. He not only isn't the pilot, he's never even done this before. No problem, though. He did stay at a Holiday Inn Express last night.

Figure 6.6 HIE's "Not the Pilot." (STAY SMART® ad appears courtesy of InterContinental Hotels Group.)

The punch line in the HIE spots is consistent with two contrasting scripts—Raskin's possible versus impossible contrast. What's possible and expected in both these settings is that credible-looking experts are able to disclose critical information or perform technical skills (such as flying a helicopter) in potentially life-threatening situations due to their training or experience. What's impossible is that they possess their knowledge or abilities not because of their training or experience but because they stayed at an HIE the night before. It is the resolution of this incongruity—the *Ah ha!*—that produces the pleasurable psychological arousal and release that we experience as humor.

But the humor is also generated by arousal-safety. Almost all the spots in the campaign—from a bicyclist with a dislocated patella to a wilderness park visitor confronting a grizzly bear—present characters in potentially life-threatening situations. But in most cases, the spots' pseudoexperts, whose advice sounds completely credible, provide the play cue viewers need to make a safety judgment that the victims of these disasters are going to be all right.

It's not immediately obvious why the HIE TV spots are humor dominant, especially since they lack a play cue at the beginning, signaling HIE's intent to be funny and entertain. But the ads' product-related elements (which are admittedly few) are presented within a mainly humorous message structure that shapes our overall experience. The initial scenes are part of that humor structure. They not only signal the ads are to be processed as fantasy and not reality (an important precursor to humor[20]), they also cue or set up the punch line ("But I did stay at a Holiday Inn Express last night"). So it's clear that the humor could not be removed from the ads without eliminating the meaning of the STAY SMART® message.

In humor-dominant ads, structural relatedness refers to how functionally integrated the message elements are with the humor. For example, in the case of incongruity-resolution, is the product message part of the incongruity? The message in the HIE spots is completely integrated with the humor. In this case, the "But I did stay at a Holiday Inn Express last night" punch line makes it possible to recognize and resolve the incongruity between the possible (scientific expert) versus impossible (HIE expert) contrast. So it's also clear why the humor couldn't be removed from the spots without destroying the meaning of the message (i.e., why they are humor dominant). We need to process the brand claim in the punch line (HIE is a smart choice) in order to recognize the contrast and get the joke.

Finally, although advertising critic Bob Garfield criticized the campaign's humor for not being related or relevant, it is somewhat thematically related. As he notes: "The campaign is three jokes in search of a premise, and none too close to finding it. . . . Presumably what they mean is that you're a smarter consumer for staying there, but, besides the flashing mention of a free breakfast bar, they don't say why."[21] But they don't have to explain why HIE is a smart choice for the humor to be thematically related. That would be evidence to support the STAY SMART® claim. All the spots need to do is relate the humor to a positive claim about staying at HIE, which they do.

Effectiveness

By 2001, HIE's campaign had been credited with increasing brand awareness by 40 percent, increasing advertising awareness by 96 percent, and helping HIE become one of the fastest-growing hotel brands.[22] A survey that tracks advertising impact showed in 2001 that about 20 percent of the sample said HIE ranked as one of the top three brands they would consider when planning their next trip.[23] Although the spots scored about average in a 2001 *USA Today* AdTrack poll,[24] the poll showed that men liked the ads much more than women did.

HIE also experienced sales success during the campaign. HIE credited the campaign with the company's growth in 1998 and 1999 and for enabling it to achieve its $1 billion sales goal ahead of schedule.[25] Company executives reported in 1999 that HIE's revenue-per-available-room rate (called RevPAR), a key industry indicator, grew by 6.75 percent, compared with 1.2 percent for Hampton Inn and 0.1 percent at Fairfield by Marriott, and they specifically credited the campaign for the success.[26] The same indicator for 2001 showed an increase of 5.2 percent compared with an average of 4.7 percent for its competitors. A 2001 survey also showed the number of people who stayed at HIE was up 8 percent over the previous year.[27] The success continued in 2003, when HIE achieved RevPAR growth nearly twice that of the segment, and another survey showed guest loyalty had doubled.[28]

Moreover, the talk value associated with the campaign clearly shows how much it resonated with audiences. As one source notes: "Holiday Inn Express' 'Stay Smart' ads have been a free media dream. The tagline has gotten so much buzz that it has 'crossed over' into pop culture, on late-night talk shows, in political cartoons, on the street and even in commercial airline cockpits. It was even repeated by Al Gore in his campaign."[29]

The campaign also received its share of awards, earning a Gold EFFIE in 1999, 2000, and 2001 and a Silver EFFIE in 2002. HIE reports they're the first hotel brand ever to be awarded an EFFIE in the category.

Did It Have Legs?

Absolutely. The original ads continued to run in national markets through 2005. And the campaign was still going strong in 2006, when HIE and Fallon Worldwide delivered new STAY SMART® ads based on the same theme.

UNILEVER BESTFOOD'S POT NOODLE: "SLAGGY" HUMOR

People had often complained about advertising for Unilever Bestfood's Pot Noodle even before the company decided in 2002 to take its advertising down a road rarely traveled by a packaged goods marketer. That's when Pot Noodle's brand managers got together with longtime ad agency United London (formerly HHCL/Red Cell, London) to controversially position Pot Noodle—precooked, dehydrated noodles combined with boiling water and eaten directly from the plastic pot—as the "slag of all snacks."

Most people outside the U.K. probably don't recognize the term *slag* as another name for "prostitute or promiscuous woman,"[30] but U.K. residents do, and a lot of them didn't appreciate the racy, aggressive humor. More than 300 people complained about the first TV ad containing the "slag of all snacks" slogan, which was more than for any other ad in the U.K. in 2002. The U.K.'s Advertising Standards Authority also upheld 288 complaints about posters displaying the same tagline. Consumers later complained that a poster headline—"Hurt me, you slag"—encouraged violence.[31]

Even the company appeared to be at least a little concerned about the campaign. Unilever cochairman Niall FitzGerald pointedly told an audience of food and grocery executives: "It is my role . . . to provide a culture supportive of innovation and risk taking, but at the same time [be] willing to step in when there is danger of us causing unnecessary offence that might tarnish our overall reputation. There is a very fine line between the slag of all snacks and being regarded by opinion formers as irresponsible corporate slags."[32]

The U.K.'s Independent Television Commission (ITC, whose duties were assumed by the Office of Communications in late 2003) ruled that the word *slag*, which it considers the 16th most offensive word in the English language, is unsuitable for broadcast and banned it.[33] The ITC's special research report on sexual imagery and offensive language in advertising, available online, makes some pretty interesting reading.[34] But despite the ban, the "slag of all snacks" slogan remained in cinema advertising and still appears on some Pot Noodle Web pages.

The Advertising: Goals, Theme, Humor Type, and Relatedness

Pot Noodle was supported early on with the long-running "Ned Noodle" campaign. Audiences enjoyed 2002's similarly irreverent "Not Poodle" promotion. Ads supporting the promotion—such as one featuring fictitious lawyer "Ewan Court," who promised to sue Pot Noodle on behalf of viewers if they found a poodle in their Pot Noodle—produced high Adwatch recall scores.[35]

But it was late in 2002 when Pot Noodle exploited its "heritage as a quick and rather embarrassing snack"[36] with imagery that metaphorically compared its appeal to illicit sex, prostitution, and raunchy pornography. According to an agency account director: "Pot Noodle is a bit like a dirty secret—most consumers will probably deny eating the stuff, or at least be a bit embarrassed about it, but the truth is they can't get enough of it."[37] The brand's manager similarly praised the campaign for unlocking "a real truth at the heart of the brand—that it satisfies an unhealthy urge—in a way that the target audience will love."[38]

And who's the target audience? Pot Noodle is mainly consumed by 16- to 24-year-old males who haven't got the time or motivation to prepare something a little more wholesome.[39] The young target audience for the campaign is particularly media savvy and "always on the look out for hidden messages and in-crowd codes."[40]

The full comedy in the Pot Noodle campaign is generated by all three of the classical humor mechanisms. The Pot Noodle spot shown in Figure 6.7 (titled "Desperate Dan") and the Web site shown in Figure 6.8 demonstrate the humor very clearly. You can also find "Desperate Dan" online (e.g., at www.absolutelyandy .com/tvadverts) or, of course, on YouTube.

In the spot, Dan calls a friend to complain about his wife's bland and unadventurous sandwiches. *Sandwich*, of course, is a metaphor for sex. The friend sends him in search of what he really wants, "something filthy, like a kebab, but harder." This

Figure 6.7   Pot Noodle's "Desperate Dan." (Ad appears courtesy of Unilever, Ltd.)

turns out to be Pot Noodle. Sleazy shop owners—offering "live food shows," "exotic food videos," and "snack mags"[41]—reject him (in some cases, actually slapping him) because the Pot Noodle he craves is too raunchy and disgusting even for them. Dan finally meets a woman who agrees to satisfy his lust. They indulge in a Pot Noodle eating frenzy in a grungy backroom, where he delivers the punch line that enables viewers to recognize and resolve the incongruity: "That felt so wrong, and yet it felt so right!"

The incongruity in the spot is consistent with a different type of Raskin contrast than in the CDW and HIE campaigns—the actual versus nonactual contrast. The first script is that the desire to consume Pot Noodle is *actually* the same as an obsessive urge to indulge in illicit sex and pornography. But it also overlaps in meaning, or contrasts, with a second script, in which it is *not actually* the case that eating Pot Noodle is the same as consuming sex and pornography, but that it's only similar to it. But there's also aggressive arousal-safety humor in the Pot Noodle campaign, with its metaphorical violation of society's sexual taboos. Arousal-safety humor is especially obvious in the "Noodle Web" Web portal, which is clearly designed to look like a pornographic Web site, in Figure 6.8.

Finally, disparagement contributes to the advertising's humor. Pot Noodle's "It's dirty and you want it" slogan satirizes some people's obsessive desire for sleazy sex and raunchy pornography and uses it to make a point about eating Pot Noodle. The key to recognizing the satire in "Desperate Dan" is that we are not encouraged to empathize or sympathize with Dan.

Figure 6.8   Pot Noodle's Web portal. (Web image appears courtesy of Unilever, Ltd.)

Like the HIE ads, it's not immediately obvious why "Desperate Dan" is humor dominant. But also like the HIE ads, the product-related elements are presented within a humorous message structure that signals the ads should be processed as fantasy and not serious communication. The initial scenes are part of that humor structure, and they cue or set up the punch line ("That felt so wrong, and yet it felt so right!"). Once again, it's clear the humor could not be removed from the ads without eliminating the meaning of the "naughty but nice" brand message[42]—that eating Pot Noodle is something shameful but irresistible.

In terms of structural relatedness, the brand message is completely integrated with the humor, as it is in the HIE spots. The message is that eating Pot Noodle is something consumers should be embarrassed about but can't resist because it feels so good. The brand-related promise is delivered in the punch line of the joke, which enables us to recognize the sexual metaphor. The humor in the spot is also somewhat thematically related. The aggressive humor reinforces the edgy and risqué brand image of Pot Noodle and supports its claim that eating Pot Noodle is a shameful indulgence.

Effectiveness

Individual ads in the campaign, such as "Desperate Dan," achieved very high levels of awareness.[43] More important, for the campaign overall, an industry tracking study showed an awareness index of 20 (the average is only 4!) and advertising recognition of 74 percent. Pot Noodle already dominated the U.K.'s instant hot snacks market when the campaign began, with close to 80 percent market share. But, incredibly, its share grew another 15 percent in the four months after the start of the campaign.[44] See some other astounding factoids about Pot Noodle in Box 6.3, which shows how popular it is.

There's also evidence Pot Noodle's humorous campaign resonated with audiences. Some claim the brand has achieved near-cultlike status among the U.K.'s youth. "Pot Noodle is an iconic brand for teens and represents a rebellious and irreverent attitude towards life. It has always been known for its willingness to push the boundaries."[45] Finally, and despite the controversy, the "slag of all snacks" campaign was recognized in 2003 with one of the U.K.'s most prestigious marketing honors—the *Marketing Week* Campaign of the Year Effectiveness Award.

Did It Have Legs?

Despite its success, and as I mentioned earlier, it looks as though Unilever and Pot Noodle mainly distanced themselves from the "slag of all snacks" advertising. Still, the campaign was immediately followed with new and similarly racy advertising, such as the "Mariachi's Shame" spot for the Seedy Sanchez Mexican flavor (which received several creative awards, as well) and the "Office Bike" campaign. Racy advertising continued after that with an ad taglined "Have you got the Pot Noodle horn?" in which the main character enters a bar with a giant brass horn stuffed down the front of his pants.

> **Funny Business**
>
> ### Box 6.3. ASTOUNDING POT NOODLE FACTOIDS
> - Unilever's Crumlin factory in South Wales annually produces 175 million pots of Pot Noodle.
> - According to a 2002 U.K. survey, 44.6 percent of 11- to 19-year-olds named Pot Noodle as their favorite food.
> - Five Pot Noodles are eaten every second in Britain.
> - A survey found that only McDonald's surpasses Pot Noodle as the favorite hot snack food of U.K. teens.
>
> *Sources:* United London, "Pot Noodle," http://www.hhclunited.com (accessed July 31, 2006); Zentropy Partners Advertising, "Pot Noodle," http://www.zentropypartners.co.uk/03_ourwork/webadvertising/potnoodle.stm (accessed May 10, 2005).

CROSS-CASE FINDINGS AND OVERALL CONCLUSIONS

One thing you've learned in previous chapters is that advertisers figured out a long time ago that humor can fail for lots of reasons. But you've also discovered a substantial body of theoretical and practical knowledge about humor and how it works in advertising. Based on generalizations from this body of knowledge, what predictable patterns of humor characteristics and contextual factors explain the success of the CDW, HIE, and Pot Noodle campaigns?

As you've learned, advertising professionals and researchers almost unanimously agree that humor attracts attention and generates awareness. Similarly, the pros generally believe humor is an effective way to gain name registration and message retention and to register simple copy points. Academic research also supports the proposition that the use of humor doesn't necessarily harm recall and comprehension. The data from the case studies show that all three campaigns gained high levels of awareness and successfully established or reinforced brand images. Individual ads also achieved high levels of recognition and recall. It's important to recognize, too, that all three campaigns won industry awards that included effectiveness as an award criterion.

What explains the apparent bottom-line success—increases in customers, sales, and market share—of the three campaigns? The *affect-transfer hypothesis* we talked about in Chapter 4 seems a likely explanation. People like funny advertising, and they often transfer their liking to the products, brands, and even the advertisers. Several studies we looked at in Chapter 4 confirmed a positive relationship between incongruity-resolution humor and attitude toward the ad, attitude toward the brand, and purchase intention. So people probably transferred their liking of the funny, entertaining, and *memorable* advertising to the advertisers and their brands, which, in turn, enhanced purchase intention and, ultimately, sales.

There may be no stronger agreement among professionals and researchers than the proposition that the effects of advertising humor depend on audience characteristics. Advertising pros, especially, believe that youthful, better-educated, upscale, and male audiences respond best to funny ads. In addition, research we reviewed in Chapters 3 and 4 confirms that certain kinds of humor appeal more to men than to women. How does this apply here? The target audiences for all three campaigns were either male or predominantly male.

It's even more revealing, though, to consider audience type together with humor type, another factor that both researchers and creative pros believe affects humor and responses to it. The arousal-safety component of the CDW campaign and its empathy-generating potential was paired perfectly with the empathy message strategy. Pot Noodle's extremely aggressive full comedy was a similarly potent match with their media-savvy and arousal-seeking yet apathetic youthful male audience. And in the case of the HIE STAY SMART® campaign, *USA Today* AdTrack data confirmed that men enjoyed the spots a lot more than women did. Synergistic matches between humor type and audience type help explain why the humor in the campaigns not only resonated with their target audiences but, in HIE's case, also became a near-cultural phenomenon.

As we've talked about elsewhere in this book, researchers and ad pros believe effective humor is relevant or thematically related. The findings from these case studies show the humor in all three campaigns was at least somewhat thematically related.

Other straightforward propositions based on the body of knowledge we explored elsewhere in this book also help explain the success of the campaigns. Product type is believed by both researchers and professionals to be an important factor, with humor thought to be especially appropriate for consumer nondurables and business services. Pot Noodle is, of course, a consumer nondurable. HIE (for the campaign's target audience, anyway) is a business service, and CDW offers both business products and services. Advertising practitioners believe that radio and TV are the media best suited to humor. TV, of course, was used as the primary medium in all three of the campaigns.

And finally, a conclusion or two regarding the funny campaign cases we looked at in this chapter as well as the exploration of advertising humor I've attempted in this book. As I pointed out in the Introduction, humor is undeniably a complicated phenomenon. But as I also promised, once the findings of academic research and theory were combined with the experience and insights of successful advertising professionals, a body of knowledge emerged that revealed many of the secrets behind the successful use of humor in advertising. Related to that, the findings of this chapter's multiple case study once more confirm that the beliefs of these two types of advertising expert—academics and professionals—overlap in more ways than many of them probably thought.

NOTES

1. Robert Y. Yin, *Case Study Research: Design and Methods*, 2nd ed. (Thousand Oaks, CA: Sage, 1994).

2. Yin, *Case Study Research*; Adri Smaling, "Inductive, Analogical, and Communicative Generalization," *International Journal of Qualitative Methods* 2, no 1 (2003), http://www.ualberta.ca/~iiqm/backissues/2_1/html/smaling.html (accessed July 27, 2006).

3. Yin, *Case Study Research*, 102–103.

4. Mark Veverka, "Motivated!" *Barron's* 82, no. 29 (2002): 24.

5. Fred Beard, "Successful Humorous Advertising Campaigns: A Case Study," *Southwestern Mass Communication Journal* 20, no. 1 (2005): 41–52.

6. Ed Lawler, "19th Annual Sawyer Awards: Integrated Campaign Winner: CDW Computer Centers," *B to B* 87, no. 13 (2002): 20.

7. John E. Frook, "2001 Marketer of the Year: Joseph Kremer," *B to B* 86, no. 22 (2001): 17.

8. CDW, "'Fred, the I.T. Guy' Returns as CDW Launches New National Ad Campaign," http://www.cdw.com/webcontent/inside/press/2003/press020603.asp (accessed May 10, 2005).

9. Viktor Raskin, *Semantic Mechanisms of Humor* (Boston: Reidel, 1985).

10. Frook, "2001 Marketer of the Year."

11. Paul S. Speck, "On Humor and Humor in Advertising" (PhD diss., Texas Tech University, 1987).

12. Frook, "2001 Marketer of the Year."

13. Lawler, "19th Annual Sawyer Awards."

14. "New Campaigns," *B to B* 87, June 10 (2002): 14.

15. "CDW Launches New Version of 'Fred's Corner' Web Page," http://www.cdw.com/webcontent/inside/press/2003/press020603.asp (accessed May 6, 2004).

16. Joe Kremer, cited in "It's a Marketer's Dream: 'Fred' Gets Feedback," *B to B* 86, no. 12 (2001): 4.

17. Aaron Baar, "Fallon Gets Smart as Holiday Inn Takes on Budget Hotel Segment," *Adweek* (Midwest Edition) 39, no. 18 (1998): 3.

18. Holiday Inn Express, "Holiday Inn Express Wins Gold Effie Award for 'Stay Smart' Campaign. Hotel Brand Is First Ever to Receive Top Honors," http://www.pressoffice.hiexpress.com/pressreleases.cfm?ID=895&CID=5 (accessed May 6, 2004).

19. "Stay Smart Campaign Delivers for Express," *Hotels* 35, no. 9 (2001): 26.

20. Paul S. Speck, "The Humorous Message Taxonomy: A Framework for the Study of Humorous Ads," in *Current Issues and Research in Advertising*, eds. James H. Leigh and Claude R. Martin Jr. (Ann Arbor: University of Michigan, 1991), 1–44.

21. Bob Garfield, "No Room for Logic at Holiday Inn Express," *Advertising Age* (Midwest Edition) 69, no. 19 (1998): 65.

22. Holiday Inn Express, "Holiday Inn Express Wins Gold Effie Award."

23. "Stay Smart Campaign Delivers for Express."

24. "Effectiveness of Holiday Inn Express's 'Stay Smart' Marketing Campaign," *USA Today* 19, no. 212 (2001): 4B.

25. Mike Beirne, "HI Express Seeks 'Smart' Creative," *Brandweek* 42, no. 22 (2001): 8; Motoko Rich, "Holiday Inn Express Aims to Hone Image," *Wall Street Journal* (Eastern Edition) July 24, 2000, B12; Carlo Wolff, "Keeping on Keeping On," *Lodging Hospitality* 55, no. 4 (1999): 39–41.

26. Rich, "Holiday Inn Express."

27. "Stay Smart Campaign Delivers for Express."

28. Holiday Inn Express, "Holiday Inn Express Wins Gold Effie Award."

29. "Slogan's Buzz Fuels Hotel's Biz," *USA Today*, http://www.usatoday.com/money/advertising/adtrack/2001-07-16-ad-track-holiday-inn-express.htm (accessed May 15, 2005).

30. Ted Duckworth, "A Dictionary of Slang," http://www.peevish.co.uk (accessed May 12, 2005).

31. "Pot Noodle Stays Down in Dirt," *The Grocer* 226, no. 7633 (2003): 52.

32. "Pot Noodle Stays Down in Dirt."

33. Poppy Brech, "Pot Noodle Tops ITC's Catalogue of Ad Complaints," *Marketing* (UK) January 2, 2003, 1.

34. The Fuse Group on Behalf of Ofcom, "Language and Sexual Imagery in Broadcasting: A Contextual Investigation Research Study," http://www.ofcom.org.uk (accessed April 15, 2006).

35. Jules Grant, "Pot Noodle Sticks with Humour for 'Poodle' Promotion," *Marketing* (UK) March 28, 2002, 20.

36. Grant, "Pot Noodle Sticks with Humour."

37. Tanya Livesey, cited in Grant, "Pot Noodle Sticks with Humour."

38. Atif Sheikh, cited in Suzanne Bidlake, "Unilever Uses Sex to Sell 'Trashy' Noodles," *Euromarketing* V, no. 18 (2002): n.p.

39. Bidlake, "Unilever Uses Sex to Sell 'Trashy' Noodles."

40. Ross Diamond and Frances Stonor Saunders, "A Dirty Business," *New Statesman* 131, no. 4599 (2002): 28.

41. Bidlake, "Unilever Uses Sex to Sell 'Trashy' Noodles."

42. Diamond and Saunders. "A Dirty Business."

43. Grant, "Pot Noodle Sticks with Humour."

44. Mad.co.uk, "Campaign of the Year," http://www.mad.co.uk/publication/mw/awards03/categories/campaign.html (accessed May 10, 2004).

45. "It's Such a Slag," *The Grocer* 225, no. 7556 (2002): 54.

Selected Bibliography

AdAge.com. "The Advertising Century." http://www.adage.com/century/campaigns
.html.

Alden, Dana L., and Wayne D. Hoyer. "An Examination of Cognitive Factors Related to Humorousness in Television Advertising." *Journal of Advertising* 22, no. 2 (1993): 29–37.

Alden, Dana L., Wayne D. Hoyer, and Choi Lee. "Identifying Global and Culture-Specific Dimensions of Humor in Advertising: A Multinational Analysis." *Journal of Marketing* 57, no. 2 (1993): 64–75.

Alden, Dana L., Wayne D. Hoyer, Choi Lee, and G. Wechasara. "The Use of Humor in Asian and Western Television Advertising: A Four Country Comparison." *Journal of Asia-Pacific Business* 1, no. 2 (1995): 2–23.

Alden, Dana L., and Drew Martin. "Global and Cultural Characteristics of Humor in Advertising: The Case of Japan." *Journal of Global Marketing* 9, no. 1/2 (1995): 121–143.

Alden, Dana L., A. Mukherjee, and Wayne D. Hoyer. "The Effects of Incongruity, Surprise and Positive Moderators on Perceived Humor in Television Advertising." *Journal of Advertising* 29, no. 2 (2000): 1–16.

Alden, Dana L., A. Mukherjee, and Wayne D. Hoyer. "Extending a Contrast Resolution Model of Humor in Television Advertising: The Role of Surprise." *Humor* 13, no. 2 (2000): 193–217.

Beard, Fred. "Humor in Advertising: A Review of the Research Literature, 1993–2003." In *Proceedings of the 9th International Conference on Corporate and Marketing Communications (CMC)*, edited by T. C. Melewar. Coventry, U.K.: University of Warwick, 2004.

Beard, Fred. "One Hundred Years of Humor in American Advertising." *Journal of Macromarketing* 25, no. 1 (2005): 54–65.

Beard, Fred. "Practitioner Views of Humor in Advertising: A Twenty-Year Update." Paper presented at the annual conference of the Society of Marketing Advances, Nashville, TN, November 2, 2006.

Beard, Fred. "Successful Humorous Advertising Campaigns: A Case Study." *Southwestern Mass Communication Journal* 20, no. 1 (2005): 41–52.

Beard, Fred, and David Tarpenning. "What's So Funny? A Conceptual/Instructional Model of Humorous Advertising Message Factors." *Southwestern Mass Communication Journal* 17, no. 2 (2002): 14–29.

Belch, George E., and Michael A. Belch. "An Investigation of the Effects of Repetition on Cognitive and Affective Reactions to Humorous and Serious Television Commercials." *Advances in Consumer Research* 11 (1984): 4–10.

Brooker, George. "A Comparison of the Persuasive Effects of Mild Humor and Mild Fear Appeals." *Journal of Advertising* 10, no. 4 (1981): 29–40.

Buijzen, Moniek, and Patti M. Valkenburg. "Developing a Typology of Humor in Audiovisual Media." *Media Psychology* 6 (2004): 146–167.

Calkins, Earnest E. *And Hearing Not.* New York: Scribner, 1946.

Cantor, Joanne, and Pat Venus. "The Effect of Humor on Recall of a Radio Advertisement." *Journal of Broadcasting* 24, no. 1 (1980): 13–22.

Catanescu, Cordruta, and Gail Tom. "Types of Humor in Television and Magazine Advertising." *Review of Business* 22, no. 1/2 (2001): 92–96.

Chattopadhyay, Amitava, and Kunal Basu. "Prior Brand Evaluation as a Moderator of the Effects of Humor in Advertising." *Journal of Marketing Research* 24, no. 4 (1989): 466–476.

Cho, Hyongoh. "Humor Mechanisms, Perceived Humor and Their Relationships to Various Executional Types in Advertising." *Advances in Consumer Research* 22 (1995): 191–197.

Cline, Thomas W., and James J. Kellaris. "The Joint Impact of Humor and Argument Strength in a Print Advertising Context: A Case for Weaker Arguments." *Psychology and Marketing* 16, no. 1 (1999): 69–87.

Cline, Thomas W., Moses B. Altsech, and James J. Kellaris. "When Does Humor Enhance or Inhibit Ad Responses? The Moderating Role of the Need for Humor." *Journal of Advertising* 32, no. 3 (2003): 31–45.

Crane, Ben. "The Trade Card Place." http://www.tradecards.com.

De Pelsmacker, Patrick, and Maggie Geuens. "The Advertising Effectiveness of Different Levels of Intensity of Humour and Warmth and the Moderating Role of Top of Mind Awareness and Degree of Product Use." *Journal of Marketing Communications* 5, no. 3 (1999): 113–129.

De Pelsmacker, Patrick, and Maggie Geuens. "The Communication Effects of Warmth, Eroticism and Humour in Alcohol Advertisements." *Journal of Marketing Communications* 2, no. 4 (1996): 247–262, 256.

Duncan, Calvin P. "Humor in Advertising: A Behavioral Perspective." *Journal of the Academy of Marketing Science* 7, no. 4 (1979): 285–306.

Duncan, Calvin P., and James E. Nelson. "Effects of Humor in a Radio Advertising Experiment." *Journal of Advertising* 14, no. 2 (1985): 33–40, 64.

Duncan, Calvin P., James E. Nelson, and Nancy T. Frontezak. "The Effects of Humor on Advertising Comprehension." *Advances in Consumer Research* 11 (1984): 432–437.

Flaherty, Karen, Marc G. Weinberger, and Charles S. Gulas. "The Impact of Perceived Humor, Product Type, and Humor Style in Radio Advertising." *Journal of Current Issues and Research in Advertising* 26, no. 1 (2004): 25–36.

Fox, Stephen. *The Mirror Makers: A History of American Advertising and Its Creators.* New York: Vintage, 1984.

Freberg, Stan. *It Only Hurts When I Laugh.* New York: Times Books, 1988.

Fugate, Douglas L. "The Advertising of Services: What Is an Appropriate Role for Humor?" *Journal of Services Marketing* 12, no. 6 (1998): 453–472.

Fugate, Douglas L., Jerry B. Gotlieb, and Dawn Bolton. "Humorous Services Advertising: What Are the Roles of Sex, Appreciation of Humor, and Appropriateness of Humor?" *Journal of Professional Services Marketing* 21, no. 1 (2000): 9–23.

Garfield, Bob. *And Now a Few Words from Me: Advertising's Leading Critic Lays Down the Law, Once and for All.* New York: McGraw-Hill, 2003.

Gelb, Betsy D., and Charles M. Pickett. "Attitude-Toward-the-Ad: Links to Humor and to Advertising Effectiveness." *Journal of Advertising* 12, no. 2 (1983): 34–42.

Gelb, Betsy D., and George M. Zinkhan. "The Effect of Repetition on Humor in a Radio Advertising Study." *Journal of Advertising* 14, no. 4 (1985): 13–20, 68.

Gelb, Betsy D., and George M. Zinkhan. "Humor and Advertising Effectiveness after Repeated Exposures to a Radio Commercial." *Journal of Advertising* 15, no. 2 (1986): 15–20, 34.

Geuens, Maggie, and Patrick De Pelsmacker. "Need for Cognition and the Moderating Role of the Intensity of Warm and Humorous Advertising Appeals." *Asia Pacific Advances in Consumer Research* 3 (1998): 74–80.

Goldstein, Jeffrey H., and Paul E. McGhee. *The Psychology of Humor: Theoretical Perspectives and Empirical Issues.* New York: Academic, 1972.

Goodrum, Charles A., and Helen Dalrymple. *Advertising in America: The First 200 Years.* New York: Abrams, 1990.

Herold, Don. *Humor in Advertising and How to Make It Pay.* New York: McGraw-Hill, 1963.

Keith-Spiegel, Patricia. "Early Conception of Humor: Varieties and Issues." In *The Psychology of Humor*, edited by Jeffrey H. Goldstein, Hans J. Eyesenck, and Paul E. McGhee, 3–39. New York: Academic, 1972.

Kelly, J. Patrick, and Paul J. Solomon. "Humor in Television Advertising." *Journal of Advertising* 4, no. 3 (1975): 31–35.

Laird, Pamela. *Advertising Progress: American Business and the Rise of Consumer Marketing.* Baltimore: Johns Hopkins University Press, 1998.

Lammers, H. Bruce, Laura Liebowitz, George Edward Seymour, and Judith E. Hennessey. "Humor and Cognitive Responses to Advertising Stimuli: A Trace Consolidation Approach." *Journal of Business Research* 11, no. 2 (1983): 173–185.

Madden, Tom, and Marc G. Weinberger. "The Effects of Humor on Attention in Magazine Advertising." *Journal of Advertising* 11, no. 3 (1982): 8–14.

Madden, Tom, and Marc G. Weinberger. "Humor in Advertising: A Practitioner View." *Journal of Advertising* 24, no. 4 (1984): 23–29.

Marchand, Roland. *Advertising the American Dream: Making Way for Modernity, 1920–1940.* Berkeley: University of California Press, 1985.

Markiewicz, Dorothy. "The Effects of Humor on Persuasion." PhD diss., Ohio State University, 1972.

McCullough, Lynette S., and Ronald K. Taylor. "Humor in American, British, and German Ads." *Industrial Marketing Management* 22, no. 1 (1993): 17–29.

McGhee, Paul E. *Humour: Its Origin and Development.* San Francisco: Freeman, 1979.

Meyers, William. *The Image-Makers: Power and Persuasion on Madison Avenue.* New York: Times Books, 1984.

Monro, D. H. *Argument of Laughter.* Melbourne: Melbourne University Press, 1951.

Morreall, John E. *Taking Laughter Seriously.* Albany: State University of New York Press, 1983.

Murphy, John H., Isabella C. M. Cunningham, and Gary Wilcox. "The Impact of Program Environment on Recall of Humorous Television Commercials." *Journal of Advertising Research* 8, no. 2 (1979): 17–21.

Nelson, James E. "Comment on 'Humor and Advertising Effectiveness after Repeated Exposures to a Radio Commercial.'" *Journal of Advertising* 16, no. 1 (1987): 63–68.

Oakner, Larry. *And Now a Few Laughs from Our Sponsor.* New York: Wiley, 2002.

Ogilvy, David. *Confessions of an Advertising Man.* New York: Atheneum, 1964.

Ogilvy, David. *Ogilvy on Advertising.* New York: Vintage, 1985.

Petty, Richard E., and John T. Cacioppo. *The Elaboration Likelihood Model of Persuasion.* New York: Springer-Verlag, 1986.

Pollay, Richard W. "The Subsiding Sizzle: A Descriptive History of Print Advertising, 1900–1980." *Journal of Marketing* 49 (Summer 1985): 24–37.

Pope, Daniel. *The Making of Modern Advertising.* New York: Basic, 1983.

Pornpitakpan, Chanthika, and Tze Ke Jason Tan. "The Influence of Incongruity on the Effectiveness of Humorous Advertisements: The Case of Singaporeans." *Journal of International Consumer Marketing* 12, no. 1 (2000): 27–46.

Presbrey, Frank. *The History and Development of Advertising.* Garden City, NY: Doubleday, 1929.

Raskin, Viktor. *Semantic Mechanisms of Humor.* Boston: Reidel, 1985.

Ries, Al, and Jack Trout. *Positioning: The Battle for Your Mind.* Rev. ed. New York: McGraw-Hill, 1981.

Rowsome, Frank, Jr. *They Laughed When I Sat Down: An Informal History of Advertising in Words and Pictures.* New York: McGraw-Hill, 1970.

Schudson, Michael. *Advertising: The Uneasy Persuasion*. New York: Basic, 1984.

Schwartz, Tony. *The Responsive Chord*. Garden City, NY: Anchor, 1973.

Scott, Cliff, David M. Klein, and Jennings Bryant. "Consumer Response to Humor in Advertising: A Series of Field Studies Using Behavioral Observation." *Journal of Consumer Research* 16, March (1990): 498–501.

Smith, Stephen M. "Does Humor in Advertising Enhance Systematic Processing?" *Advances in Consumer Research* 20, no. 1 (1993): 155–159.

Speck, Paul S. "The Humorous Message Taxonomy: A Framework for the Study of Humorous Ads." In *Current Issues and Research in Advertising*, edited by James H. Leigh and Claude R. Martin, Jr., 1–44. Ann Arbor: University of Michigan, 1991.

Speck, Paul S. "On Humor and Humor in Advertising." PhD diss., Texas Tech University, 1987.

Spotts, Harlan E., Marc G. Weinberger, and A. L. Parsons. "Assessing the Use and Impact of Humor on Advertising Effectiveness: A Contingency Approach." *Journal of Advertising* 26, no. 3 (1997): 17–32.

Stern, Barbara B. "Advertising Comedy in Electronic Drama." *European Journal of Marketing* 30, no. 9 (1996): 37–60.

Sternthal, Brian, and Samuel C. Craig. "Humor in Advertising." *Journal of Marketing* 37, no. 4 (1973): 12–18.

Suls, Jerry M. "A Two-Stage Model for the Appreciation of Jokes and Cartoons: An Information-Processing Analysis." In *The Psychology of Humor: Theoretical Perspectives and Empirical Issues*, edited by Jeffrey H. Goldstein and Paul E. McGhee, 81–100. New York: Academic, 1972.

Sutherland, John C., and Lisa A. Middleton. "The Effect of Humor on Advertising Credibility and Recall of the Advertising Message." In *Proceedings of the 1983 Convention of the American Academy of Advertising*, edited by Donald W. Jugenheimer, 17–21. Lawrence: University of Kansas, 1983.

Toncar, Mark F. "The Use of Humour in Television Advertising: Revisiting the US-UK Comparison." *International Journal of Advertising* 20, no. 4 (2001): 521–540.

Unger, Lynette S. "Observations: A Cross-Cultural Study on the Affect-Based Model of Humor in Advertising." *Journal of Advertising Research* 35, no. 1 (1995): 66–72.

Unger, Lynette S. "The Potential for Using Humor in Global Advertising." *Humor* 9, no. 2 (1996): 133–168.

Weinberger, Marc G., and Leland Campbell. "The Use and Impact of Humor in Radio Advertising." *Journal of Advertising Research* 31, (December–January 1991): 44–52.

Weinberger, Marc G., and Charles Gulas. "The Impact of Humor in Advertising: A Review." *Journal of Advertising* 21, no. 4 (1992): 35–59.

Weinberger, Marc G., and Harlan Spotts. "Humor in U.S. versus U.K. TV Advertising." *Journal of Advertising* 18, no. 2 (1989): 39–44.

Weinberger, Marc G., Harlan Spotts, Leland Campbell, and Amy L. Parsons. "The Use and Effect of Humor in Different Advertising Media." *Journal of Advertising Research* 35, no. 3 (1995): 44–56.

Whipple, Thomas W., and Alice E. Courtney. "How Men and Women Judge Humor: Advertising Guidelines for Action and Research." In *Current Issues and Research in Advertising*, edited by James H. Leigh and Claude R. Martin, Jr., 43–56. Ann Arbor: University of Michigan, 1981.

Zhang, Yong. "Responses to Humorous Advertising: The Moderating Effect of Need for Cognition." *Journal of Advertising* 25, no. 1 (1996): 15–33.

Zillman, Dolf, and Joanne R. Cantor. "A Disposition Theory of Humour and Mirth." In *Humour and Laughter: Theory Research and Application*, edited by Antony J. Chapman and Hugh C. Foot, 93–116. London: Wiley, 1976.

Zinkhan, George M., and Betsy D. Gelb. "Humor and Advertising Effectiveness Reexamined." *Journal of Advertising* 18, no. 1 (1987): 66–68.

Zinkhan, George M., and Betsy D. Gelb. "Repetition, Social Settings, Perceived Humor and Wearout." *Advances in Consumer Research* 17 (1990): 438–441.

Selected Creative Credits and Awards

ADS: "Coverage" and "Dinner Guests"; Advertiser: The Yard Fitness Center; Agency: JC Advertising; Creative Director/Copywriter/Art Director: Josh Caplan; Production Company: Backyard Productions; Producer: Peter Keenan; Director: Kevin Smith; Director of Photography: Randy Arnold; Editor: Bob Mori/Superior Assembly; Sound Design: Loren Silber/POP Sound; Awards and Recognition: Cannes Lion, Belding, ABC's "World's Greatest Commercials"

Ad: "Joystick"; Advertiser: Northern Star Council, Boy Scouts of America; Agency: Carmichael Lynch, Inc.; Account Directors: James Clunie and Mike Fetrow; Copywriter: Brian Tierney; Account Executive: Wigton/O'Keefe; Art Buyer: Jill Kahn; Production: Christine Moe; Traffic/PM: Anita Carline; Awards: The Show Public Service Single (Bronze), The Show Public Service Campaign w/ Jablonski & Pinewood (Silver), The Show Illustration (Bronze), The One Show Public Service 2005 (Merit) for Print, Print Regional Design Campaign (Selected for Publication)*

Ad: "Frustrating"; Advertiser: Turner Classic Movies (TCM); Agency: Leo Burnett; Award: American Advertising Awards ADDY 2006 (Silver) for Magazine

Ad: "Optimist"; Advertiser: *The Economist*; Agency: Abbott Mead Vickers BBDO Ltd.; Creative Directors: Paul Belford and Nigel Roberts; Art Directors: Tony Hardcastle, Roy Hyndman, Paul Belford, and Matt Doman; Copywriters: Mark Tweddell, Tim Riley, Nigel Roberts, and Ian Heartfield; Typographer: John Tisdall; Awards: The One Show 2005 (Bronze) for Outdoor: Campaign, CLIO Awards 2005 (Bronze) for Campaign*

Ad: "E = IQ^2"; Advertiser: *The Economist*; Agency: Abbott Mead Vickers BBDO Ltd.; Executive Creative Director: Peter Souter; Art Directors: Paul Brazier, Dave Dye, and Jeremy Carr; Copywriters: Nick Worthington, Sean Doyle, and Jeremy Carr; Advertising Manager: Jacqui Kean; Awards: London International Advertising Awards 2001 (Winner) for Print: Consumer Campaign, Campaign Poster Awards 2001 (Silver) for Best 48 Sheet, Campaign Poster Awards 2001 (Gold) for Best Campaign, IPA Advertising Effectiveness Awards 2002 (Silver)*

Ad: "Hairy Chest"; Advertiser: Findlay Market Mustard; Agency: HSR Business to Business; Creative Directors: John Pattison and Laura Black; Photographer: Tony Aarasmith

Ad: "Lunch Money"; Advertiser: Hobart; Agency: HSR Business to Business; Account Directors: John Pattison and Gene Dow; Copywriter: Paul Singer; Photographer: Scott Lane

Ads: "Garbage Can," "Worker," "Gardener," "Policeman"; Advertiser: Weru AG; Agency: Scholz & Friends Berlin GmbH; Creative Directors: Jan Leube and Matthias Spaetgens; Art Director: Kay Luebke; Copywriter: Michael Haeussler; Account Supervisors: Katrin Seegers and Lili Geiger; Photographer: Ralph Baiker; Advertiser's Supervisors: Dieter Frost and Malte Hyba; Awards: The One Show 2004 (Silver) for Outdoor: Campaign, Cannes Lions International Advertising Festival 2004 (Gold Lion Campaign) for Home Appliances & Furnishings, Cannes Lions International Advertising Festival 2004 (Gold Lion Campaign) for Home Appliances/Furnishings/Electronics & Audio Visual, London International Advertising Awards 2004 (Grand Prize) for Print; London International Advertising Awards 2004 (Winner) for Print: Trade Campaign, London International Advertising Awards 2004 (Winner) for Print: Home Furnishings and Appliances* (Individual ads in this campaign also received numerous individual creative awards.)

Ad: "Cupboard"; Advertiser: H. J. Heinz (UK); Agency: Leo Burnett; Creative Director: Jim Thornton; Art Directors/Copywriters: Nick Pringle and Clark Edwards; Account Director: Jo Graham; Photographer: Kelvin Murray; Awards: Advertising Creative Circle Awards 2005 (Gold) for Best Magazine Advertisement, International Food and Beverage Creative Excellence Awards 2005 (FAB Award) for Savoury Foods, International Food and Beverage Creative Excellence Awards 2005 (FABulous Award) for Press & Poster, YoungGuns International Advertising Award 2005 (Silver) for Consumer Magazines, Campaign Press Advertising Awards 2005 (Commended), The One Show 2006 (Gold), The One Show 2006 (Silver), American Advertising Awards ADDY 2006 (Gold) for Magazine*

Ad: "Brainy"; Advertiser: *The Economist*; Agency: Ogilvy South Africa; Award: The One Show 2004 (Silver) for Outdoor: Single

Ad: "Ashtray"; Advertiser: Singapore Cancer Society; Agency: Dentsu Young & Rubicam/Singapore; Art Director/Writer: Toh Han Ming; Creative Directors: Patrick Low and Mark Fong; Award: One Show Silver Award Guerilla Advertising*

Ad: "Baseball"; Advertiser: Mount Sinai Medical Center; Agency: DeVito/Verdi; Creative Director: Sal DeVito; Award: International ANDY Awards 2006 (Silver) for Health/Medical Products and Services

Ad: "Celibate"; Advertiser: The Workshops of David T. Smith; Agency: HSR Business to Business; Account Director: John Pattison; Copywriter: Paul Singer

Ad: "Dance Party"; Advertiser: Sprint Nextel Corp.; Agency: TBWA\Chiat\Day New York; Executive Creative Director: Gerry Graf; Creative Directors: Scott Vitrone and Ian Reichenthal; Art Director: Scott Vitrone; Copywriter: Ian Reichenthal; Director: Jim Jenkins; Director of Photography: Tim Ives; Producer: Ralph Laucella; Executive Producers: Steve Orent, Dan Duffy, and Melissa Miller; Account Manager: Stephanie Retcho; Agency Executive Producer: Nathy Aviram; Editor: Dave Koza; Editing Company: MacKenzie Cutler; Awards: D&AD Awards 2005 (Silver) for TV & Cinema Advertising: TV Commercials/Individual up to and including 30 sec., Cannes Lions International Advertising Festival 2005 (Bronze Lion) for Commercial Public Services*

Ad: "Surprise Dinner"; Advertiser: Ameriquest Mortgage Company Inc.; Agency: DDB Los Angeles; Executive Creative Director: Mark Monteiro; Creative Director: Helene Cote; Art Director: Feh Tarty; Copywriter: Pat McKay; Director: Craig Gillespie; Director of Photography: Rodrigo Prieto; Producer: Deb Tietjen; Executive Producers: Vanessa MacAdam, David Zander, Lisa Rich, David Glean, and Darlene Gorzela; Account Director: Ingrida Nasvytis; Managing Director: David Hennagin; Editor: Haines Hall; Management Supervisor: Shawn Heintz-Mackoff; Production Supervisor: Janet Guastalli; Awards: Emmy for Outstanding Commercial 2005, The One Show 2005 (Gold) for Consumer TV: :30/:25 – Campaign, Cannes Lions International Advertising Festival 2005 (Bronze Lion Campaign) for Banking, Investment & Insurance, The New York Festivals TV Cinema & Radio Advertising Awards 2006 (Grand Award) for Best Campaign, The New York Festivals TV Cinema & Radio Advertising Awards 2006 (Gold WorldMedal) for Banking/Financial Services/Insurance, The New York Festivals TV Cinema & Radio Advertising Awards 2006 (Silver WorldMedal) for Banking/Financial Services/Insurance, International ANDY Awards 2006 (Bronze) for Financial Products and Services, American Advertising Awards ADDY 2006 (Gold) for Television, American Advertising

Awards ADDY 2006 (Gold) for Campaign, American Advertising Awards ADDY 2006 (Gold) for Professional Services, American Advertising Awards ADDY 2006 (Silver) for Professional Services*

Ad: "Horse's Ass"; Advertiser: SCA Australasia; Agency: Clemenger BBDO Melbourne; Award: Cannes Lions International Advertising Festival 2006 (Bronze Lion) for Toiletries*

Ad: "Tom's Mailbag"; Advertiser: Accor North America/Motel 6; Agency: The Richards Group; Brand Manager: Eric Studer; Copywriter: Chris Smitt; Producer: Sheri Cartwright

Ads: "Split Up," "Big Meeting," "I'm Hungover"; Advertiser: Tate Britain; Agency: Fallon London, Ltd.; Creative Directors: Richard Flintham and Andy McLeod; Art Director and Copywriter: Juan Cabral; Account Supervisor: Chris Kay; Advertiser's Supervisor: Will Gompertz; Award: Cannes Lions International Advertising Festival 2006 (Grand Prix Campaign) for Corporate Image*

Ad: "If Cisco Invented the Wheel"; Advertiser: Juniper Networks; Agency: Ackerman McQueen; Cocreative Directors: Tim Oden and Bruce Parks; Cartoonist: Kevin Pope

Ad: "Pro Hockey Players"; Advertiser: St. Michael's Majors hockey club; Agency: Downtown Partners/Toronto; Creative Director: Dan Pawych; Writers: Kevin Rathgeber and Brent Wheeler; Agency Producer: Janice Crondahl; Production Company: Griffiths, Gibson & Ramsay Productions; Award: The One Show 2002 (Silver) Consumer Radio: Campaign**

Ads: "Blister Pods," "Bone-Head Lawyers," "High-Dollar Paraphernalia"; Advertiser: 3rd Lair Skatepark/Skateshop; Agency: Wowza; Art Director: Steve Pederson; Writer: Jeff Rabkin; Awards: The One Show 2004 (Bronze) for Collateral: Campaign (Point of Purchase & In-Store), The Show 2003 (two golds, one silver) Collateral Point of Purchase.

Ad: "Epidemic"; Advertiser: Miller Brewing Company; Agency: Y&R Chicago; Executive Creative Director: Mark Figliulo; Creative Directors: David Loew and Jon Wyville; Art Directors: Jon Wyville and Mollie Wilkie; Copywriters: Tim Cawley and David Loew; Director: Traktor; Agency Producer: Brian Smego; Agency Executive Producer: Matt Bijarchi; Award: Cannes Lions International Advertising Festival 2004 (Shortlist) for Alcoholic Drinks*

Ad: "Two Dancers Die"; Advertiser: Atlanta Ballet; Agency: Sawyer Riley Compton/Atlanta; Art Director: Kevin Thoem; Writers: Kevin Thoem and Ari Weiss; Creative Director: Bart Cleveland; Award: One Show Merit Award Public Service/Political Newspaper or Magazine Single*

Ad: "Karaoke"; Advertiser: National Thoroughbred Racing Association; Agency: DeVito/Verdi; Creative Director: Sal DeVito; Awards: The One Show 2005 (Gold)

for Consumer Radio: Single, CLIO Award 2005 (Silver) for Campaign, Cannes Lions International Advertising Festival 2005 (Gold Lion Campaign) for Travel, Entertainment & Leisure

Ad: "Golf"; Advertiser: National Thoroughbred Racing Association; Agency: DeVito/Verdi; Creative Director: Sal DeVito; Awards: Art Directors Annual Awards 2004 (Gold) for Radio Advertising – Campaign, The One Show 2004 (Gold) for Consumer Radio: Campaign, American Advertising Awards ADDY 2004 (Gold) for Regional/National Campaign, London International Advertising Awards 2004 (Winner) for Radio: Campaign

Ad: "New Word"; Advertiser: Auto Crime Police and Insurance Corporation of B.C.; Agency: DDB Canada; Award: Cannes Lions International Advertising Festival 2006 (Bronze Lion)*

Ads: "Custom Config." and "Responsiveness"; Advertiser: CDW Corporation; Agency: JWT Technology; Copywriters: David Sokolik and Harry Hayes; Art Director and Creative Director: Roy Trimble; Producer: Mark Wagner; Account Director: Ken Cohen; Director: Jeff Gorman; Client Representatives: Don Gordon and Janine Walgren

Ad: "Ebola"; Advertiser: Holiday Inn Express; Agency: Fallon Worldwide; Creative Director: David Lubars (now at BBDO); Art Director: Dave Damman; Copywriter: Tom Rosen; Director: David Kellogg; Director of Photography: Neil Shapiro; Agency Producer: John Haggerty*

Ad: "Desperate Dan"; Advertiser: Unilever UK, Ltd.; Agency: United London; Creative Directors: Jonathan Thake and Lee Tan; Art Director: Lee Tan; Copywriter: Jonathan Thake; Director: Traktor; Producer: Jim Bouvet; Account Director: Tanya Livesey; Advertiser's Supervisor: Chris Springford; Awards: British Television Advertising Awards 2003 (Silver) for Canned, Frozen, Dried Food, Advertising Creative Circle Awards 2003 (Silver) for Best Campaign or Series, Advertising Creative Circle Awards 2003 (Bronze) for Best TV Commercial, Advertising Creative Circle Awards 2003 (Bronze) for Best Idea in 30 seconds*

SOURCES
   * Adforum.com
   ** The One Show

Index